HOW ARE YOU FEELING?

AT THE CENTRE OF THE INSIDE OF THE HUMAN BRAIN'S MIND

DAVID SHRIGLEY
B.A. (HONS)

W.W. NORTON & COMPANY
NEW YORK · LONDON

THE BRAIN

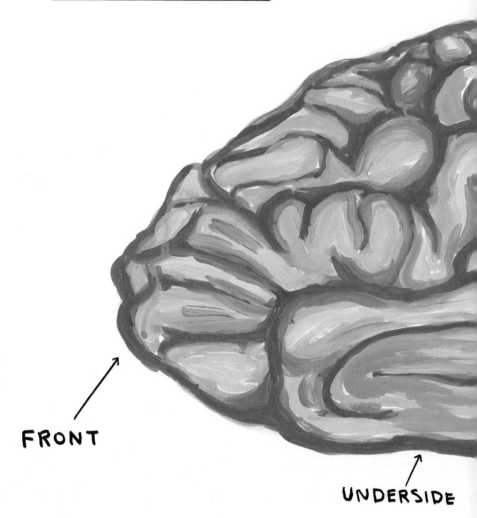

FRONT

UNDERSIDE

TOP (OR SUMMIT)

SEP 26 2013

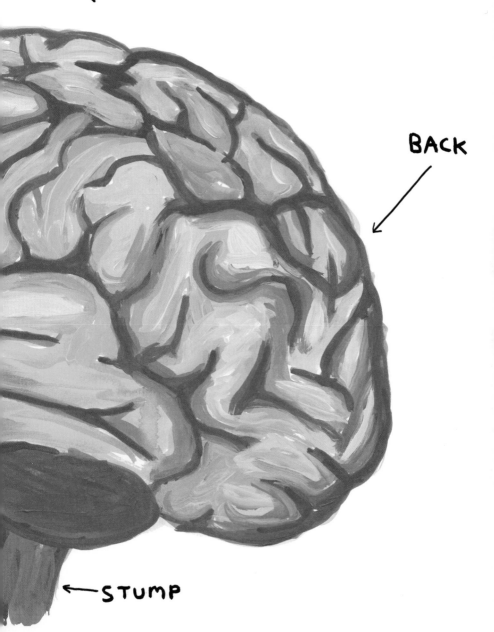

BACK

STUMP

FIRST AMERICAN EDITION 2013

PRINTED IN CHINA

FOR INFORMATION ABOUT PERMISSION TO REPRODUCE SELECTIONS FROM THIS BOOK,
WRITE TO PERMISSIONS, W.W. NORTON & COMPANY, INC.
500 FIFTH AVENUE, NEW YORK, NY 10110

FOR INFORMATION ABOUT SPECIAL DISCOUNTS FOR BULK PURCHASES,
PLEASE CONTACT W.W. NORTON SPECIAL SALES
AT SPECIALSALES@WWNORTON.COM OR 800-233-4830

MANUFACTURING BY ASIA PACIFIC OFFSET
PRODUCTION MANAGER : DEVON ZAHN

ISBN 978-0-393-24039-9

W.W. NORTON & COMPANY, INC.
500 FIFTH AVENUE, NEW YORK, N.Y. 10110
WWW.WWNORTON.COM

W.W. NORTON & COMPANY LTD.
CASTLE HOUSE, 75/76 WELLS STREET, LONDON WIT 3QT

1 2 3 4 5 6 7 8 9 0

Q. WHAT IF THIS BOOK DOESN'T WORK?
A. IT WILL WORK
Q. IS IT GUARANTEED TO WORK?
A. NO.
Q. BUT I CANNOT STAND THE NOT-KNOWING
   -FOR-SURE
A. THIS BOOK WILL HELP WITH THE
   NOT-KNOWING-FOR-SURE
Q. IS IT GUARANTEED TO HELP WITH THE
   NOT-KNOWING-FOR-SURE?
A. NO.

MIRROR

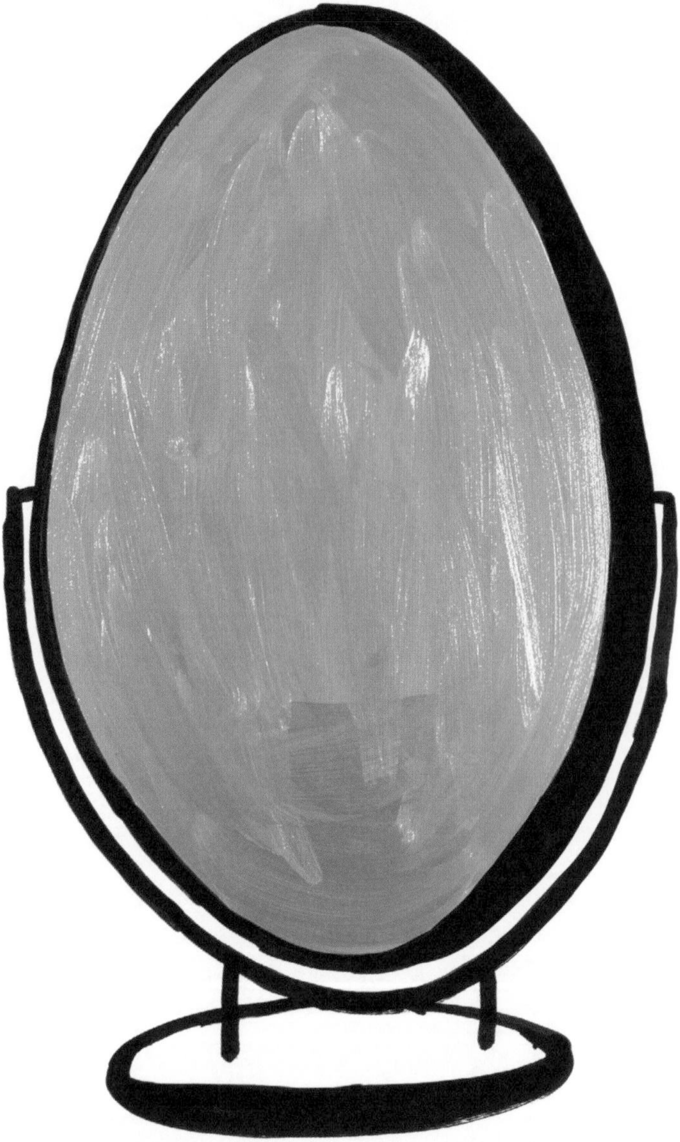

YOUR BRAIN

YOU CANNOT SEE YOUR BRAIN IN
THE MIRROR BUT YOU CAN BE
SURE THAT IT IS THERE.
~~YOUR~~ BRAIN IS EXTRAORDINARY
BUT IT IS NOT LIKE A HAIR DRYER:
WHEN IT GOES WRONG YOU CANNOT
JUST THROW IT IN THE RIVER AND
GET ANOTHER ONE.
WHEN IT GOES WRONG YOU MUST
GET IT FIXED.

EYE WASH
USED TO WASH THE WORMS OUT OF YOUR EYES

WORMS

WORMS IN YOUR EYES: **EYE WORMS**
WORMS IN SIDE YOU
WORMS IN YOUR BRAIN: **BRAIN WORMS**
WORMS IN YOUR FOOD: **WORMS IN YOUR FOOD**

YOU ARE DESCRIBED BY A SUPPOSED FRIEND AS A WORM.
YOUR NAME WRITTEN IN WORMS.
YOU TURN INTO A WORM: YOUR HEAD, YOUR LIMBS FALL OFF, ETC.
YOU BEFRIEND A GROUP OF WORMS JOIN THEIR GROUP/GANG/ORGANIZATION (PLAYING AN ACTIVE ROLE)
NEW LIFE AS A WORM/WITH WORMS
THEN:
YOU ARE EJECTED FROM THE ~~████~~ WORM-GROUP WITHOUT EXPLANATION
WHY?
IT'S UNFAIR: SO UNFAIR: WHY?
JUST TELL ME **WHY?**
(NO EXPLANATION)

EYE TEST

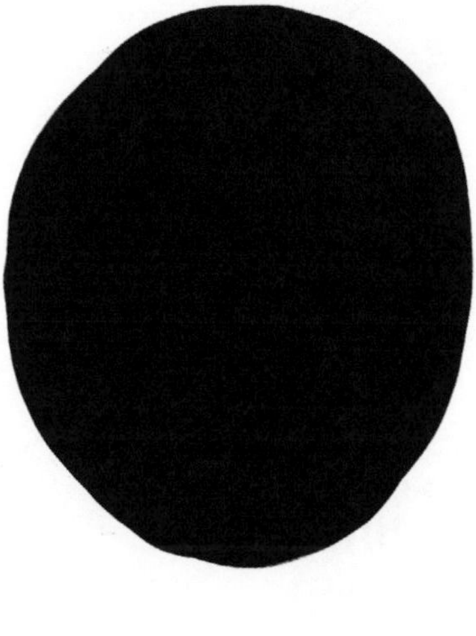

LOOK

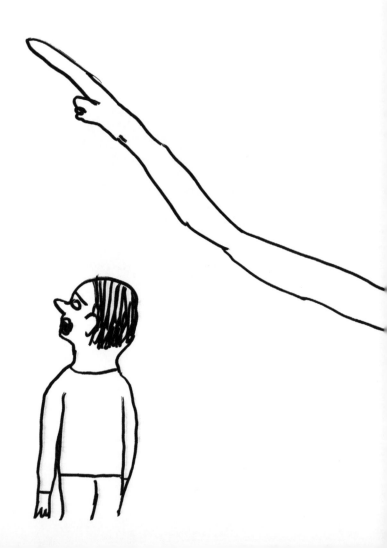

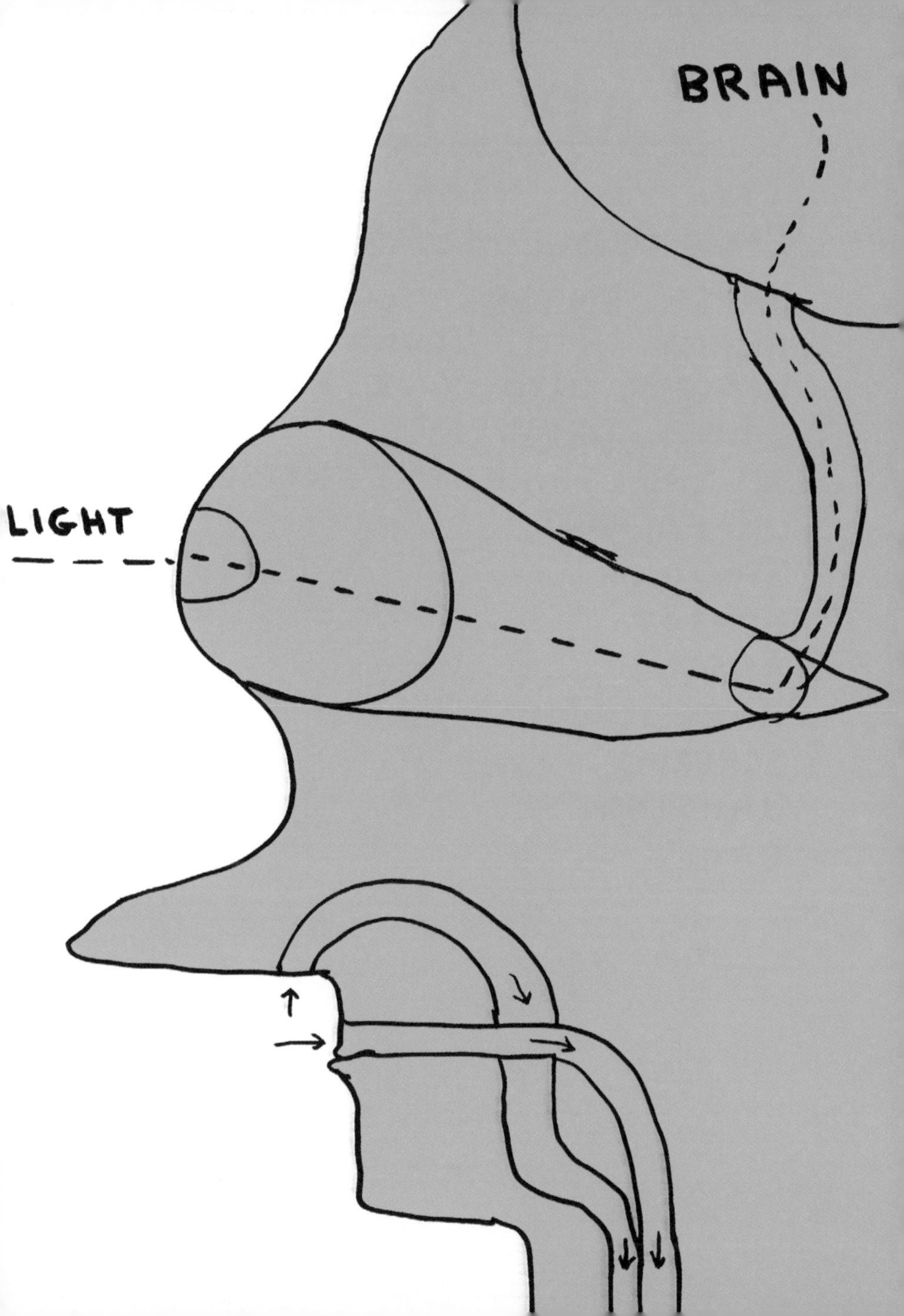
BRAIN
LIGHT

EAR TEST

CAN YOU HEAR NOISE?

CAN YOU HEAR NOISE?

NOISE ENTERS YOUR EARS AND
FORMS INTO SOUND-CLODS AND
TRAVELS INTO YOUR BRAIN UP
SMALL DRAINPIPES.

IN THE BRAIN THE NOISES ARE
SORTED OUT:

SHOUTING

PARROT

RADIO

HARPSICHORD

SCREAMS

BANGING

ETC.

SHOOOOOOOSH!

HOW I FEEL

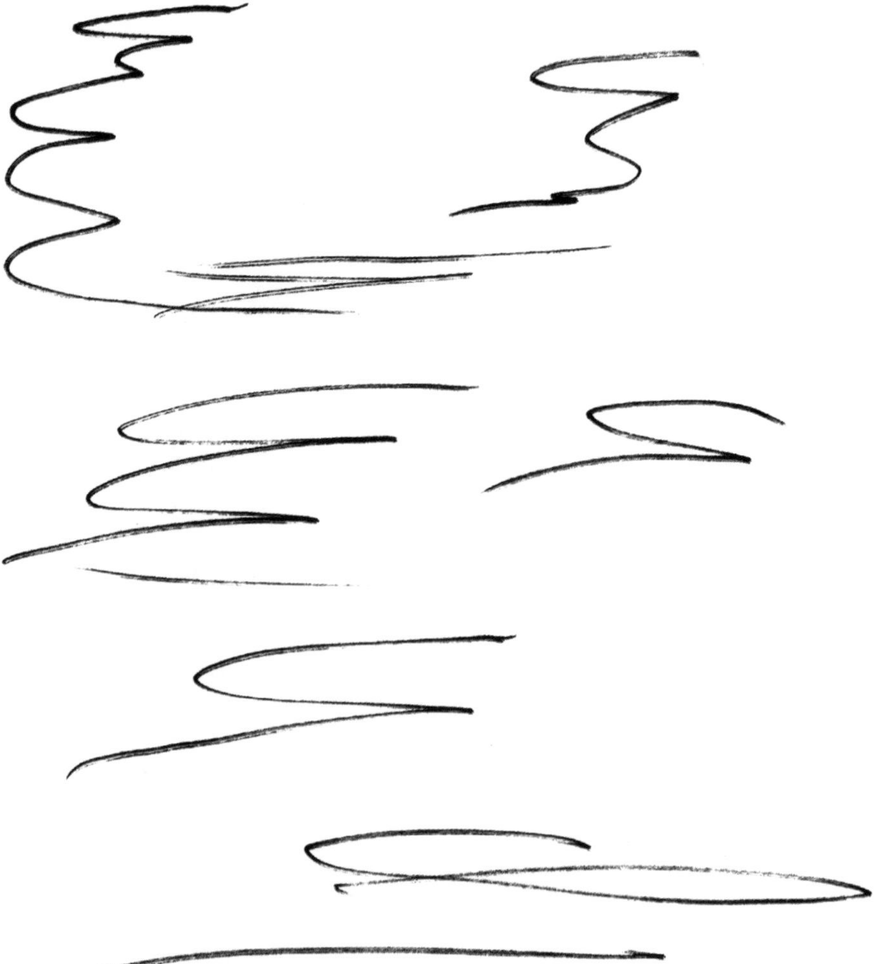

CHAPTER ONE:
IDENTIFYING THE PROBLEM

TYPES OF PERSONALITY:

WITHDRAWN

OBSESSIVE

CONFRONTATIONAL

DEFORMED PERSON

NUDIST

TATTOOS

POLICEMAN

TRANS-SEXUAL

CORPSE

TALKATIVE

SIGNS OF STRESS

- DIFFICULTY SPEAKING INFRONT OF GROUPS
- DIFFICULTY SPEAKING INFRONT OF INDIVIDUALS
- DIFFICULTY SPEAKING INFRONT OF ANIMALS
- DIFFICULTY SPEAKING ~~████~~ INFRONT OF GROUPS OF ANIMALS

ANXIETY

I'M JUST LIKE EVERYONE ELSE
I'M ~~██~~ JUST LIKE EVERYONE ELSE
I'M JUST LIKE EVERYONE ELSE
I'M JUST LIKE EVERYONE ELSE
YOU'RE NOT LIKE EVERYONE ELSE

REMEMBER:

YOU'RE NOT LIKE EVERYONE ELSE

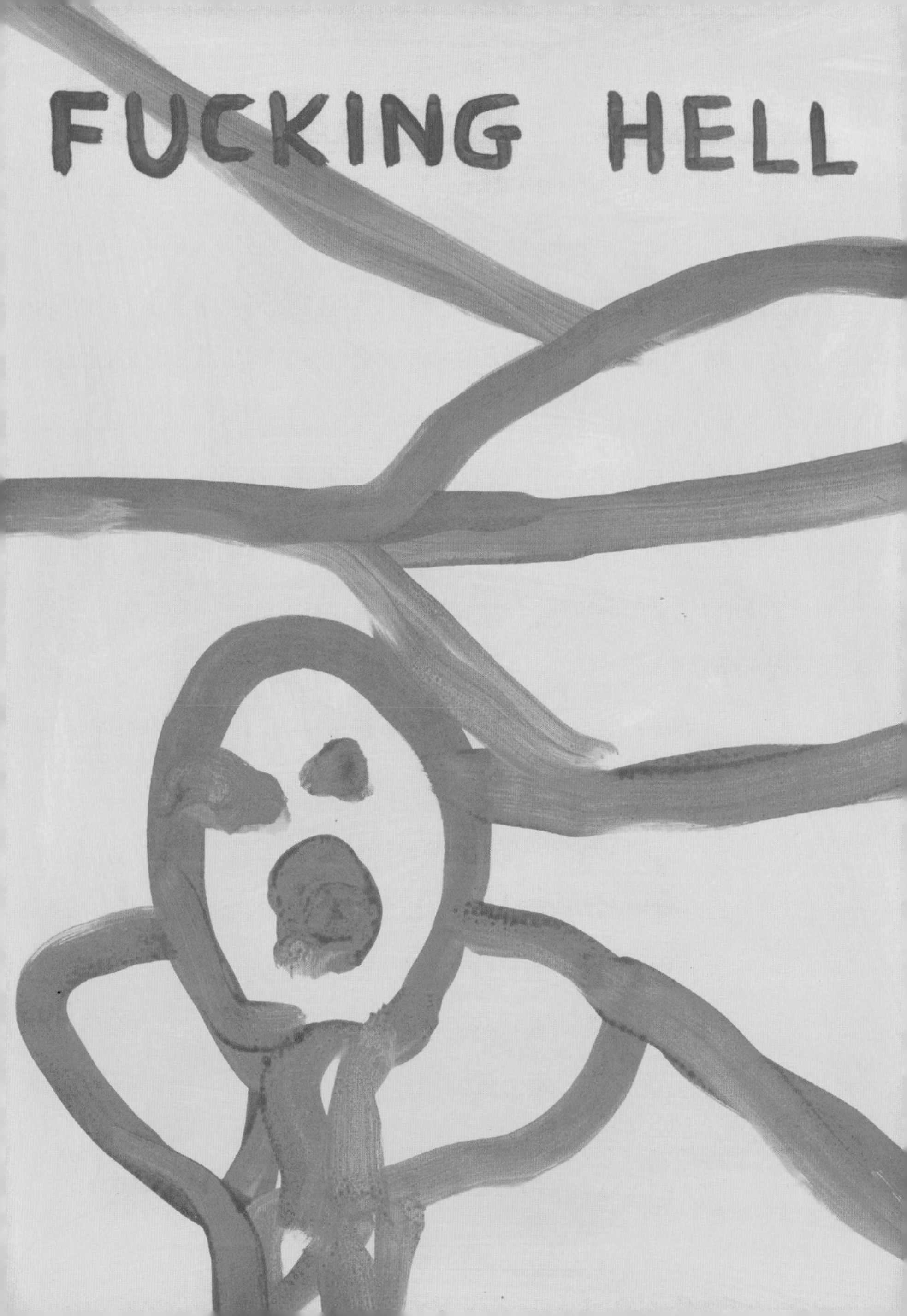
FUCKING HELL

VOICES IN YOUR HEAD

IMPOSSIBLE TO IGNORE?
THEY WON'T GO AWAY?
GIVE YOU THE SHAKES?
GIVE YOU THE FEAR?
LOSE YOUR JOB?
MAKE YOU INCONTINENT?

ADVICE :

THERE IS NO WAY OF GETTING
RID OF THE VOICES.
THEY ARE LIKE TINNITUS
TRY OBEYING THE VOICES FOR A
SHORT PERIOD.
IF THINGS IMPROVE CONTINUE
TO OBEY THE VOICES

REMEMBER :

REVIEW THE ADVICE OF THE VOICES
REGULARLY

DOCTOR'S ADVICE:

NO ADVICE: DOCTOR IS ON HOLIDAY

MASSIVE EYE IS WATCHING YOU

BUT DON'T WORRY ABOUT IT

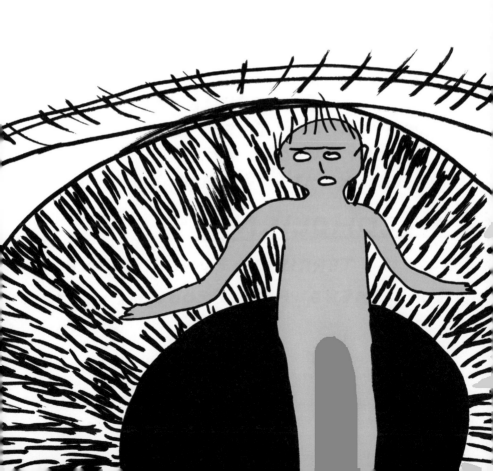

ADDICTION

ADDICTED TO:

HEROIN
TENNIS
ETC.

GAMBLING

SOMETHING IS WRONG IN THE
BRAIN
THEY CANNOT STOP IT
THEY WILL GAMBLE AWAY
EVERYTHING THEY OWN
I DON'T KNOW WHY
I THINK IT'S BORING

ALCOHOLISM

IT IS TERRIFIC FUN OF COURSE
BUT THERE ARE PROBLEMS WITH IT

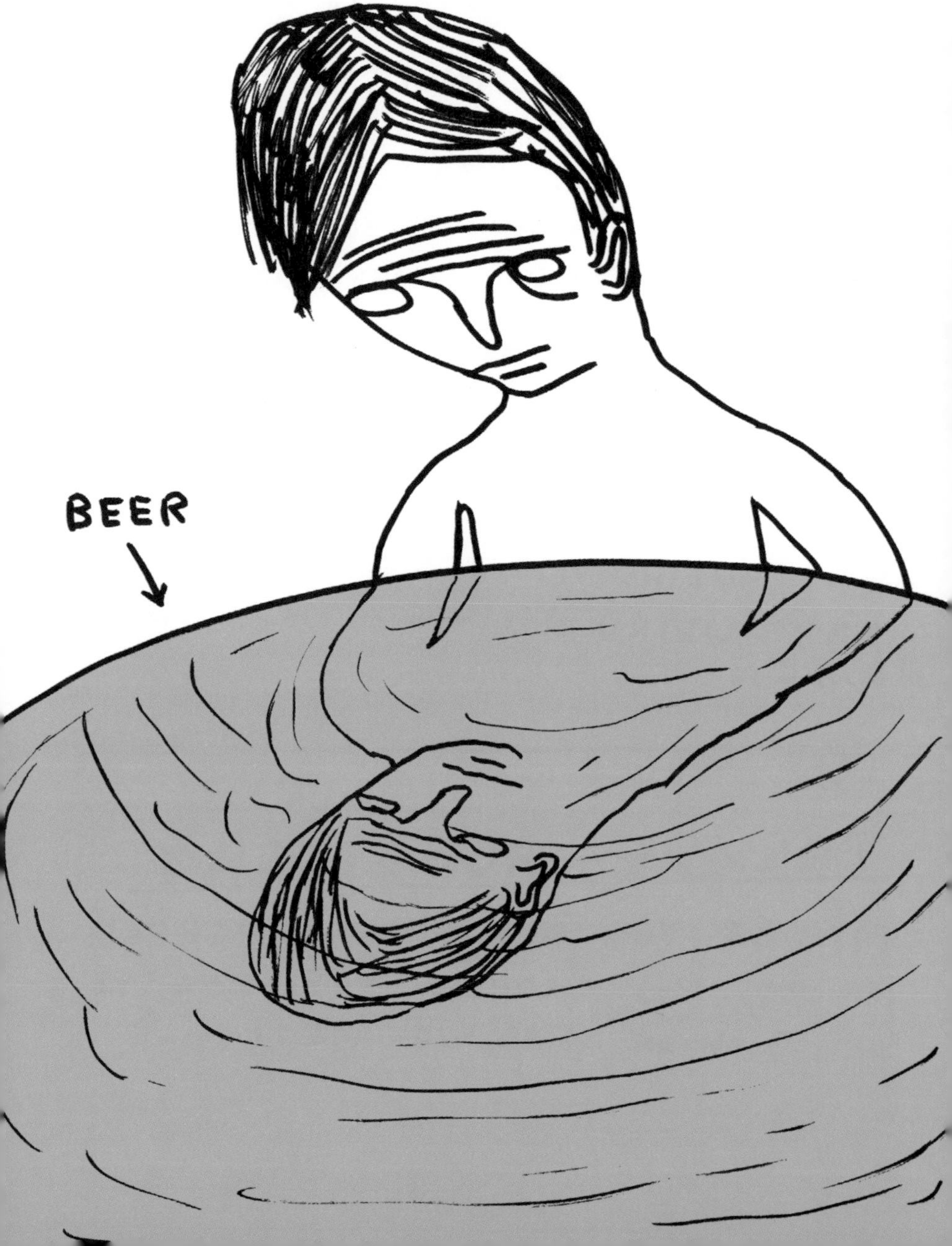
BEER

EATING DISORDERS

THEY ARE CONNECTED WITH
FEELINGS :

EAT TOO MUCH THEN VOMIT
EAT TOO MUCH THEN DON'T VOMIT

DON'T EAT AT ALL THEN TRY TO
VOMIT
DON'T EAT AT ALL THEN DON'T
TRY TO VOMIT

EAT WEIRD THINGS THEN VOMIT
EAT WEIRD THINGS THEN DON'T
VOMIT

PASSIVE - AGGRESSIVE

MAYBE YOU ARE PASSIVE-AGGRESSIVE?
MAYBE YOU SHOULD TRY NOT TO BE
SO FUCKING PASSIVE-AGGRESSIVE

FUCK YOU AND

FUCK TEA TIME

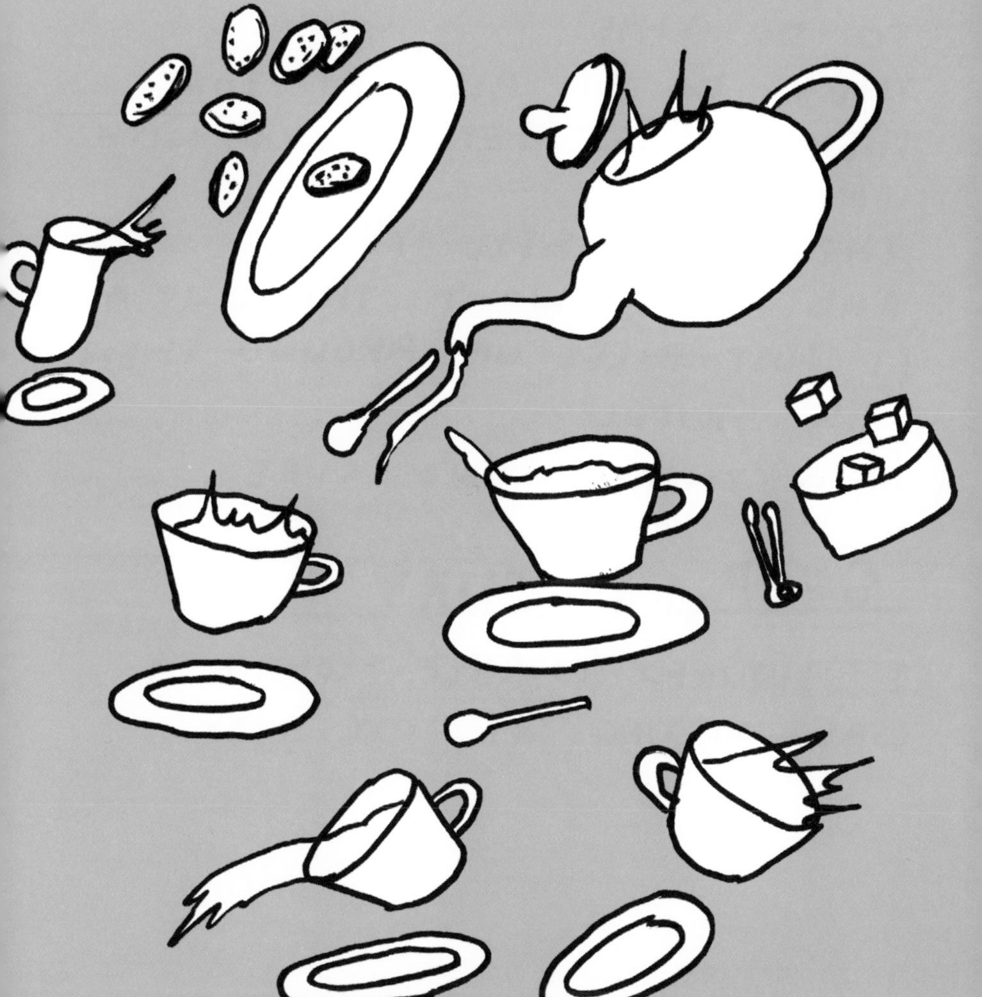

KLEPTOMANIA

WE ALL STEAL THINGS: MONEY,
CLOTHING, PETS, ETC. BUT SOME
PEOPLE HAVE NO CHOICE BUT
TO DO THIS
THEY DO IT ALL DAY LONG
THEIR HOUSES GET FULL UP WITH
THINGS
THEY CAN'T SELL IT
AND THEY WON'T THROW IT AWAY
IT JUST PILES UP AROUND THEM
IT'S AWFUL
AND THERE IS NO CURE

SELF-INJURY

I INJURED MYSELF WHILE I
WAS SITTING AT MY DESK

IT IS WRONG TO BECOME ATTACHED TO MATERIAL THINGS

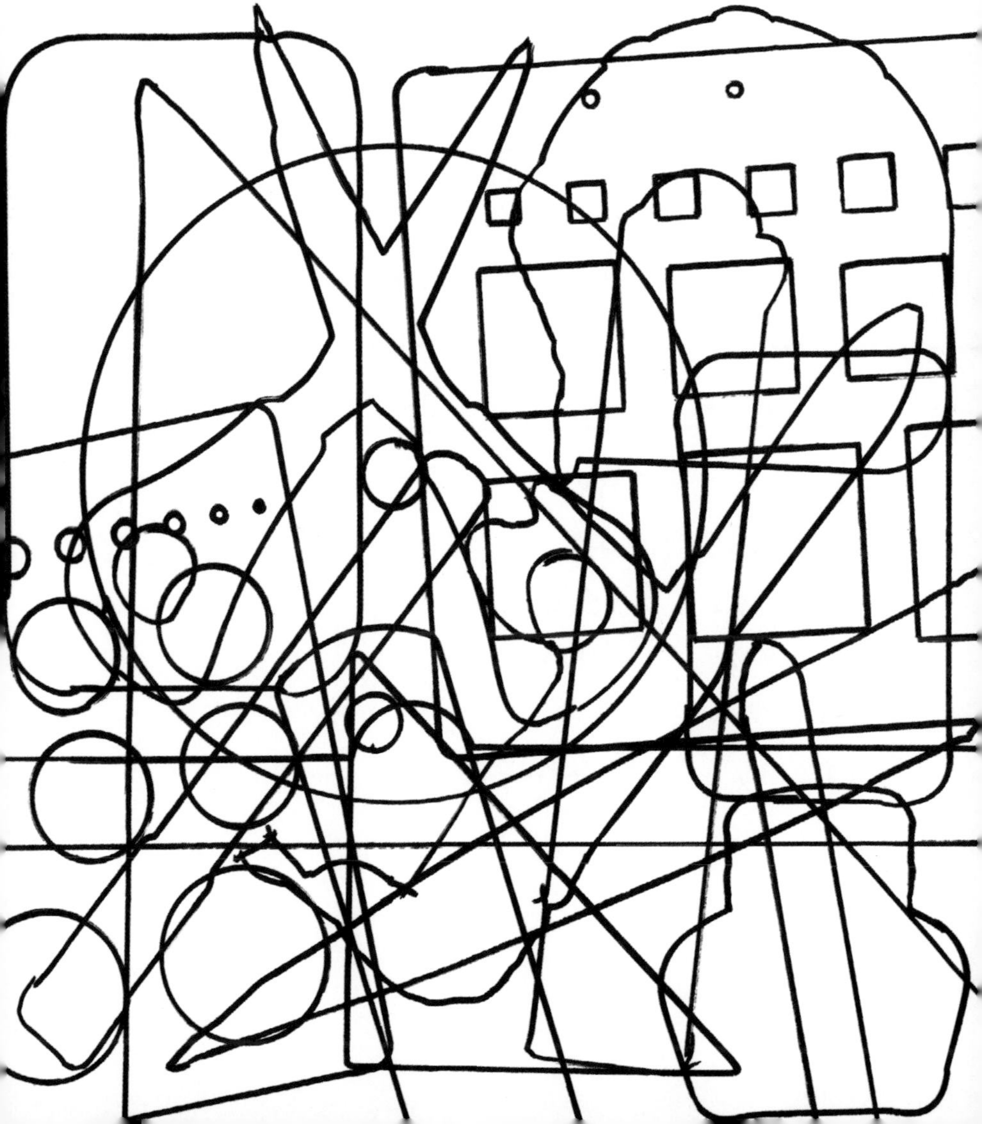

YOUR FAT FRIEND

YOU FEED HIM WITH YOUR
BAD ATTITUDE
YOUR BAD ATTITUDE IS LIKE
BISCUITS TO HIM
HE GROWS FAT ON YOUR BISCUITS
HE IS FAT
IT IS YOUR FAULT

REAL VS. IMAGINED

IT IS REAL
IT IS REAL
IT IS REAL
IT IS REAL
NO
IT IS IMAGINED

I AM A HUGE SNAKE

I AM KEPT IN A SACK

CASSEROLE OF FEELINGS

FUCK OFF
OH HOW I LOVE YOU
FUCK OFF
OH HOW I LOVE YOU
YOU BASTARD
YOU FILTH
HOW I LOVE THE WORLD
I'LL KILL YOU
AND HOW LUCKY I AM
TO BE IN LOVE WITH YOU
FUCK OFF
AND TO LIVE IN THIS BEAUTIFUL
WORLD
I LOVE YOU
YOU DOGSHIT
FUCK OFF

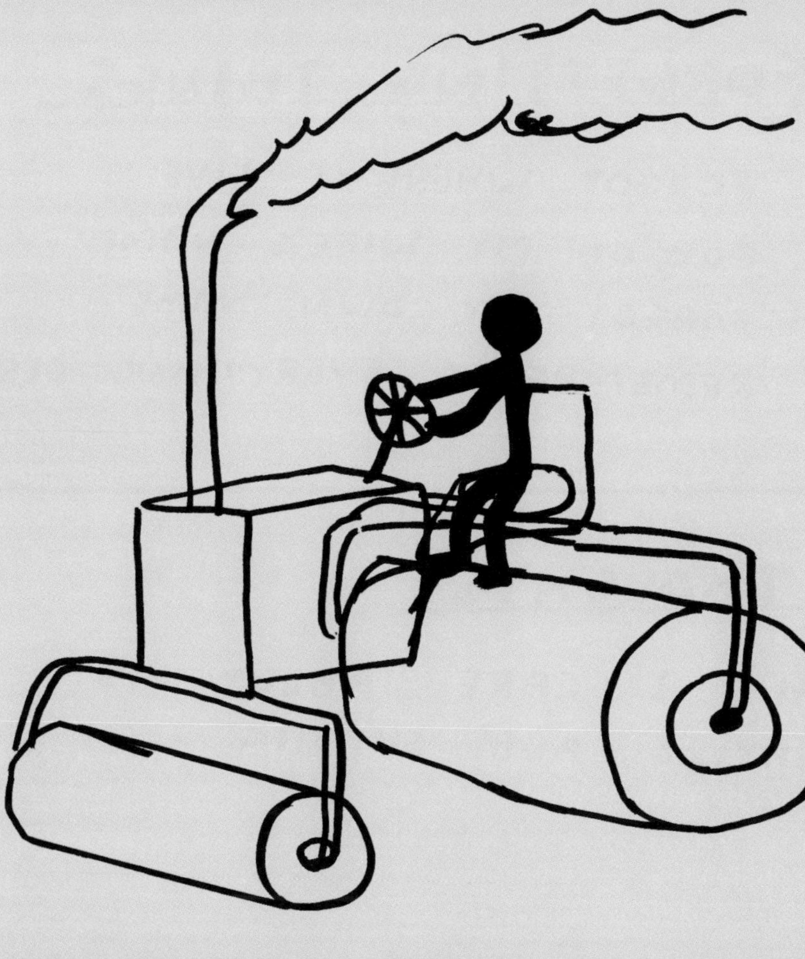

Q. WHAT DO YOU DRIVE?
A. I DRIVE A STEAM ROLLER
Q. WHERE DO YOU PARK IT?
A. I PARK IT WHEREVER I FUCKING LIKE.

FORGETTING THINGS

I FORGOT WHERE I LIVE
I FORGOT MY WIFE'S NAME
I FORGOT MY OWN NAME
I REMEMBERED EVERYTHING ELSE

THOUGHTS

ALL I CARE ABOUT IS
EATING AND SHITTING

I FIND IT HARD TO CONCENTRATE WHILST I AM PERFORMING IMPORTANT TASKS

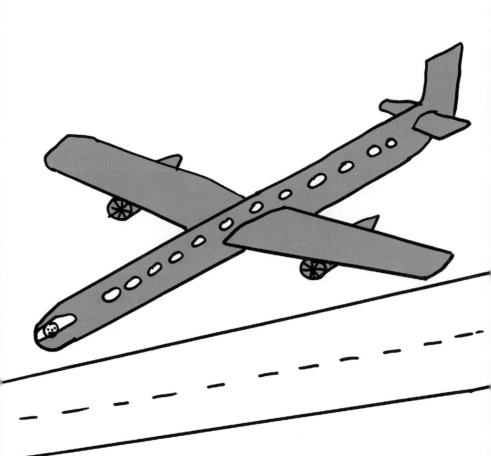

THE BRAIN AND BRAINLESSNES

THE BRAIN SAYS BE CAREFUL
BUT YOU ARE NOT CAREFUL
YOU ARE RECKLESS
AND YOU CAUSE YOURSELF INJURY
THE BRAIN SAYS TO LEARN FROM
THIS
BUT YOU DO NOT LEARN FROM
THIS
AND YOU ACCIDENTALLY CUT OFF
YOUR RIGHT ARM
BRAIN SAYS TO LEARN FROM THIS
YOU FUCKING IDIOT
AND YOU DO LEARN FROM THIS
AND WITH THE BRAIN'S HELP
YOU LEARN TO WRITE LEFT-HANDED
YOU FUCKING IDIOT

IMPROPRIETY

IT IS IMPROPER TO LOOK AT
A LADY THROUGH A PAIR OF
BINOCULARS
AFTER MANY BEATINGS I
HAVE AT LAST LEARNED MY
LESSON
SHE WAS ONLY WEARING A
THIN BLOUSE

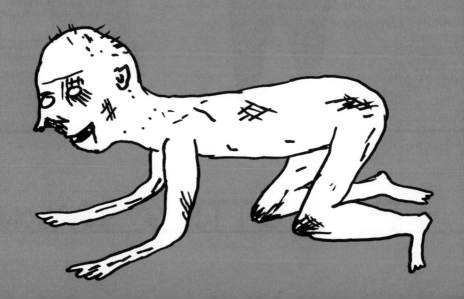

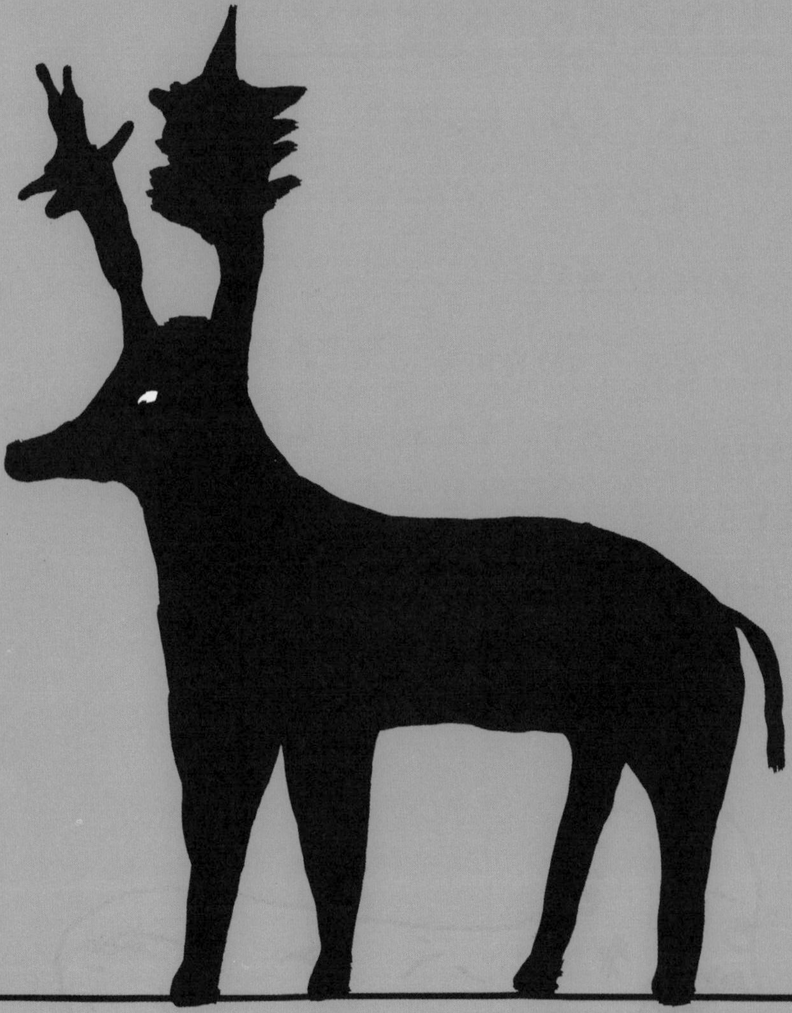

IT'S RUTTING SEASON

CHAPTER TWO: RELATIONSHIPS

HAVING A RELATIONSHIP WITH ANOTHER PERSON IS VERY VERY VERY VERY VERY DIFFICULT EVEN IF YOU COULD DUPLICATE YOURSELF YOU'D PROBABLY END UP HATING YOUR DUPLICATE AND WANTING TO SMASH-IN HIM/HER'S HEAD WITH A SPADE AFTER ONLY A SHORT TIME PERHAPS EVEN <u>BEFORE</u> YOU HAD SPOKEN TO HER.

REMEMBER:
DUPLICATING IS CURRENTLY ILLEGAL

SELECTING A SUITABLE PARTNER

THINGS TO LOOK FOR:
- TEETH
- CLEAR EYES : NO DISCHARGE
- SMELL OF NOTHING IN PARTICULAR
- EVEN HAIR-GROWTH
- SKIN W/OUT SCABS
- NO OPEN SORES/WOUNDS
- FULL EARS : NO PARTS MISSING
- ABILITY TO SPEAK OR COMMUNICATE
- ABILITY TO OBEY INSTRUCTIONS
- ABLE TO TOILET, ETC
- MAKE YOU LAUGH
- CAN COOK
- ████████
- THEY HAVE MONEY AND OR TRANSPORT

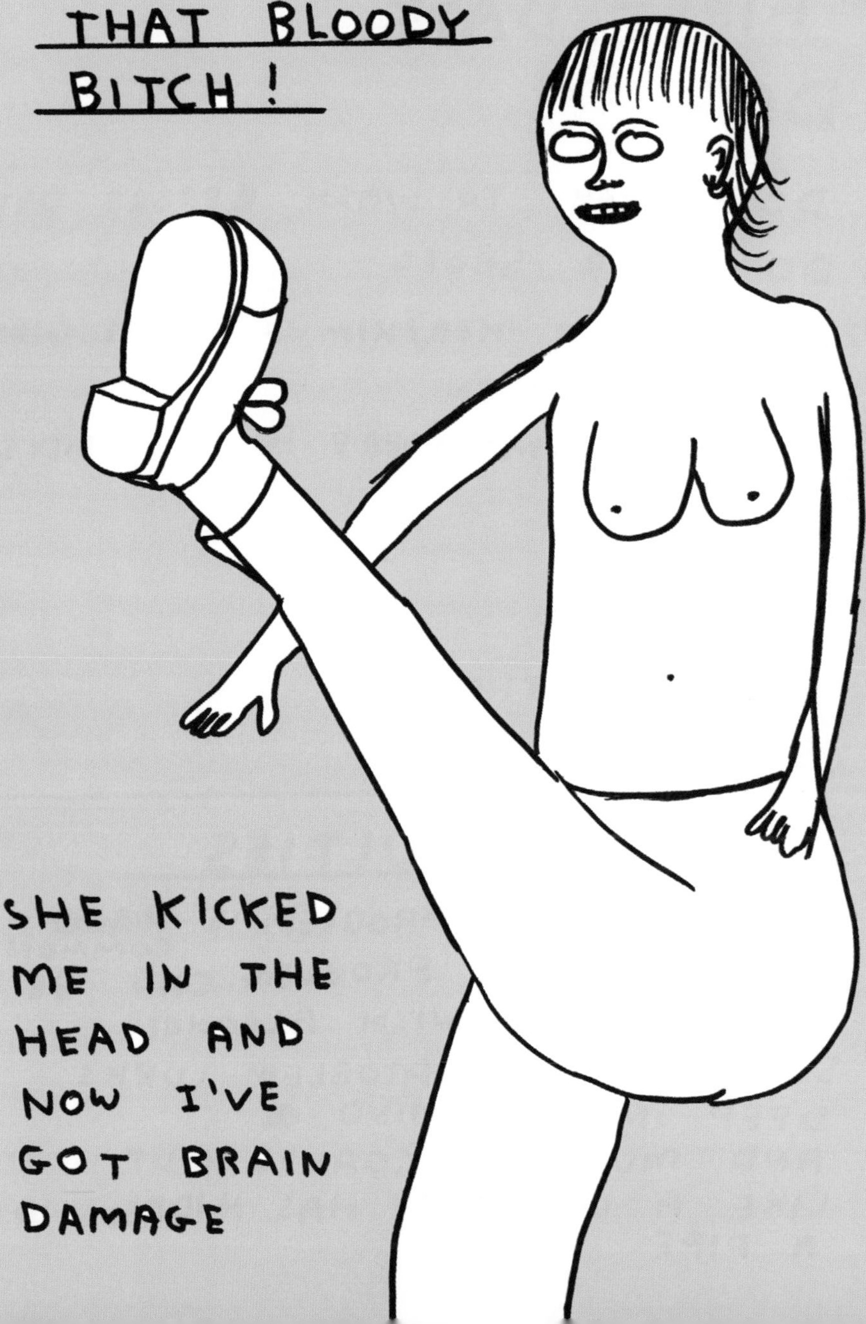
THAT BLOODY BITCH!
SHE KICKED ME IN THE HEAD AND NOW I'VE GOT BRAIN DAMAGE

FIRST DATE

DOs

DO OFFER TO WASH BEFORE DATE

DO WEAR SHOES

DO BRING HER/HIM A SMALL GIFT
EG. KITTEN

DO GO SOMEWHERE QUIET / DIMLY LIT

[redacted]

DON'TS

SHOUT AT THEM

SPIT

SEX DIFFICULTIES

THIS KIND OF PROBLEM IS [redacted] COMMON
SOMETIMES THE PROBLEM CAN BE
EASILY SOLVED WITH ALCOHOL
SOMETIMES THE PROBLEM LURKS
DEEP IN THE MIND [redacted]
AND MUST BE COAXED-OUT
LIKE A CAT THAT HAS HIDDEN IN
A PIPE

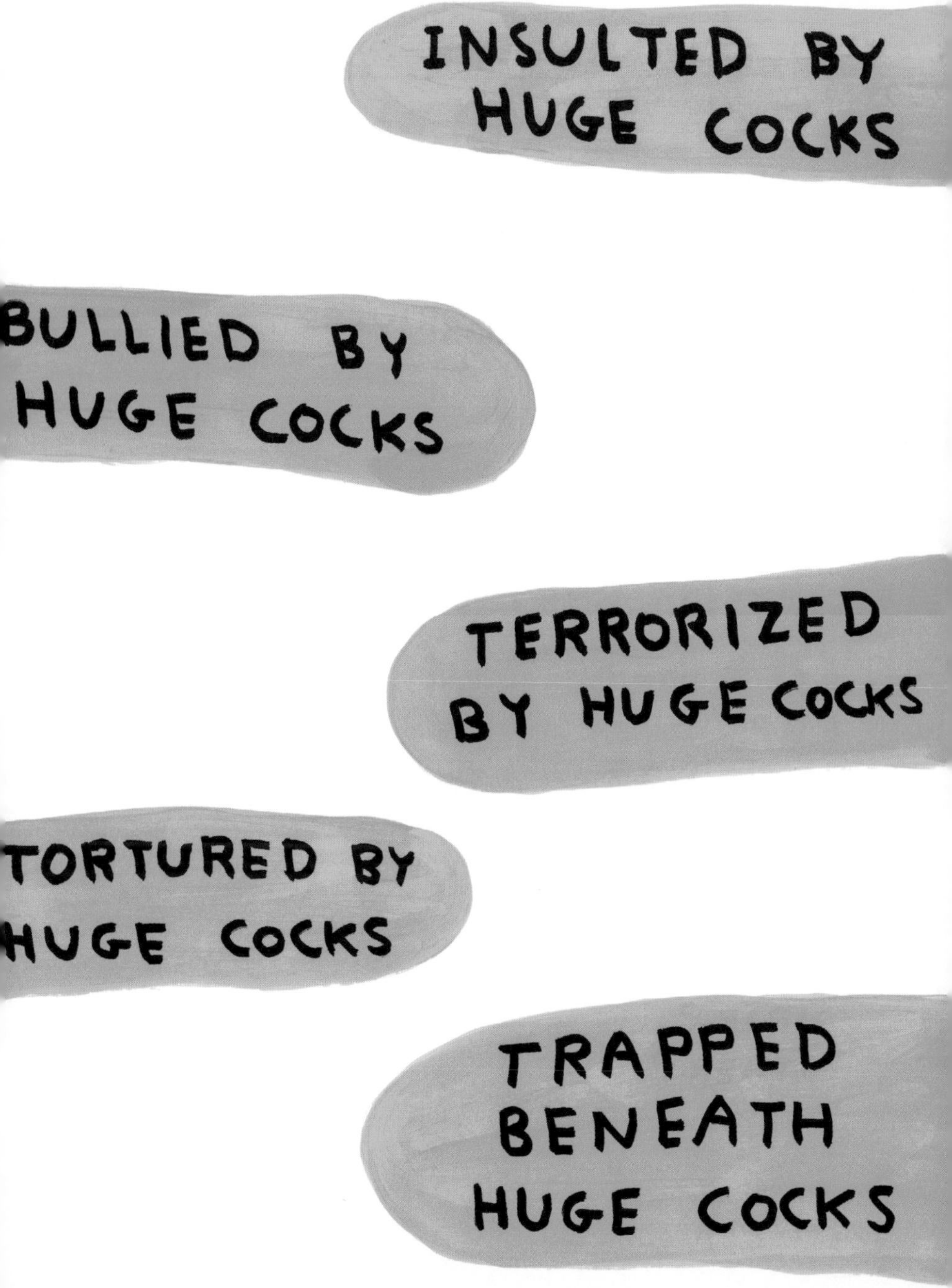
INSULTED BY HUGE COCKS
BULLIED BY HUGE COCKS
TERRORIZED BY HUGE COCKS
TORTURED BY HUGE COCKS
TRAPPED BENEATH HUGE COCKS

QUESTIONNAIRE ABOUT YOUR SEX PROBLEMS

RATE AS SEXY OUT OF 1000 :

1. MEN
2. WOMEN
3. MINERS
4. GRAVES
5. CATS
6. BOOKS
7. SLUGS
8. WINDOWS
9. INK-JET PRINTERS
10. HARMONICA PLAYING
11. RIVERS

SEXYEST PART OF THE BODY?

EYE?
EAR?
SHOULDER?
BRAIN?
KIDNEY?
JEWELS?
TOE?
HAIR?
OTHER?

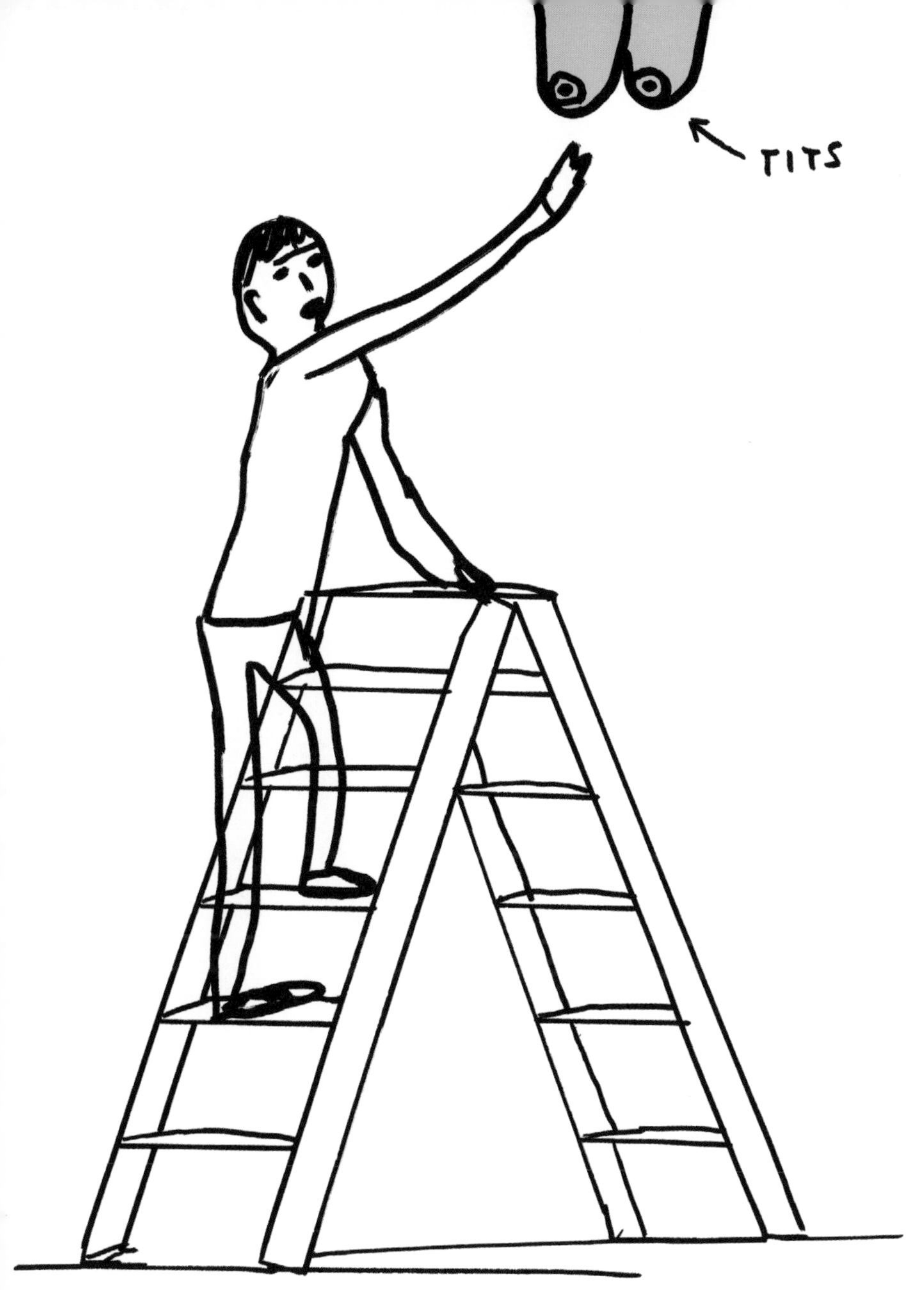
TITS

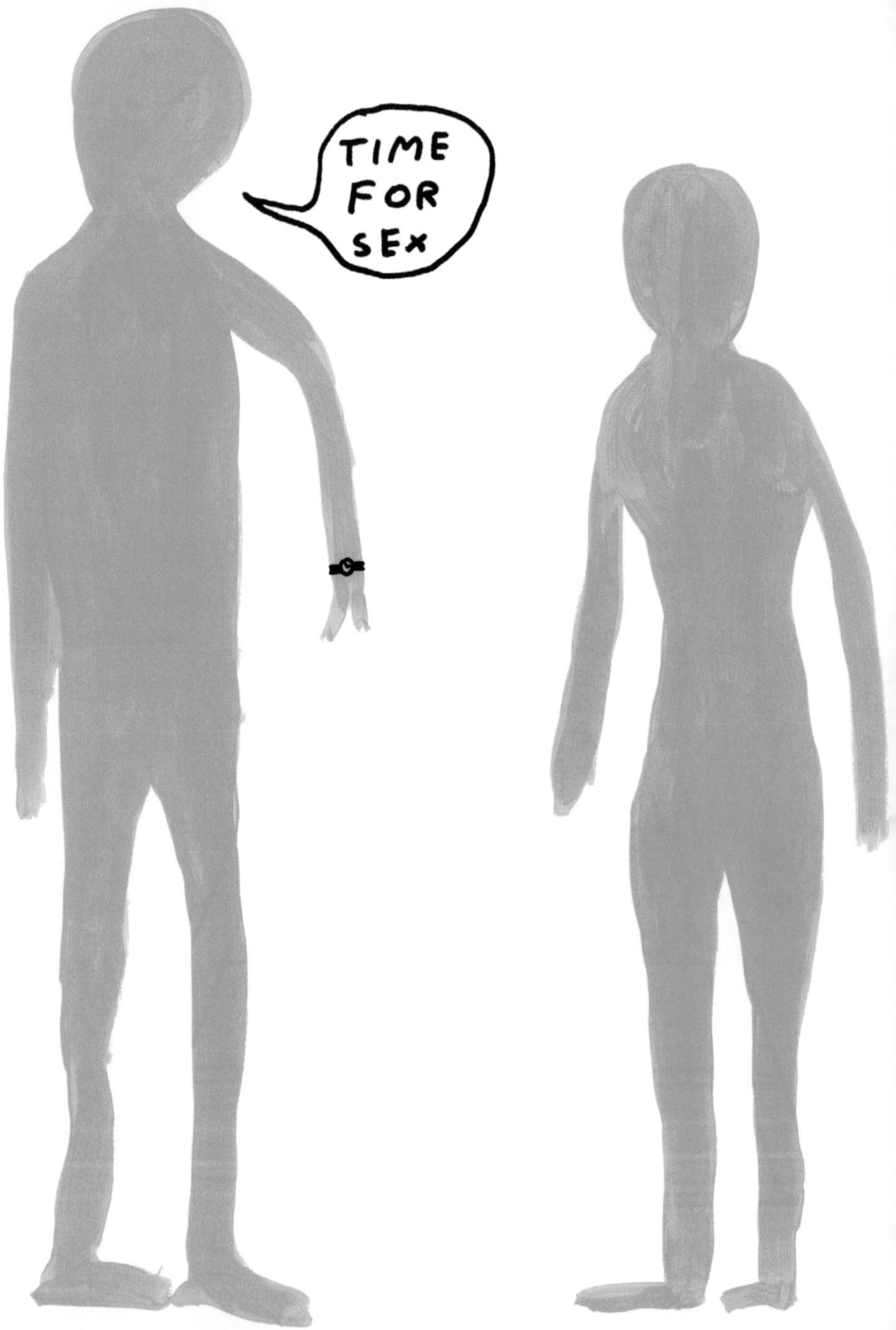
TIME FOR SEX

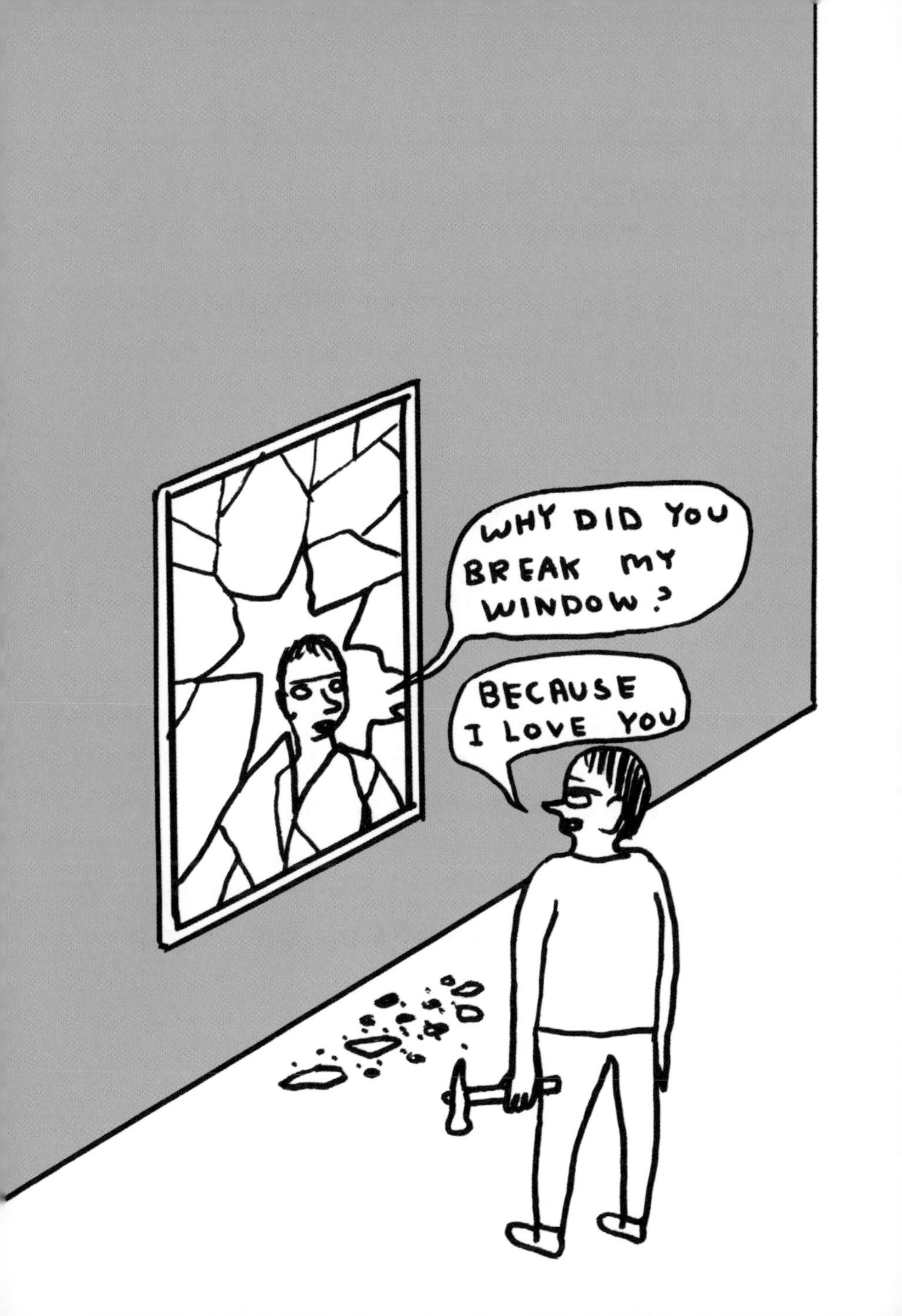
WHY DID YOU BREAK MY WINDOW?
BECAUSE I LOVE YOU

Rules of Love

LOVE DOES NOT HIT, PUNCH, BITE, STAB, ATTEMPT TO POISON, ETC.

LOVE DOES NOT USE ABUSIVE LANGUAGE WHEN TALKING ABOUT A FRIEND

LOVE DOES NOT STEAL FROM A FRIEND'S HOUSE

LOVE IS NICE TO A FRIEND'S WIFE/HUSBAND/CHILDREN/FAMILY

LOVE DOES NOT ATTEMPT TO HAVE SEXUAL RELATIONS WITH A FRIEND'S WIFE/HUSBAND/CHILDREN/FAMILY

LOVE DOES NOT LAUGH WHEN A FRIEND IS INJURED OR SAD

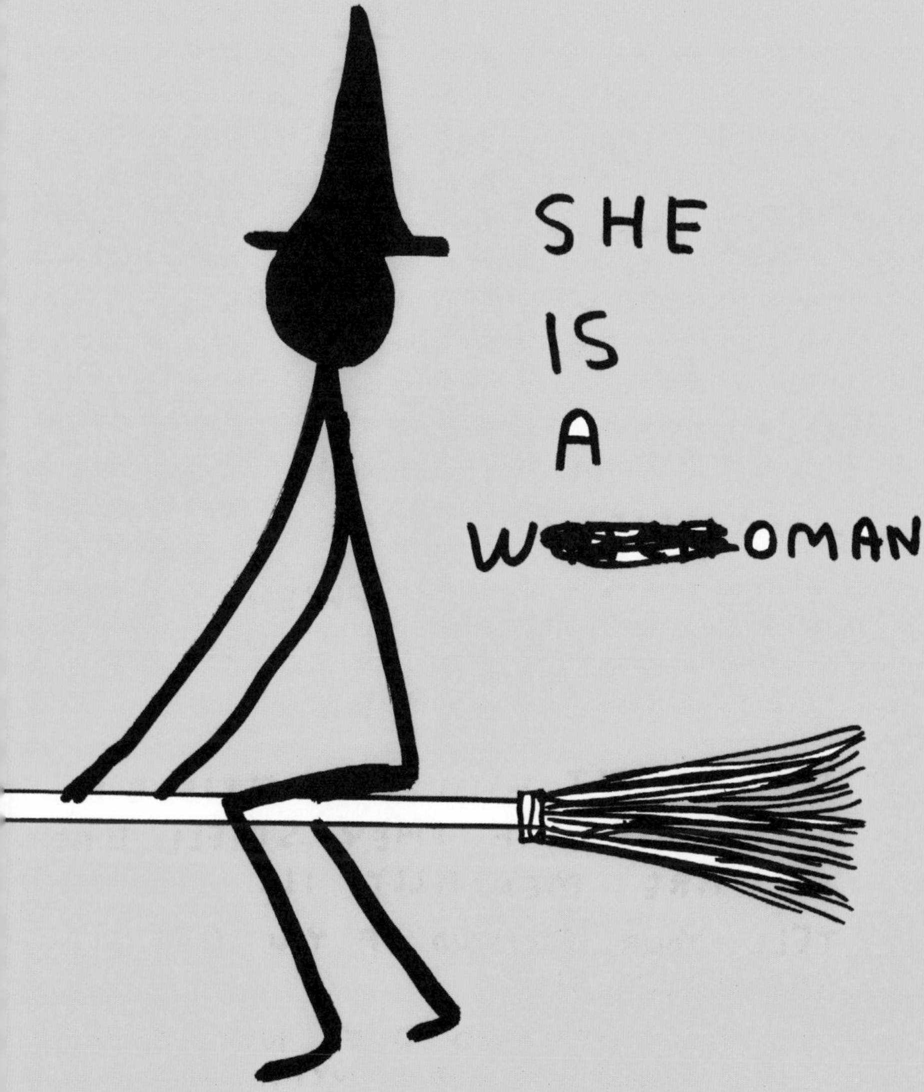
SHE
IS
A
W[redacted]OMAN

FOR A LASTING FRIENDSHIP

-BUY YOUR FRIEND EXPENSIVE FRIEND-GIFTS ON HIM/HER BIRTHDAY AND AT CHRISTMAS AND OTHER RELIGIOUS TREAT-OCCASIONS

- ATTEND EVENTS WITH YOUR FRIEND E.G. TRACTORS

- TRY TO BE ENCOURAGING TO YOUR FRIEND EVEN IF S/HE IS A WORTHLESS BASTARD

- COMPLIMENT YOUR FRIEND ON ITS/HER APPEARANCE EVEN IF THEY LOOK LIKE A RAT

- BE HONEST WITH YOUR FRIEND: TELL THEM IF THEY SMELL BAD OR ARE MENTALLY ILL

- TELL YOUR FRIEND IF YOU ARE MENTALLY ILL

- IF YOUR FRIEND DOES NOT WANT TO BE YOUR FRIEND ANYMORE YOU JUST HAVE TO FUCKING ACCEPT IT

REMEMBER:

FRIENDSHIP HAS NO LEGAL BASIS.
IF YOUR FRIEND ASKS YOU TO SIGN
A CONTRACT THEN YOU SHOULD
REFUSE AND TERMINATE THE
FRIENDSHIP IMMEDIATELY.

CASE STUDY

HE WAS MY FRIEND
I WAS VERY TENDER TOWARDS HIM
BUT HE DISLIKED TENDERNESS
SO NOW I KICK HIM
AND I BITE HIM
AND I RUB DIRT IN HIS WOUNDS
AND WE HAVE A MUCH BETTER
RELATIONSHIP

I LIVE APART [redacted]
FROM MY WIFE NOW
IT IS FOR THE [redacted] BEST

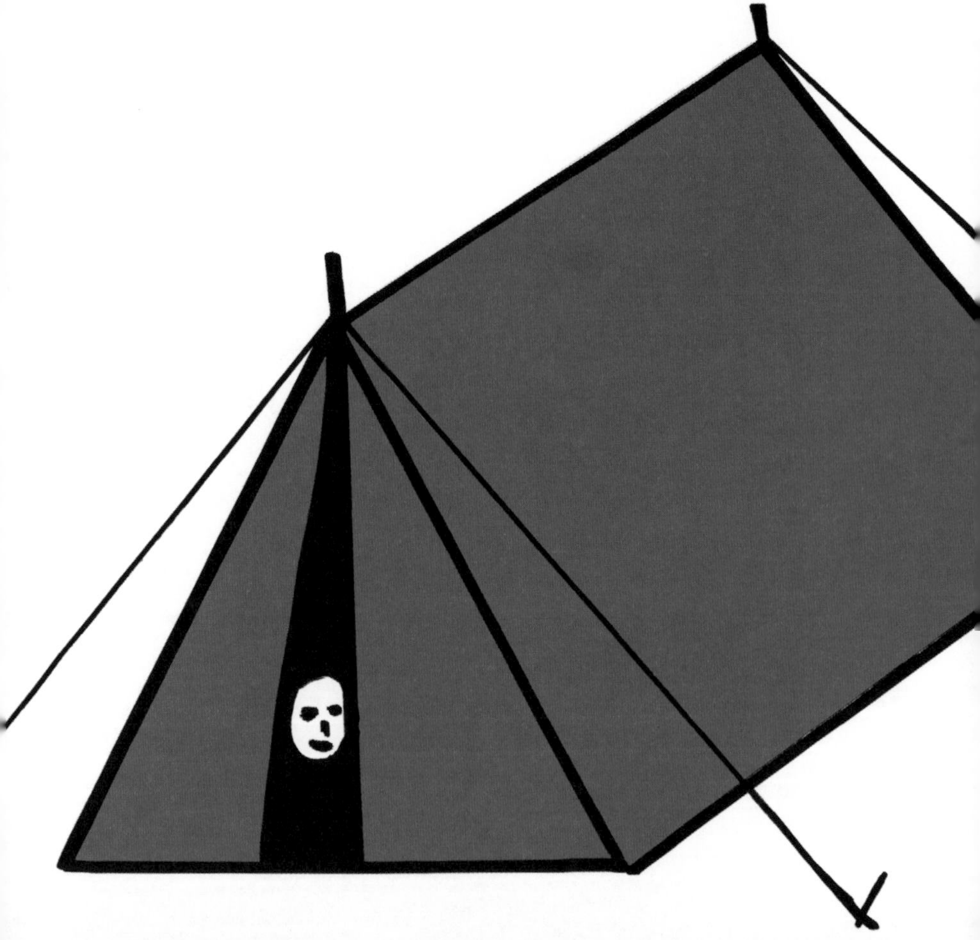

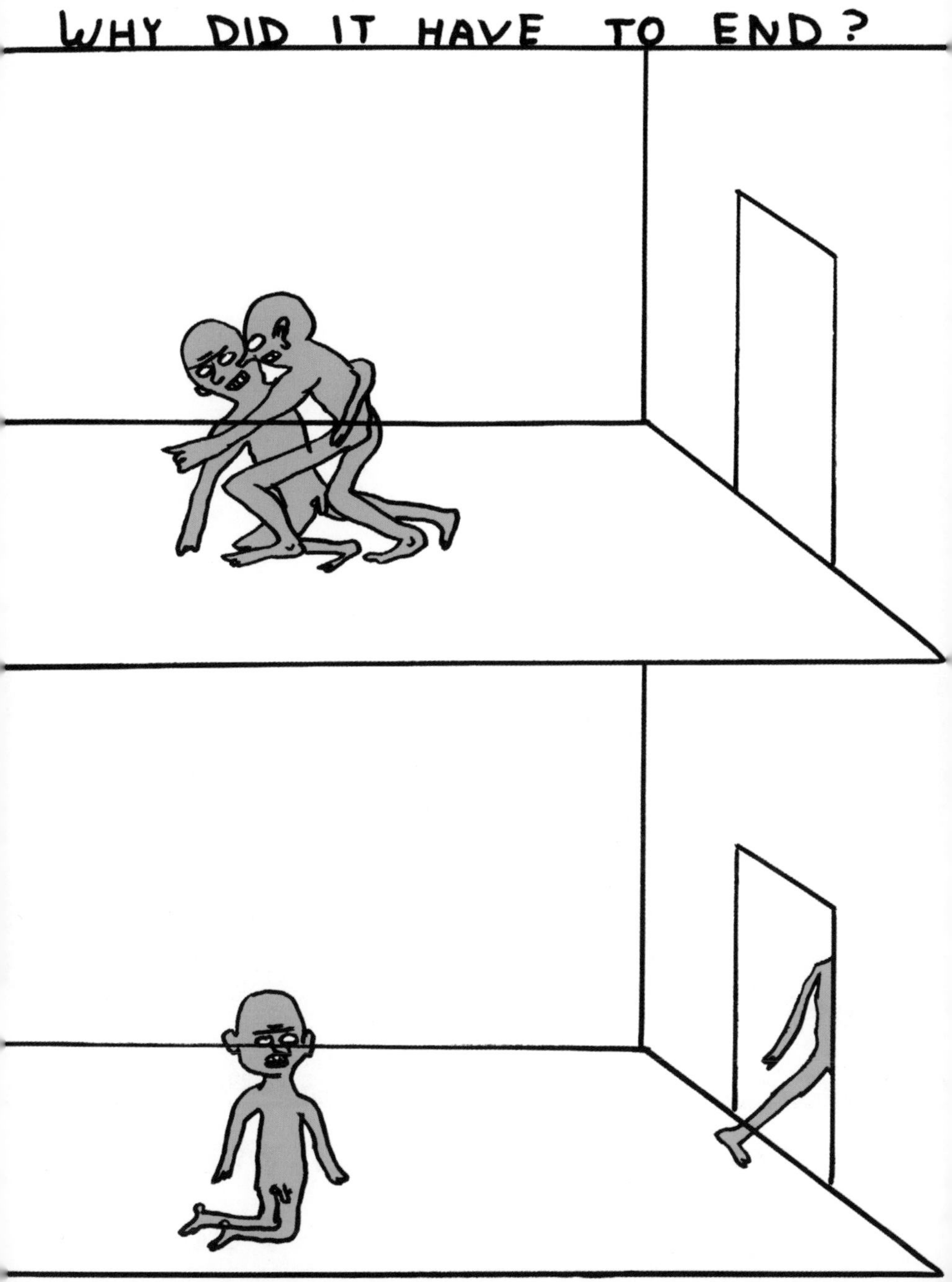
WHY DID IT HAVE TO END?

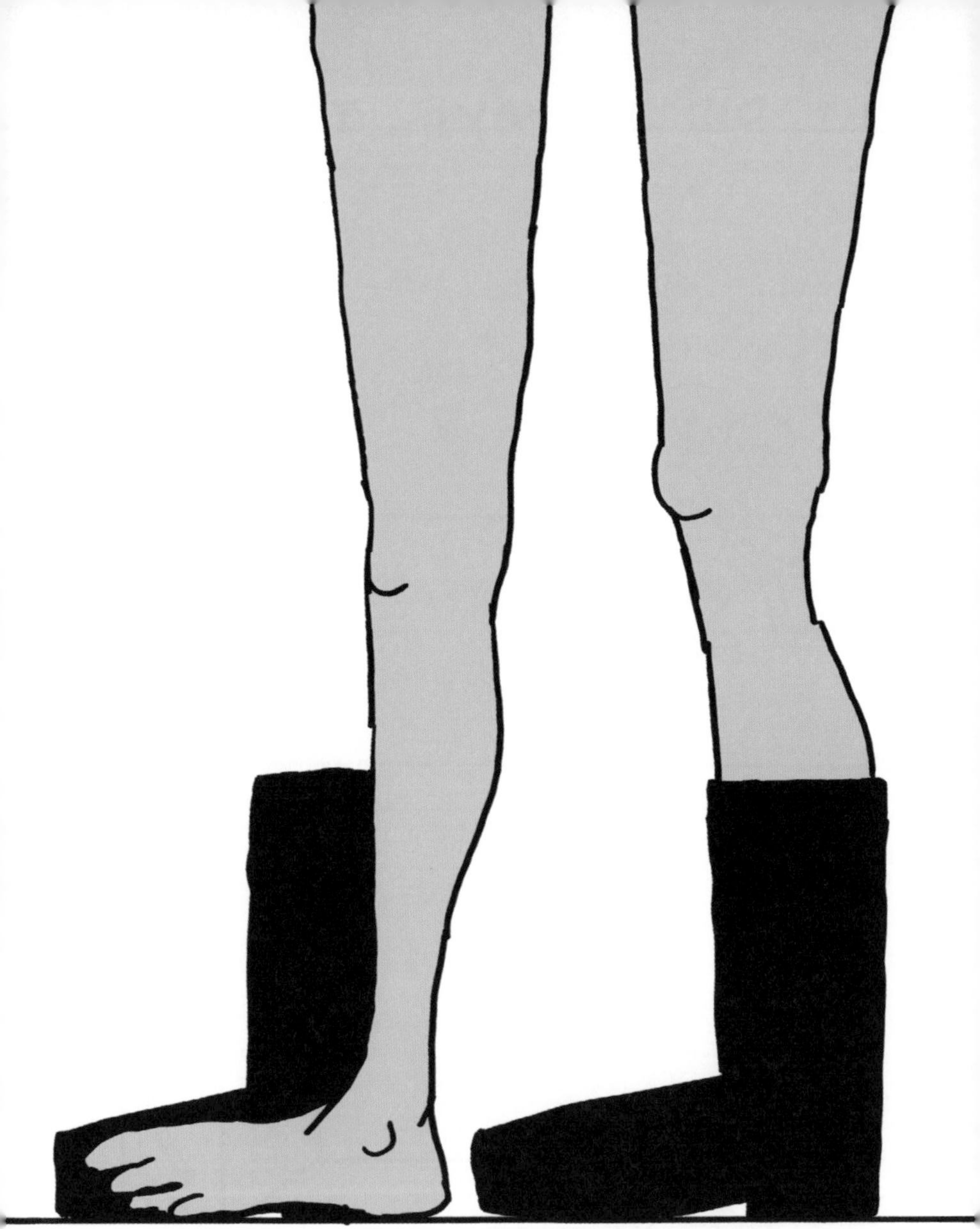

PLEASE ALLOW ME TO
SHOW YOU MY FOOT

CHAPTER THREE
TREATMENT

BEING SELF-CRITICAL

I AM AN ARSONIST

I AM A RAPIST

I AM A MURDERER

I TORTURE PEOPLE IN A SECRET DUNGEON

I DO NOT RESPECT ANYONE

I DO NOT RESPECT ANYTHING

I DO NOT EAT ENOUGH VEGETABLES

INK BLOB TEST

THE BLOBS ARE MADE AT RANDOM
THEY ARE NOT ART
THEY ARE ACCIDENTS
THEY ARE HORRIBLY UGLY
YOU WILL BE INVITED TO LOOK
AT THEM
YOU MUST THEN SAY WHAT YOU
THINK THE BLOBS ARE
YOU DON'T HAVE TO TAKE THE
TEST ▬
IF YOU DON'T WANT TO

FOOTPRINT

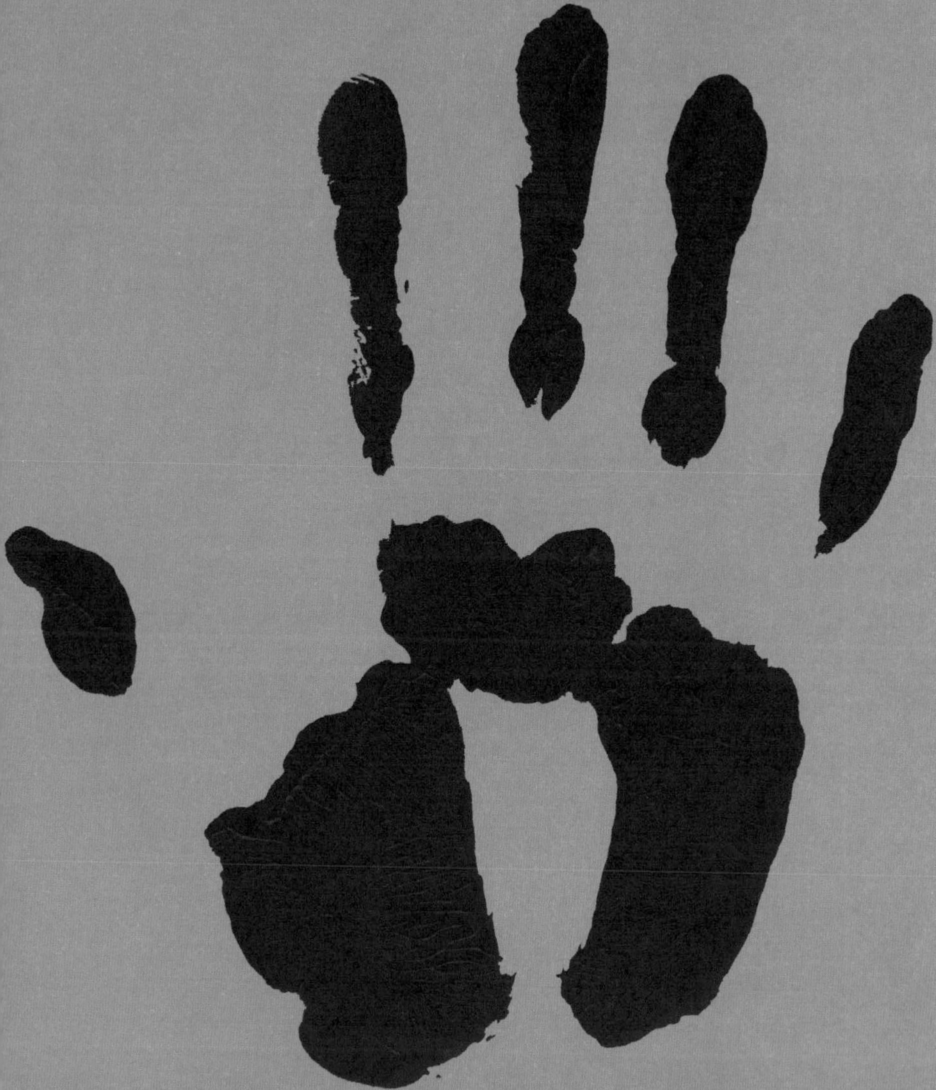

BEING PART OF A CLAN

EVERYONE WANTS TO BE PART OF
A CLAN
IT'S NORMAL
HUMAN BEINGS ARE SOCIAL
CREATURES
LIKE GOATS
BUT THERE ARE RULES TO
BEING PART OF A CLAN
THAT MUST BE FOUND-OUT
AND ADHERED-TO

E.G. PLAYING THE PIPES, ETC.

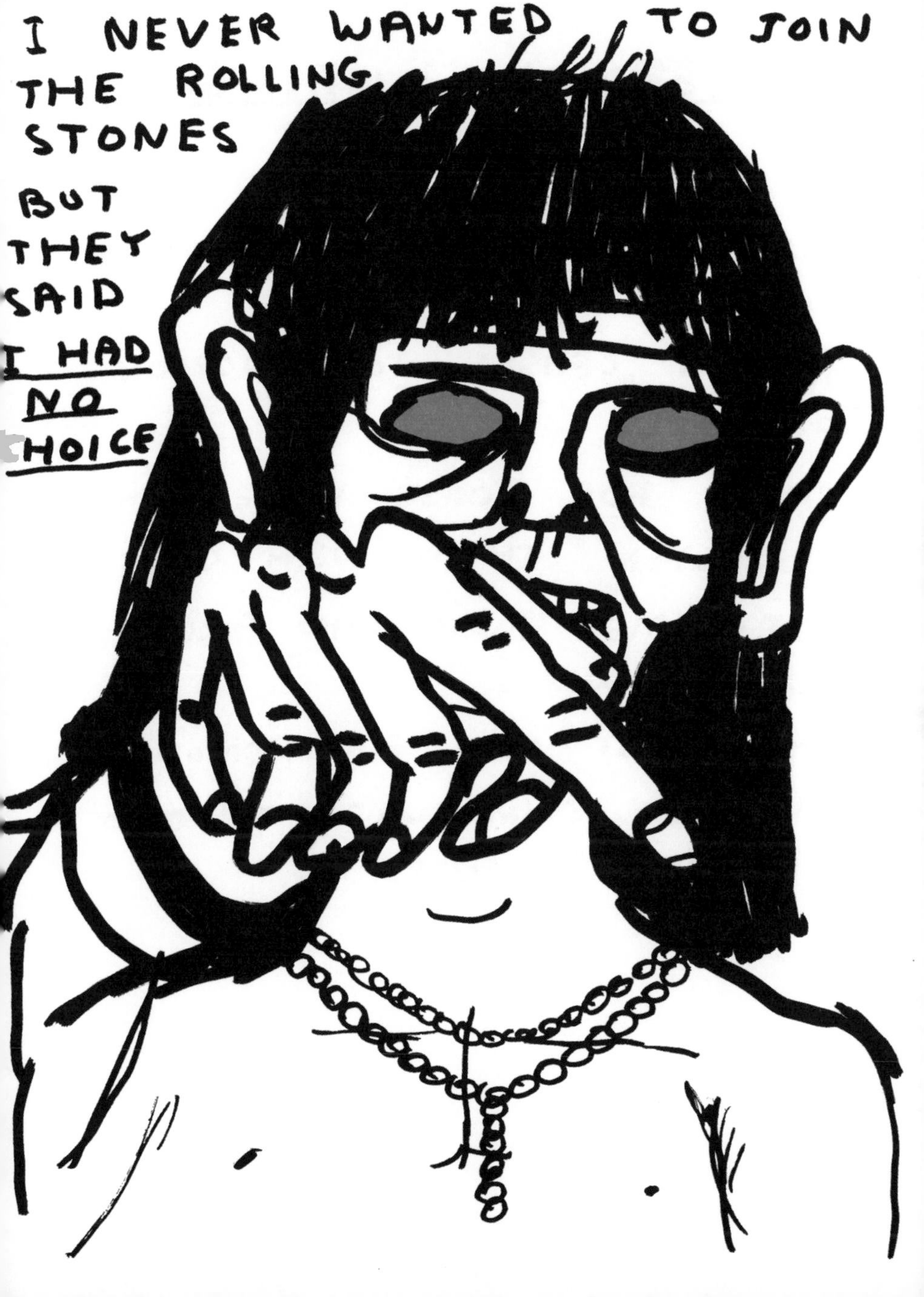
I NEVER WANTED TO JOIN THE ROLLING STONES
BUT THEY SAID I HAD NO CHOICE

INTERNAL WIRING

WE ALL HAVE INTERNAL WIRING

SOMETIMES THIS WIRING COMES
LOOSE

AND IT CEASES TO FUNCTION
PROPERLY

CHECK FOR LOOSE WIRES AND
RE-FASTEN THEM WITH GLUE

SOMETIMES DUST CAN ACCUMULATE
ON THE WIRES

THE DUST CAN BE REMOVED
WITH A MINIATURE ~~————~~
VACUUM CLEANER

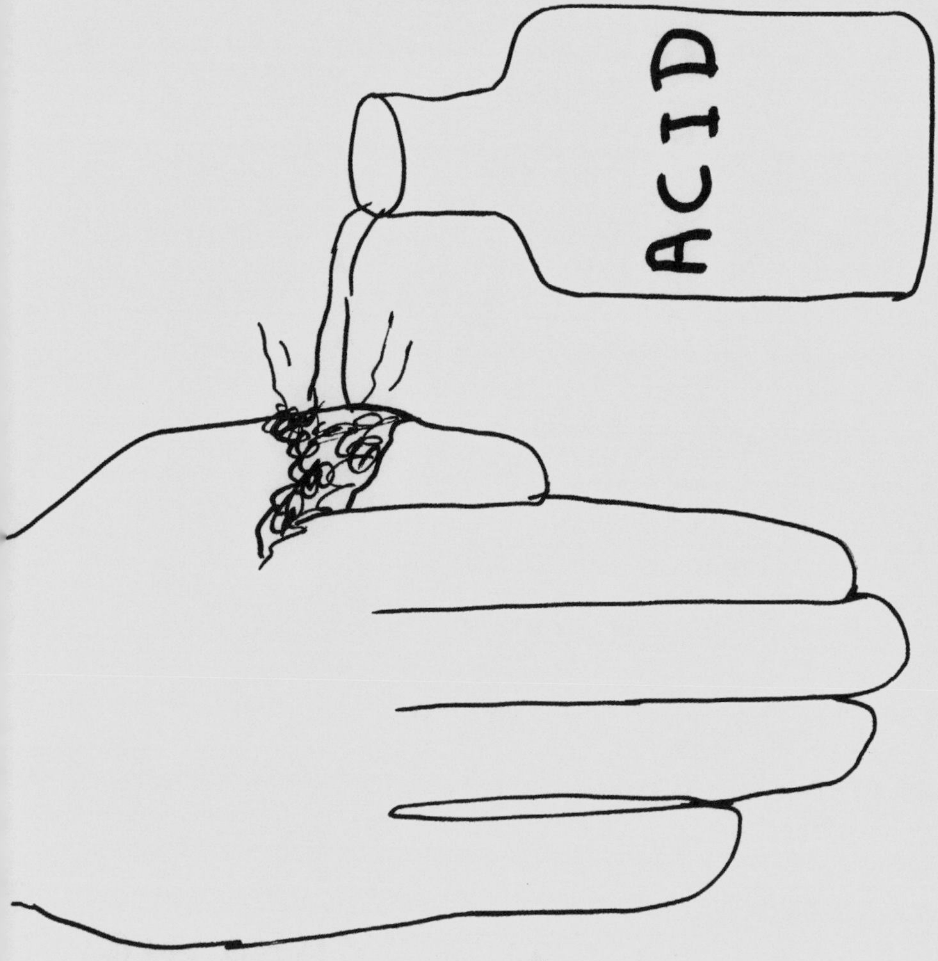
ACID

DON'T
DO THIS

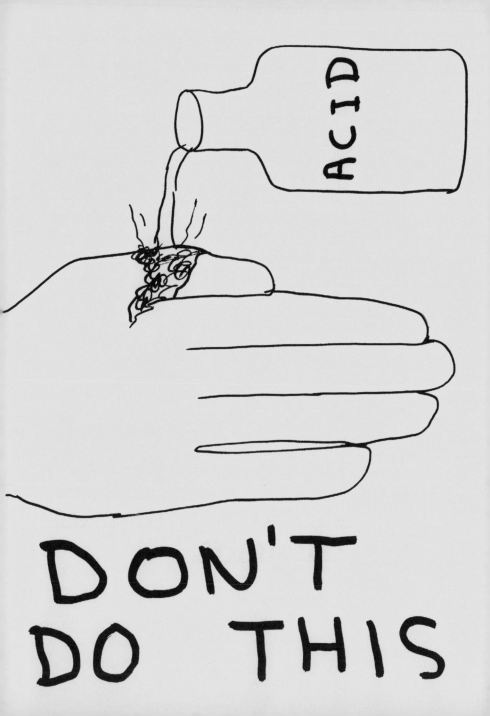

VALUES

DON'T KNOW WHAT VALUES ARE?
WE ALL HAVE VALUES:
THINGS THAT ARE IMPORTANT
TO US~~ME~~ :

LOVE
FRIENDSHIP
FAMILY
MOTORBIKES
WRESTLING
BATTLE RE-ENACTMENTS
COCK-RACING , ETC.

METHODS FOR CHANGING OUR THOUGHTS

POST-IT NOTES

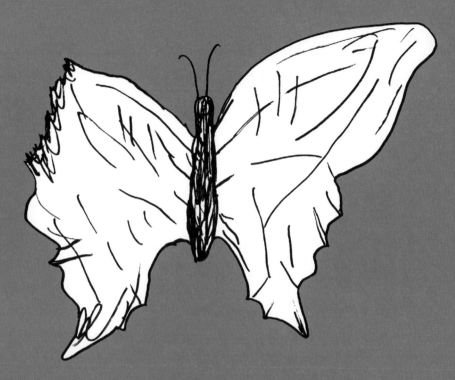

I STARTED EATING IT
BUT THEN I REALIZED
IT WAS BEAUTIFUL
AND I DECIDED TO ▬▬▬
STOP EATING IT

CONCEALED LOGIC OF OUR DOINGS

- "I HIDE SHOES OF WIFE-HUSBAND"
  - IS OK
- "I SPEAK IN SILLY VOICE"
  - IT'S OK
- "I PLAY 'CRAZY MONKEY' GAME ALL DAY WITHOUT REST PERIODS"
  - IT'S OK
- "I SNIFF GLUE AND OTHER TREAT-SOLVENTS"
  - IS OK
- "I EAT SPIDERS"
  - IS OK
- "I PUT FOREIGN BODIES IN MY CAVITY"
  - IT'S OK
- "I HIDE MEDICATION OF WIFE-HUSBAND"
  - IS OK

" I ALLOW COMPLETE SHITTING-
FREEDOM TO PET-FRIEND"
- IT'S OK
" I HOLD MY NEIGHBOUR AS
FRIEND-HOSTAGE "
- IS OK

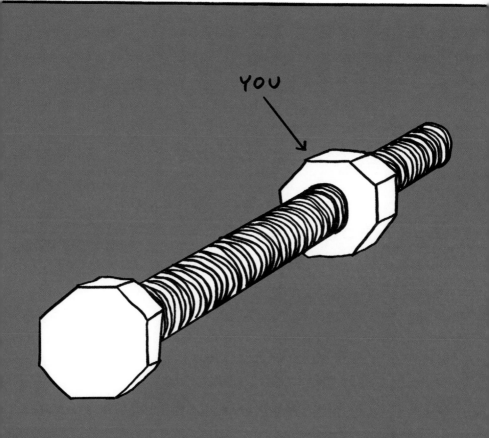

USE OF ELECTRIC SHOCKS

ARE YOU HAPPY?

YES: ADMINISTER SHOCK
NO: ADMINISTER SHOCK
DON'T KNOW: ADMINISTER SHOCK

ARE YOU SAD?

YES: ADMINISTER SHOCK
NO: ADMINISTER SHOCK
DON'T KNOW: ADMINISTER SHOCK

ARE YOU WILLING TO TORTURE PEOPLE?

YES: ADMINISTER SHOCK
NO: ADMINISTER SHOCK
DON'T KNOW: ADMINISTER SHOCK

DO YOU LIKE GETTING ELECTRIC SHOCKS?

YES: ADMINISTER SHOCK
NO: ADMINISTER SHOCK
DON'T KNOW: ADMINISTER SHOCK

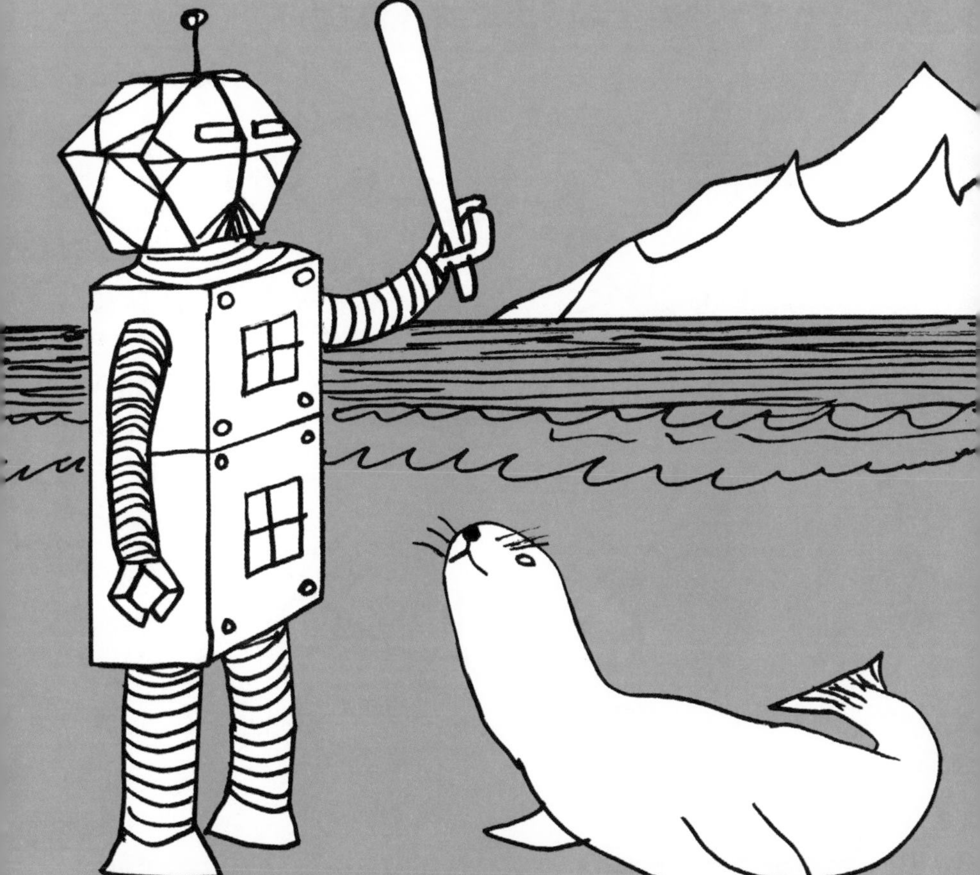

MOTHER! THE ALARM CLOCK PISSED IN MY BED AGAIN!

AND IT'S NOT EVEN TIME TO WAKE UP

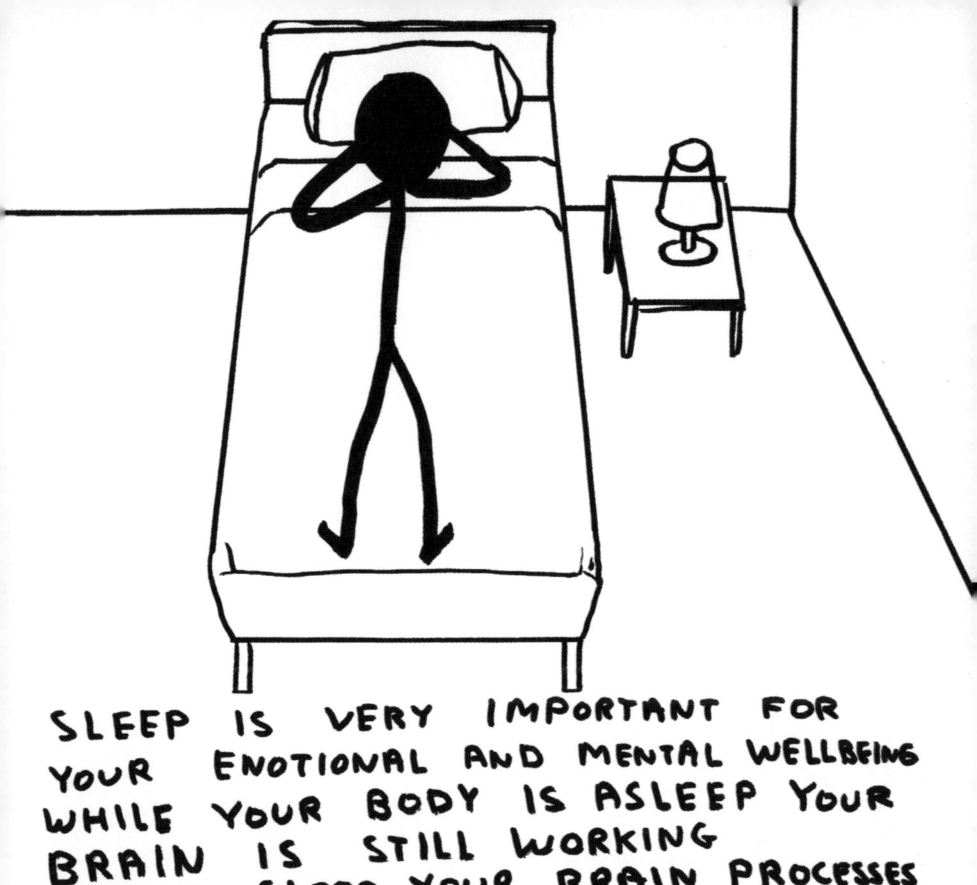

SLEEP IS VERY IMPORTANT FOR
YOUR ENOTIONAL AND MENTAL WELLBEING
WHILE YOUR BODY IS ASLEEP YOUR
BRAIN IS STILL WORKING
DURING SLEEP YOUR BRAIN PROCESSES
ALL THE INFO THAT IT HAS GATHERED
WHILE YOU WERE AWAKE
IT [redacted] DISCARDS MOST OF THIS DATA
BUT KEEPS SMALL USELESS FRAGMENTS
THAT CAN BE EASILY RECALLED.

I CAN'T SLEEP

I KEEP THINKING ABOUT THAT MOUSE WITH THE HUMAN EAR GROWING ON IT.

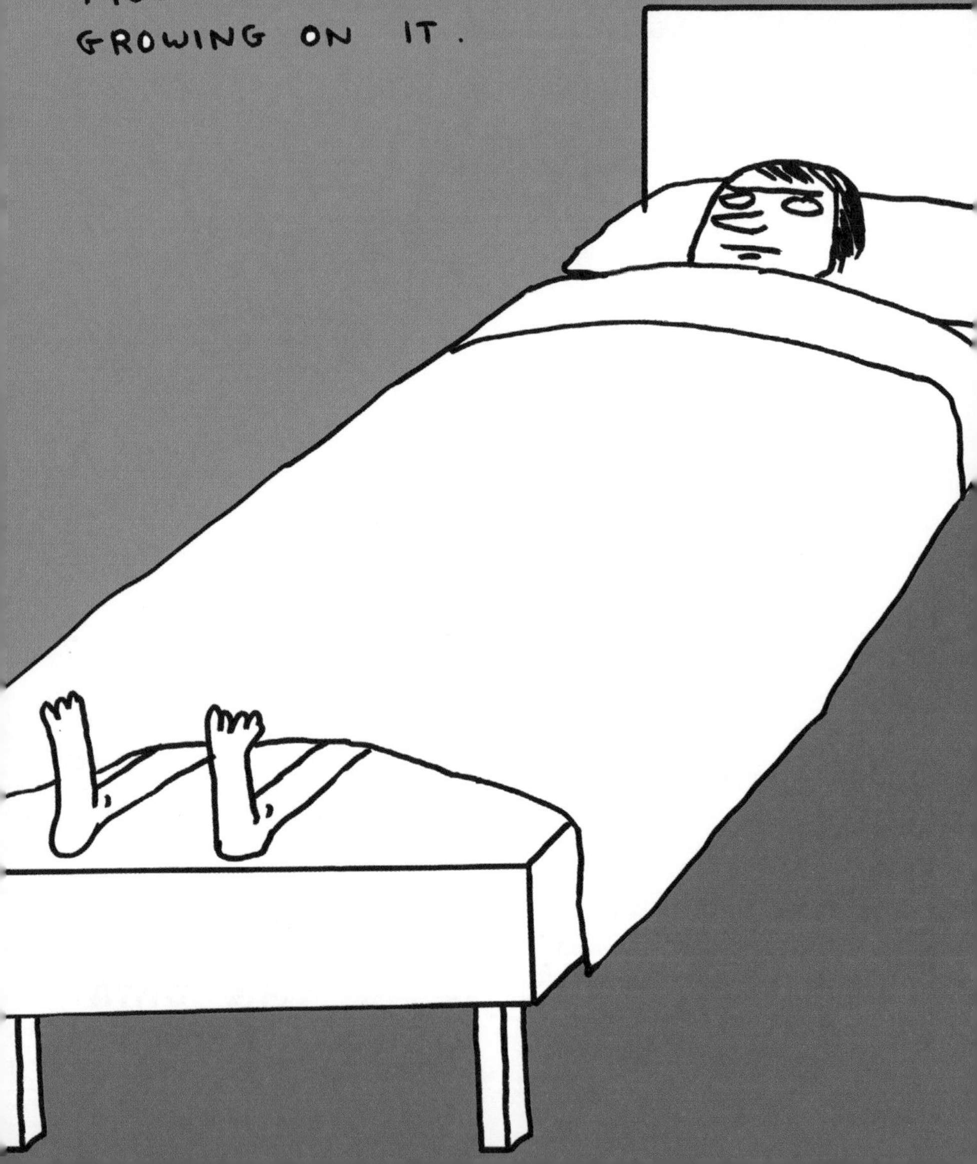

INTERPRETATION OF DREAMS

DREAM ONE

I AM LOCKED INSIDE A CABINET
THE CABINET IS MADE OF WOOD
IT IS DARK INSIDE THE CABINET
IT IS COMPLETELY SILENT

DREAM TWO

I AM A WORM
I AM TUNNELLING BENEATH THE
EARTH
I DO NOT MEET ANY OTHER
WORMS ON MY ▬▬ JOURNEY
OR ANY OTHER LIVING THINGS
IT IS COMPLETELY DARK
IT IS SILENT
APART FROM THE SOUND OF ME
TUNNELLING

DREAM THREE

I AM A PIECE OF TOAST
I AM IN A TOASTER BEING TOASTED
IT IS A NICE FEELING
I POP OUT OF THE TOASTER
AND I AM EATEN BY A
PLEASANT-LOOKING FAT WOMAN

DREAM FOUR

I AM A BUBBLE IN A GLASS
OF FIZZY WATER
IT AM REALLY HAPPY
IT IS REALLY EXCITING IN THE
FIZZY WATER
I AM HAVING A REALLY ▆▆▆
EXCELLENT TIME
I RISE TO THE SURFACE OF
THE WATER
AND I POP

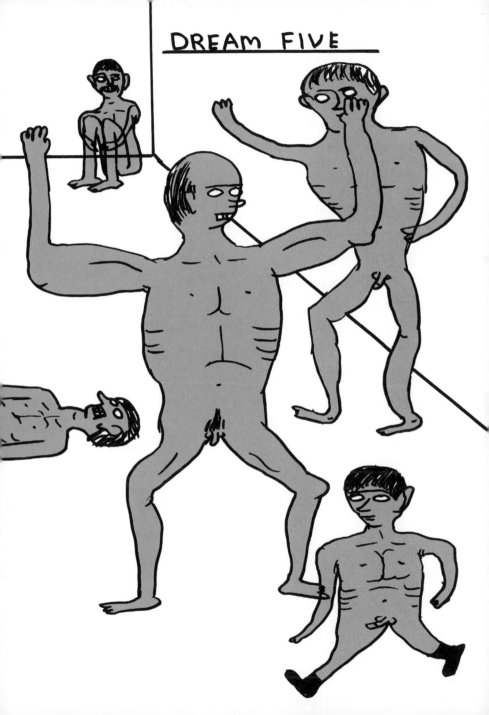

DREAM FIVE

DREAM SIX

I AM A FLEA ON A BIG DOG
I BITE THE DOG AND DRINK HIS
BLOOD
BUT THE DOG DOES NOT NOTICE
AND I AM VERY ANGRY
I BITE THE DOG AGAIN AND
DRINK MORE BLOOD
BUT STILL THE DOG DOES NOT
NOTICE
AND I AM VERY VERY ANGRY
I START SHOUTING ~~THE~~ OBSCENITIES
AT~~ES~~ THE DOG
THE DOG HEARS MY SHOUTING
AND EATS ME

DREAM SEVEN

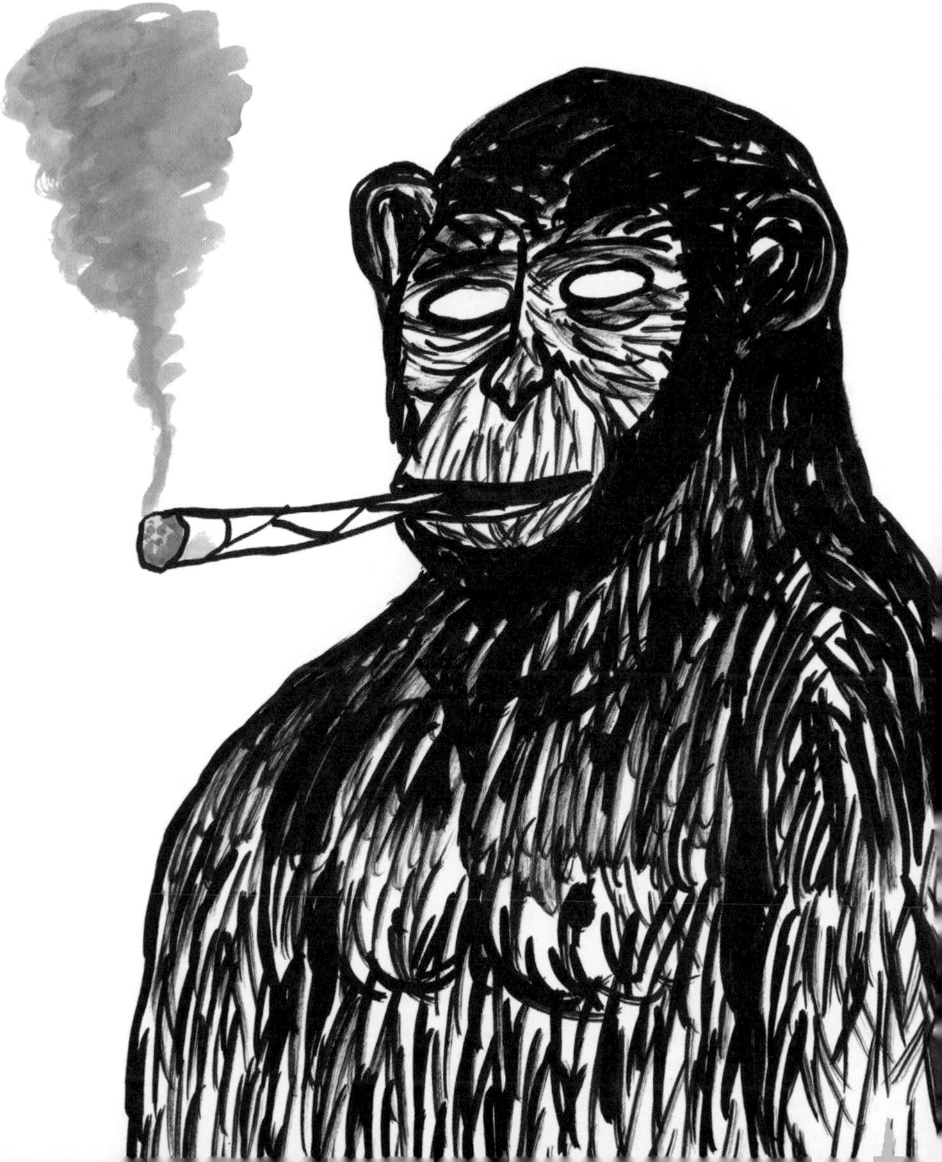

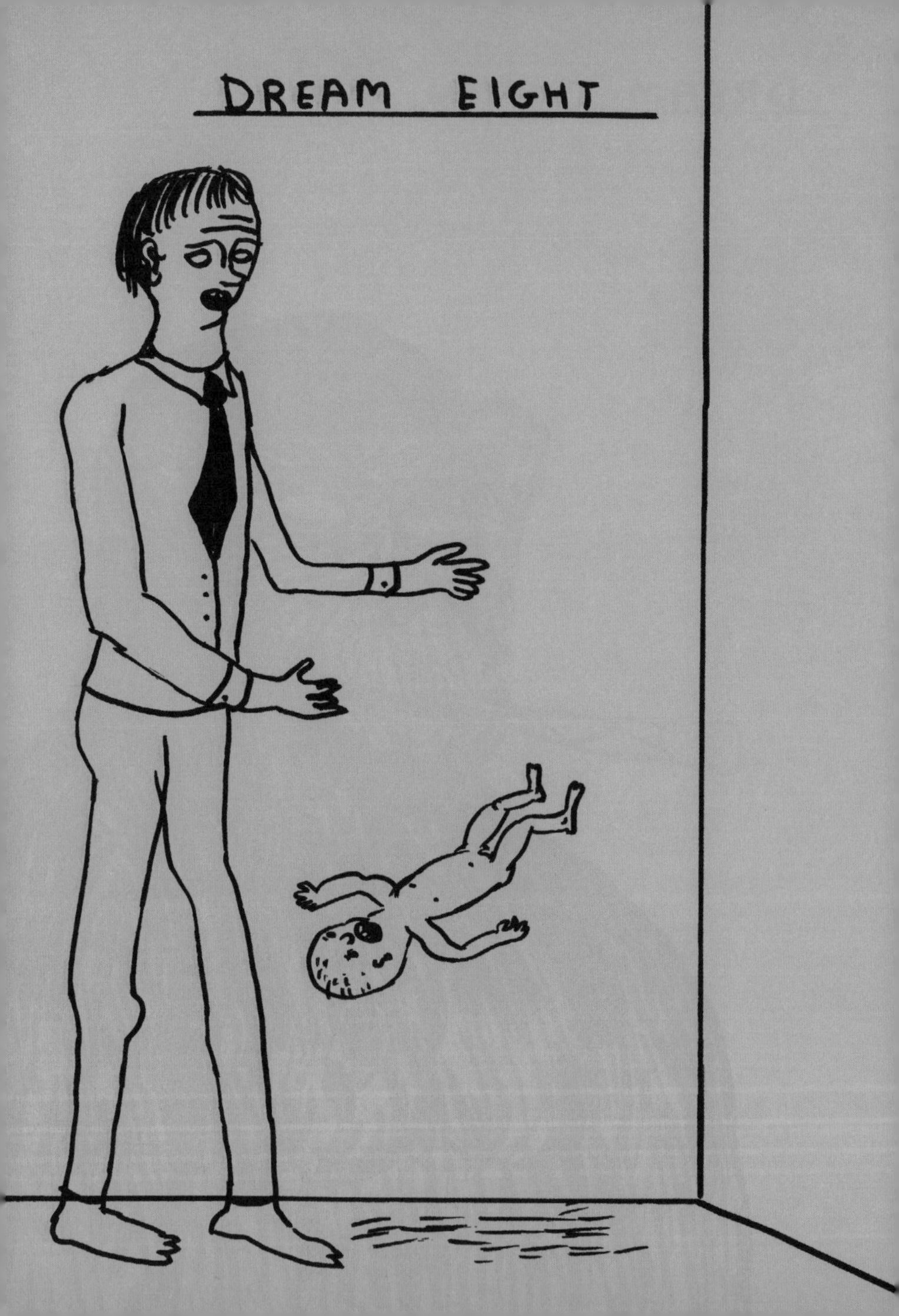
DREAM EIGHT

CHAPTER FIVE: STEPS

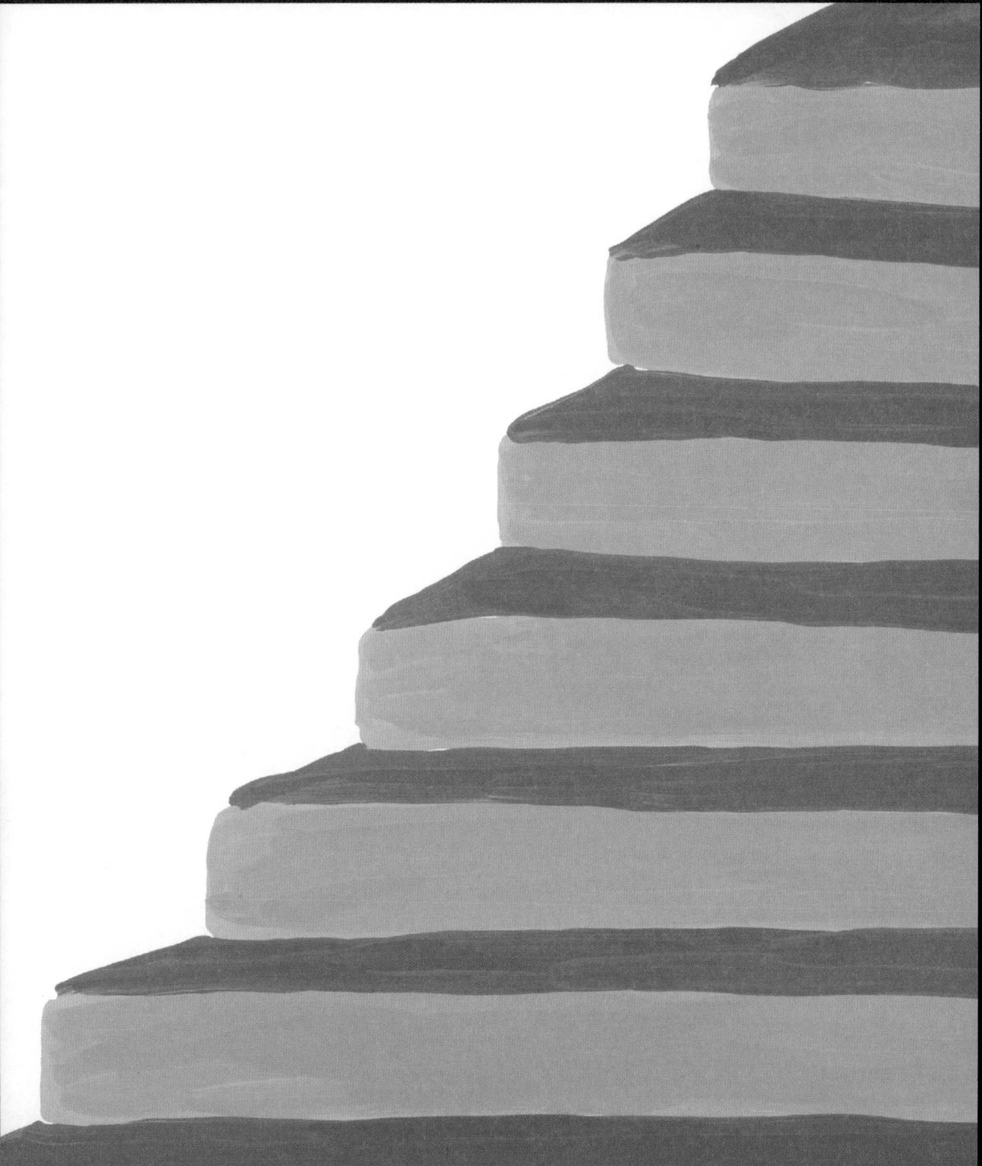

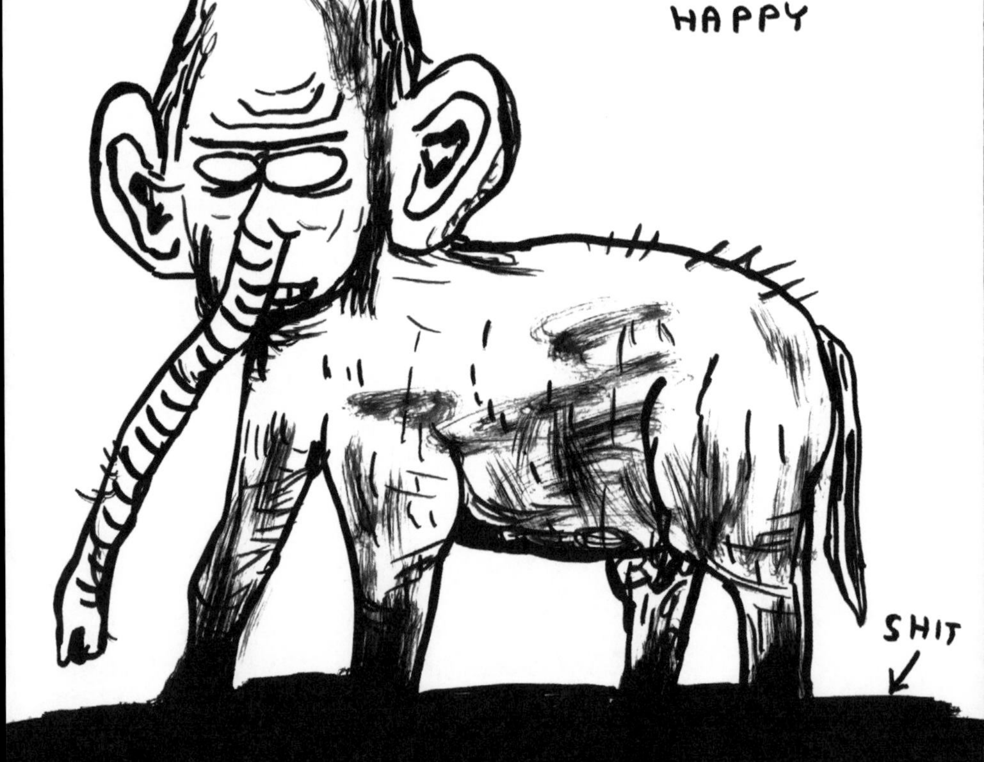
I'M SO
FUCKING
HAPPY
SHIT

12 STEPS TO EMOTIONAL WELL-BEING

1. HIGH-SPEED INTERNET
2. MASSAGE
3. T.V.
4. GET GUINEA PIG
5. DRINK COLA
6. EXPENSIVE SHOES
7. DYE YOUR HAIR
8. MAKE-UP AND/OR FACIAL
9. MOISTURIZER
10. KARAOKE
11. RELATIONSHIP
12. SLEEPING

REMEMBER:

SIX STEPS TO EMOTIONAL INTELLIGENCE

1. KNOW YOUR WORLD

YOUR WORLD MAY DIFFER FROM
THAT OF OTHER PEOPLE

2. KNOW YOURSELF

HAVE A LOOK IN THE MIRROR
DO YOU RECOGNISE THAT PERSON?
DO YOU UNDERSTAND THAT PERSON?
DO YOU FIND THAT PERSON
SEXUALLY ATTRACTIVE?

3. ███ ███

███ ███ ███ ██ ▪
▪ ▪ ███

4. BE YOURSELF

NOT AS EASY AS IT SOUNDS:
WHAT WILL YOU WEAR?
WHAT WILL YOU HAVE FOR DINNER?
WHERE WILL YOU PARK YOUR CAR?

IT'S OK, YOU LOOK FINE

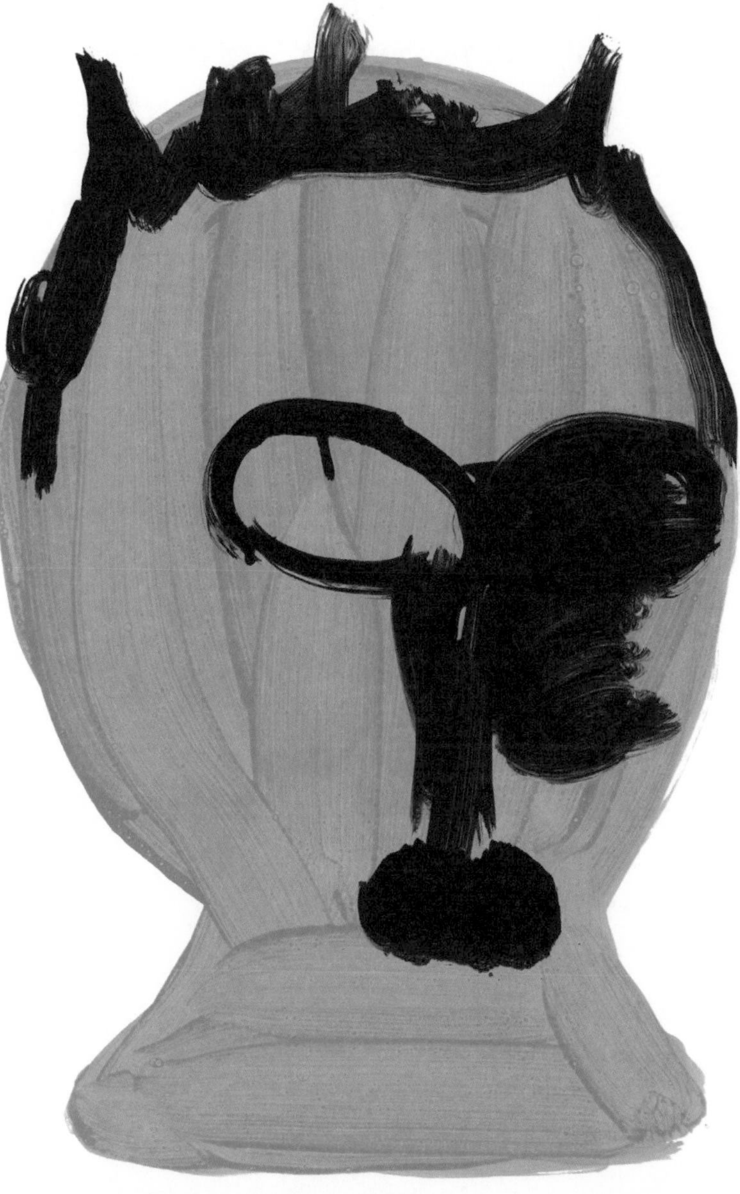

5. TELL YOURSELF THE TRUTH

I LIKE TO WEAR PARTY COSTUMES
(PARTICULARLY SMALL PAPER HATS)
I WOULD LIKE TO PLAY THE
FLUTE
I ONCE ATE A CENTIPEDE
IT TASTED OF METAL

6. CREATE YOURSELF

IF YOU DON'T LIKE YOURSELF
THEN JUST BE SOMEONE ELSE
IT'S EASY
ALL YOU NEED TO DO:
GET HOLD OF THEIR PERSONAL
INFORMATION

7. BUY YOURSELF EXPENSIVE GIFTS

SHOES
RABBIT
NEW CAR
LAWN MOWER
ANTIQUE PISTOL

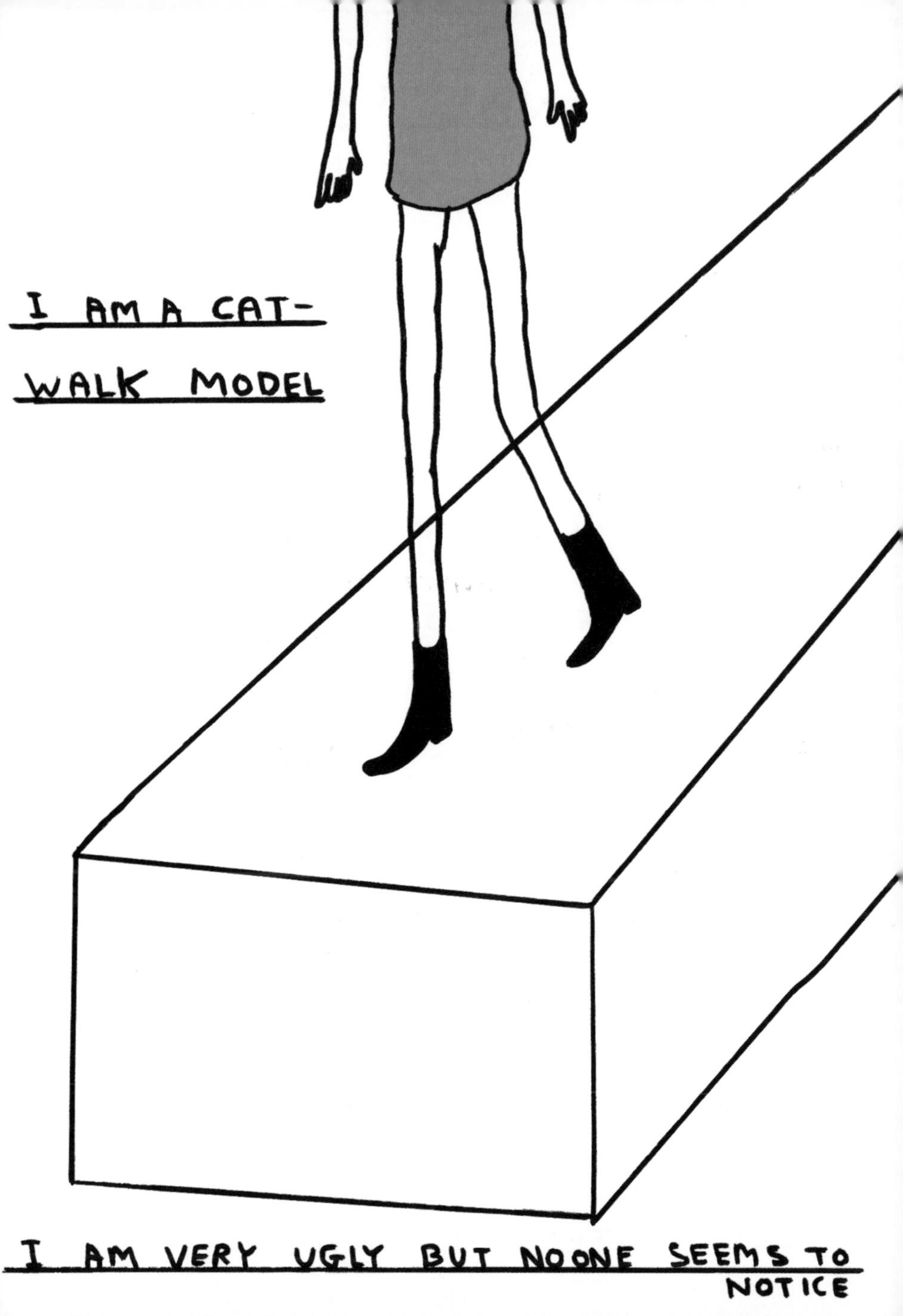
I AM A CAT-
WALK MODEL
I AM VERY UGLY BUT NOONE SEEMS TO
NOTICE

EMOTIONAL SOUP

ONIONS
EMOTIONS
SALT
PEPPER
FISH STOCK

POEM

MUMMY BEAT ME WITH A STICK
MUMMY HIT ME HARD WITH IT
I PUNCHED MUMMY IN THE TIT
MUMMY STABBED ME WITH A FORK

ELIMINATING UNHELPFUL SHIT

SOME SHIT IS HELPFUL
SOME SHIT IS UNHELPFUL
SOME SHIT IS NEITHER HELPFUL
NOR UNHELPFUL
IT IS BENIGN SHIT
TRY TO IDENTIFY DIFFERENT TYPES
OF SHIT
ELIMINATE THE UNHELPFUL SHIT

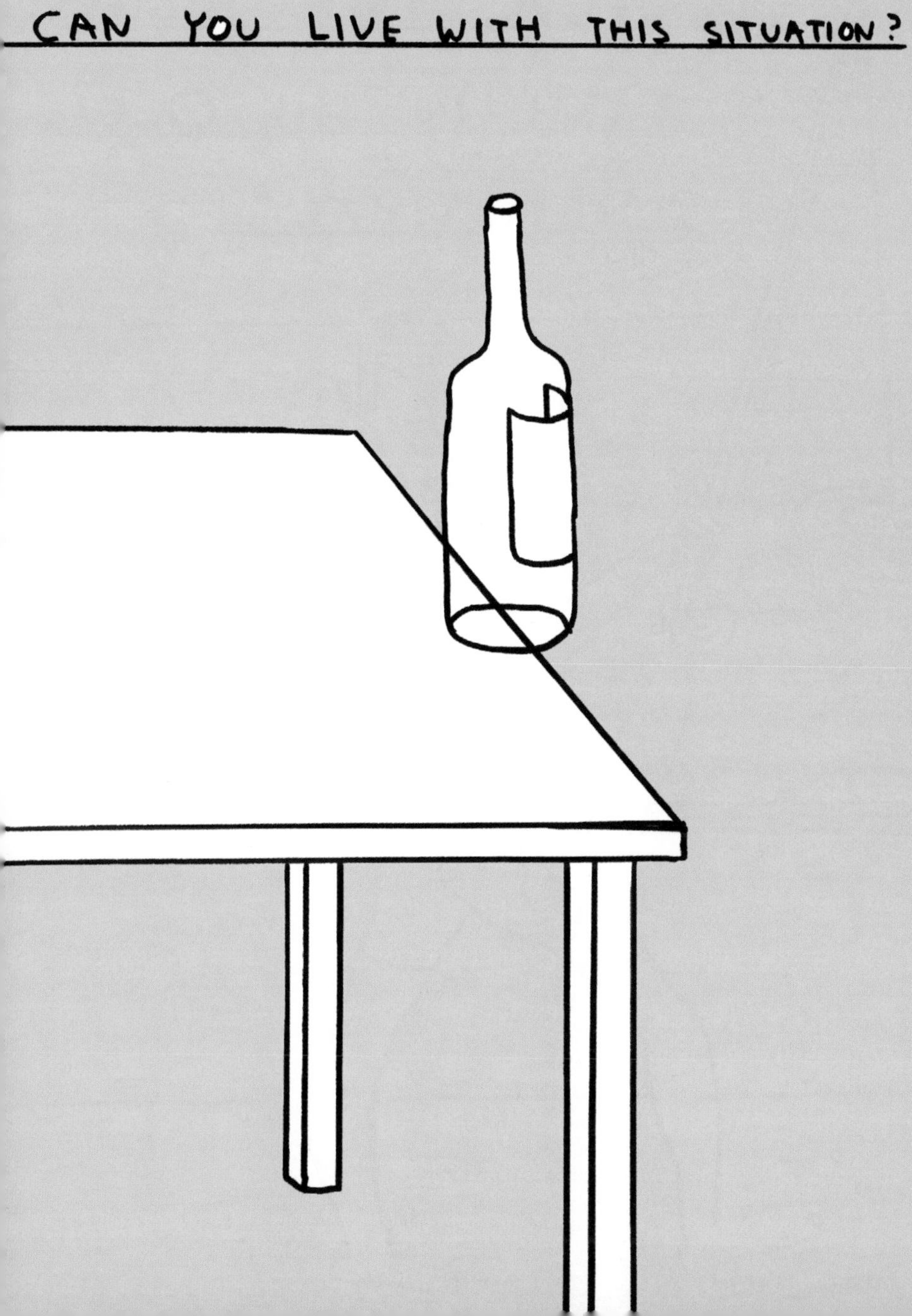
CAN YOU LIVE WITH THIS SITUATION?

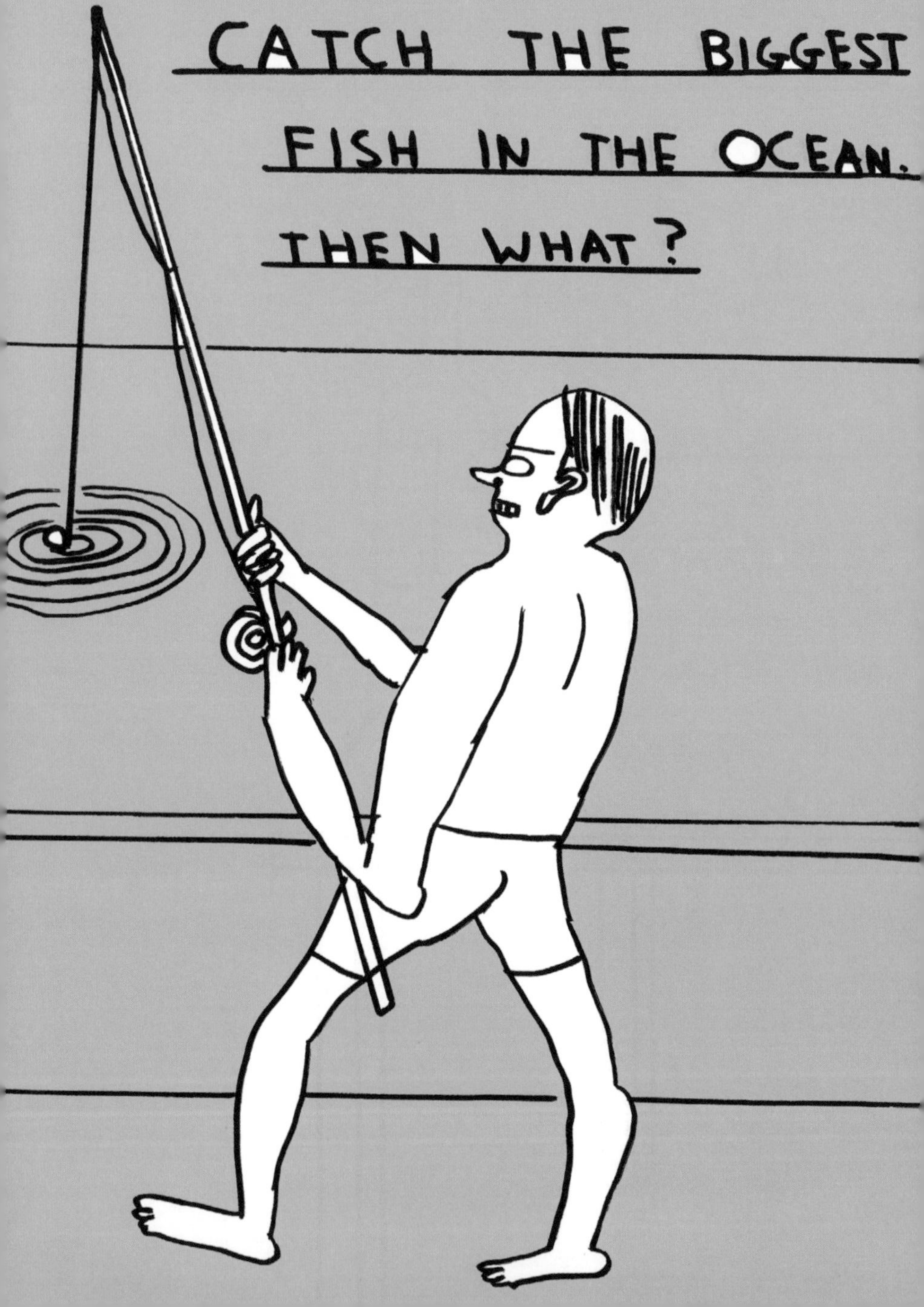
CATCH THE BIGGEST FISH IN THE OCEAN. THEN WHAT?

CHAPTER SIX
LEARNING NEW BEHAVIOUR

IN SOME WAYS WE ARE LIKE THE DOG OR THE TREE RAT OR THE OCTOPUS: WE HAVE A GREAT CAPACITY FOR LEARNING NEW BEHAVIOUR.

- THE OCTOPUS CAN GET THE THING OUT OF THE BOTTLE BECAUSE IT IS CLEVER AND DOESN'T HAVE A SKELETON.
YOU COULD ALSO GET THE THING OUT OF THE BOTTLE EVENTUALLY

- TREE RAT CAN GET NUT FROM MAZE YOU COULD PROBABLY ALSO FIND ▄ A WAY TO GET THE NUT.

- DOG CAN DO TRICKS
YOU CAN DO TRICKS

N.B.
DOG CAN SMELL BOMBS
YOU CAN'T SMELL BOMBS

BECOME A BETTER
CONVERSATIONALIST

SMILE
LISTEN WITH INTEREST
AVOID TALKING ABOUT ANYTHING
INTERESTING OR WORTHWHILE

HELPFUL ACRONYM:

FEEL
UPLIFTED
REALLY
REALLY
YES

OTHER HELPFUL ACRONYMS:

GLUE
BEANS
FLACID
CLOGS

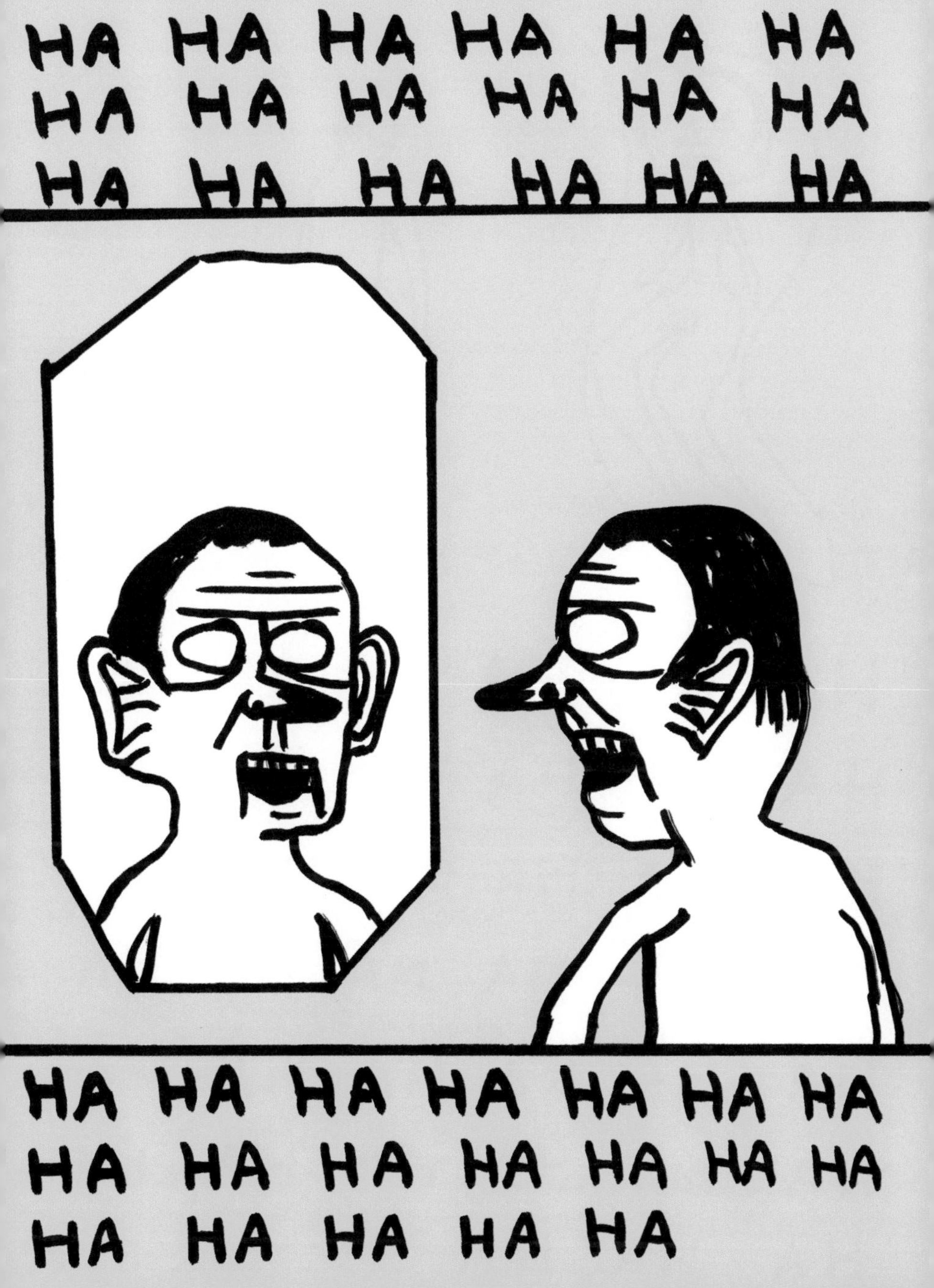
HA HA HA HA HA HA
HA HA HA HA HA HA
HA HA HA HA HA HA
HA HA HA HA HA HA HA
HA HA HA HA HA HA HA
HA HA HA HA HA

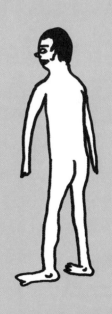

HA HA HA HA HA HA
HA HA HA HA HA HA
HA HA HA HA HA HA
HA HA HA HA HA HA
HA HA HA HA HA HA
HA HA HA HA HA HA
HA HA HA

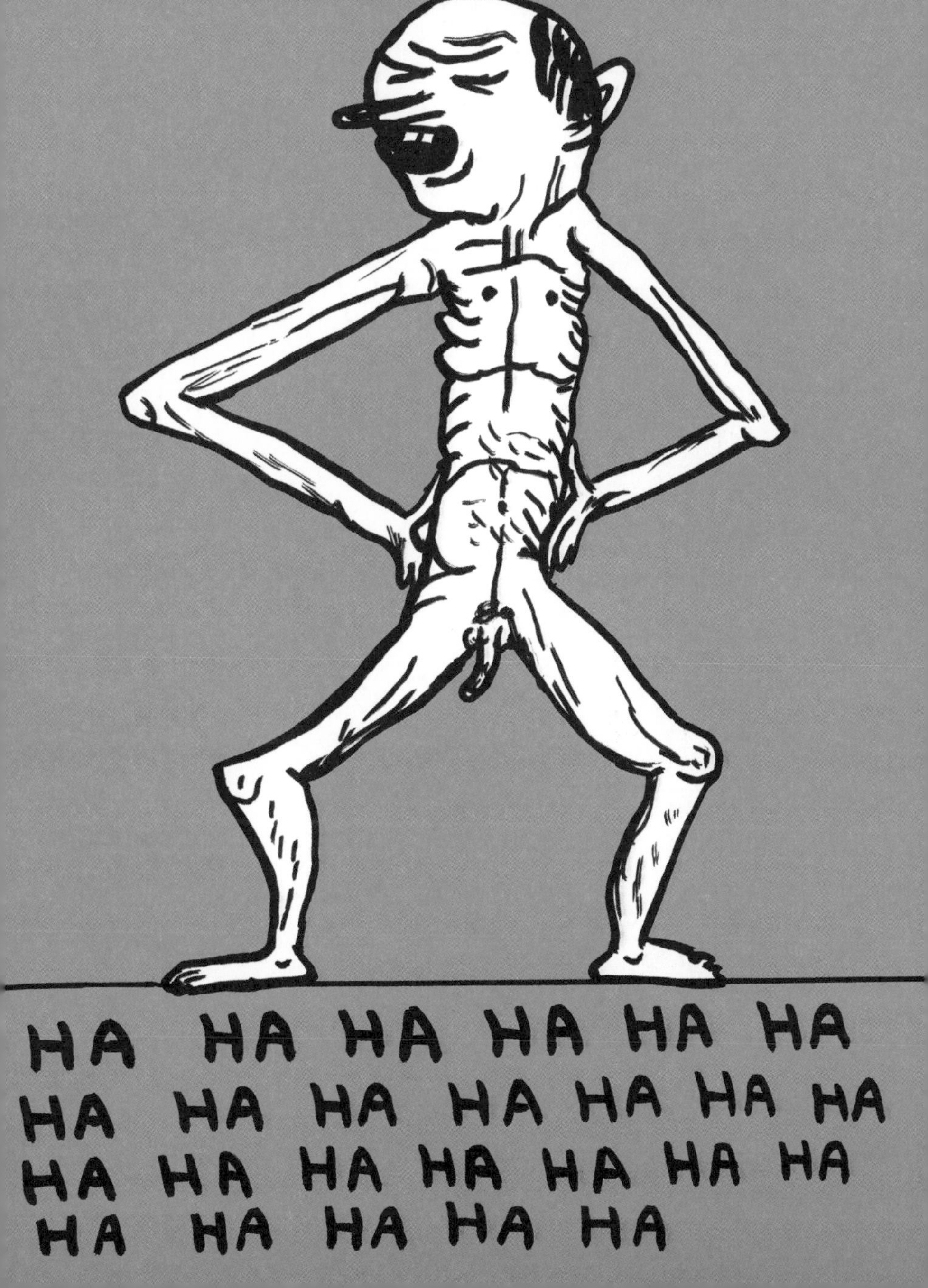
HA HA HA HA HA HA
HA HA HA HA HA HA HA
HA HA HA HA HA HA HA
HA HA HA HA HA

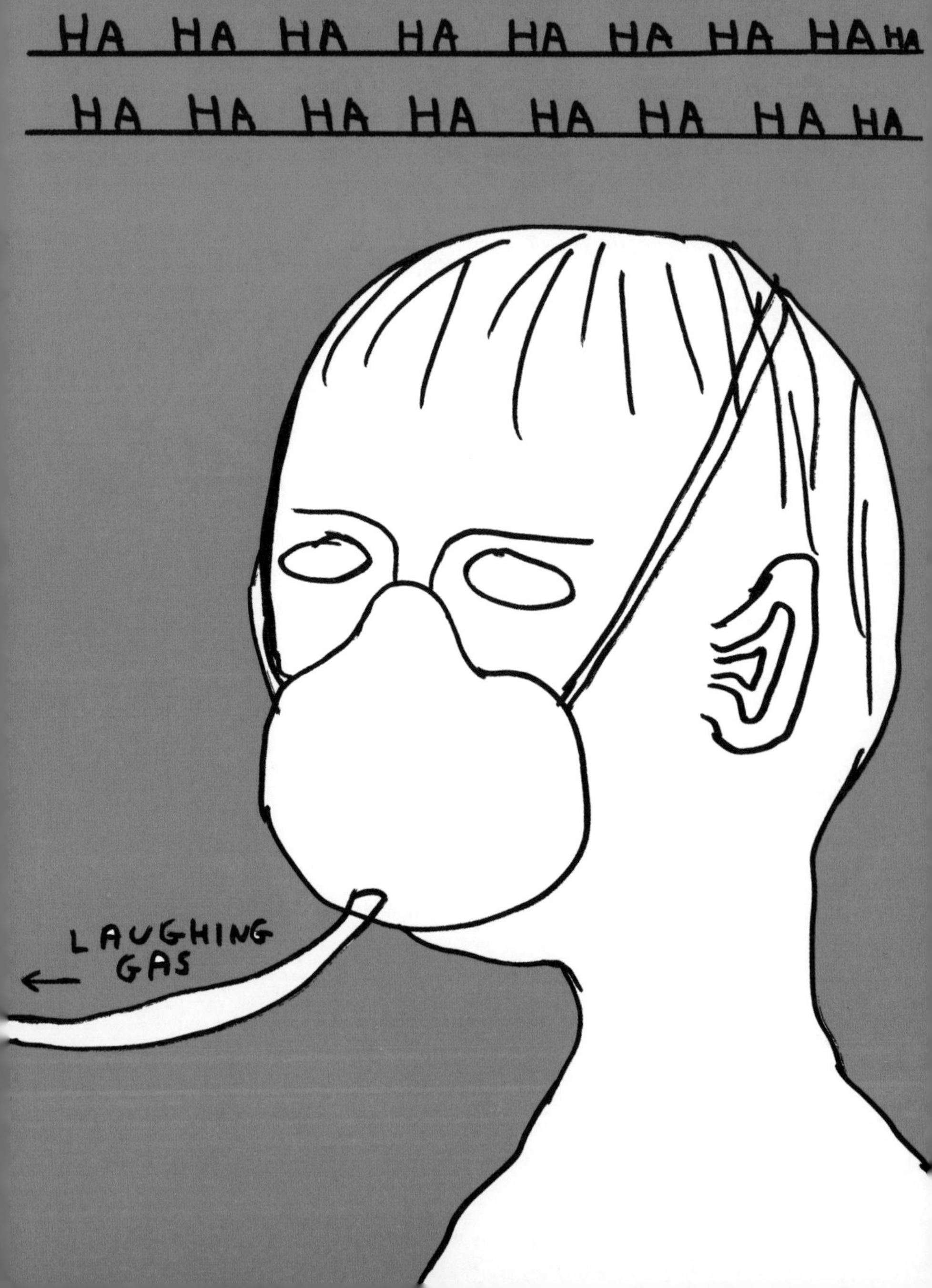
HA HA HA HA HA HA HA HAHA
HA HA HA HA HA HA HA HA
LAUGHING GAS

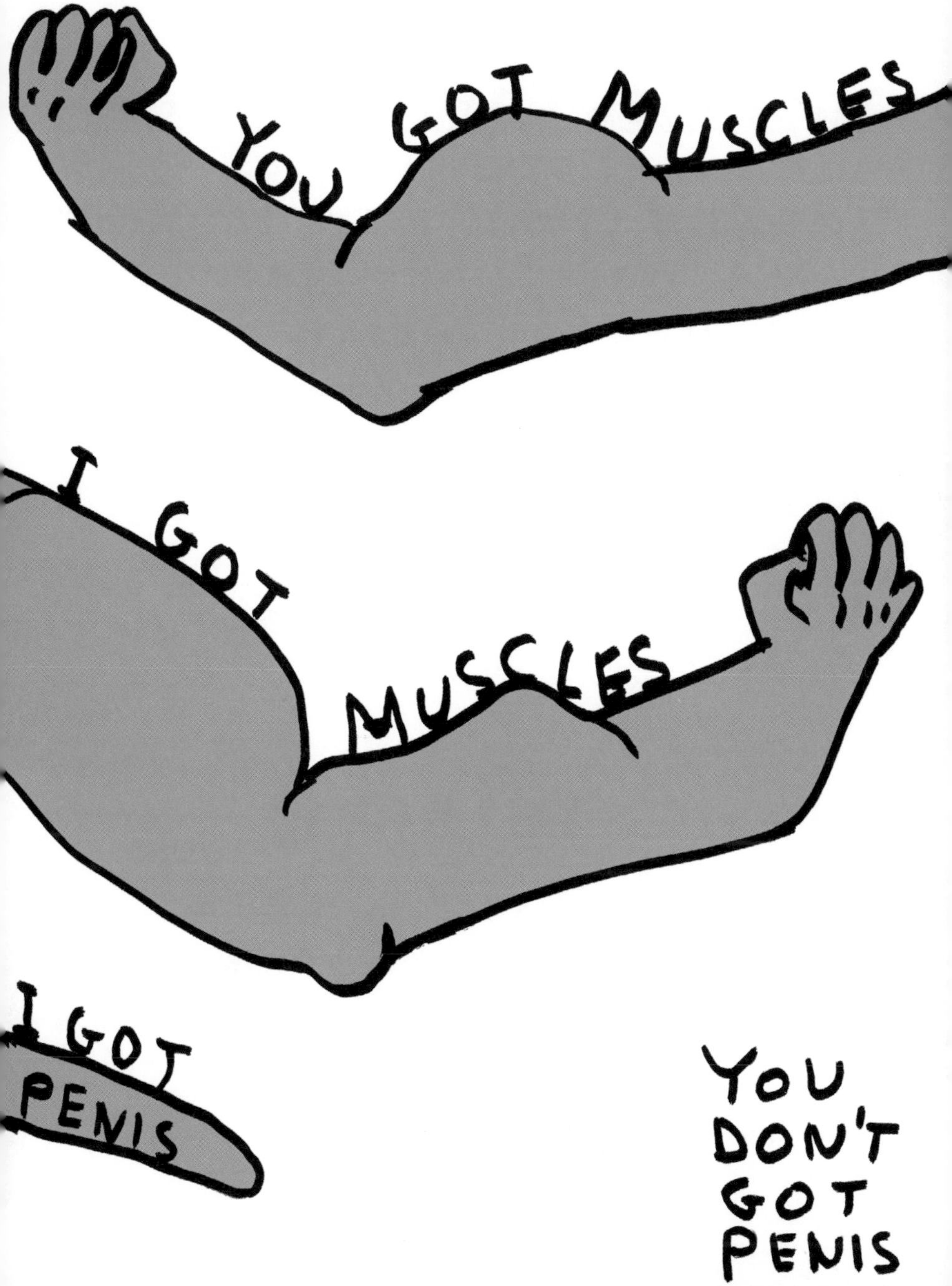
YOU GOT MUSCLES
I GOT MUSCLES
I GOT PENIS
YOU DON'T GOT PENIS

UNWANTED THOUGHTS AND WORRIES (DEALING WITH)

IMAGINE THAT THEY ARE CROCKERY
- SMASH THEM WITH A HAMMER
IMAGINE THAT THEY ARE BOOKS
- BURN THEM IN A FURNACE
IMAGINE THAT THEY ARE BALLS OF WOOL
- FLUSH THEM DOWN THE TOILET
IMAGINE THAT THEY ARE ANTS
- BURN THEM WITH A MAGNIFYING
  GLASS

MUSIC THERAPY

YOU DON'T HAVE TO BE A
MUSICIAN TO ENJOY MAKING MUSIC
YOU CAN MAKE MUSICAL INSTRUMENTS
OUT OF ANYTHING: BONES, ETC.
JUST GO FOR IT!

FUCK CREATIVITY

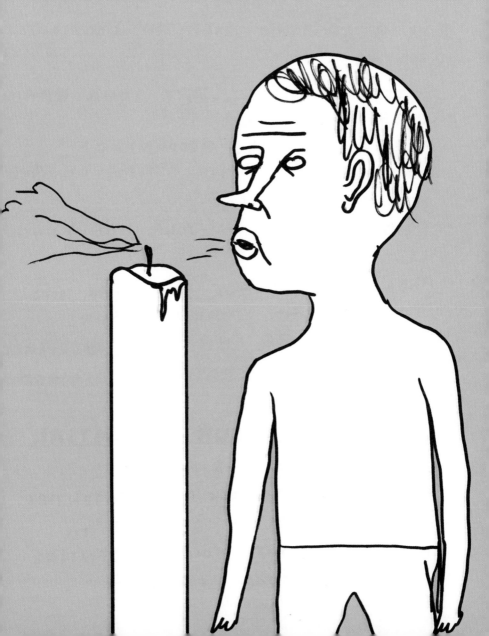

Waxing Your Brain

FOR A LASTING, HEALTHY-LOOKING BRAIN:

- AFTER WASHING, DRY YOUR BRAIN WITH A TOWEL
- PLACE A SMALL AMOUNT OF BRAIN WAX IN THE PALM OF YOUR HAND
- RUB THE WAX IN YOUR HANDS UNTIL IT BECOMES SOFT
- GENTLY MASSAGE THE WAX INTO YOUR BRAIN MAKING SURE THE ENTIRE BRAIN IS COVERED
- STYLE YOUR BRAIN AS DESIRED

Unlocking Your Potential

UNTIL THE KEY IS FOUND
YOU CANNOT UNLOCK YOUR POTENTIAL
IT IS PROBABLY BETTER TO
FORGET ABOUT YOUR POTENTIAL
FOR THE TIME BEING

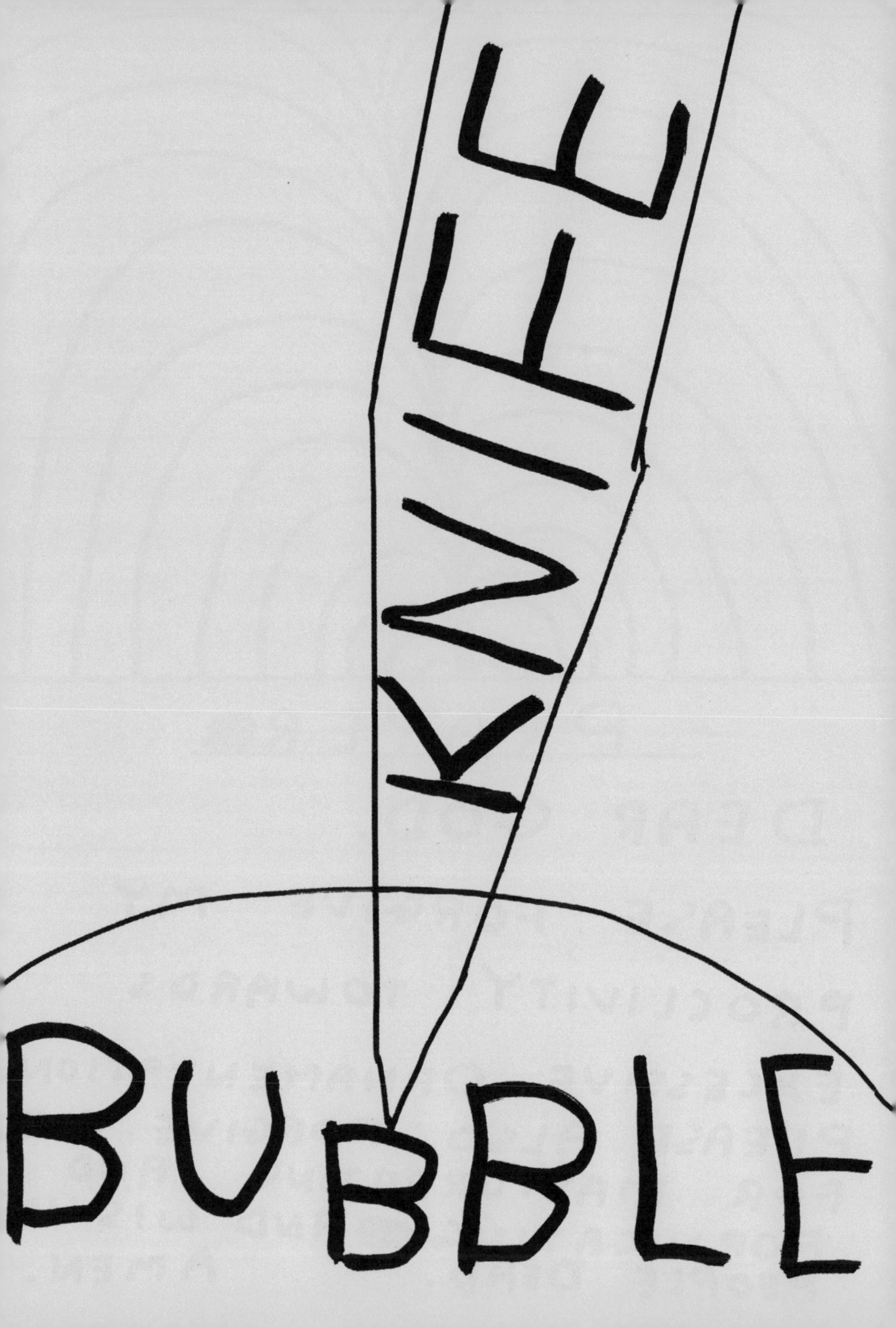
KNIFE
BUBBLE

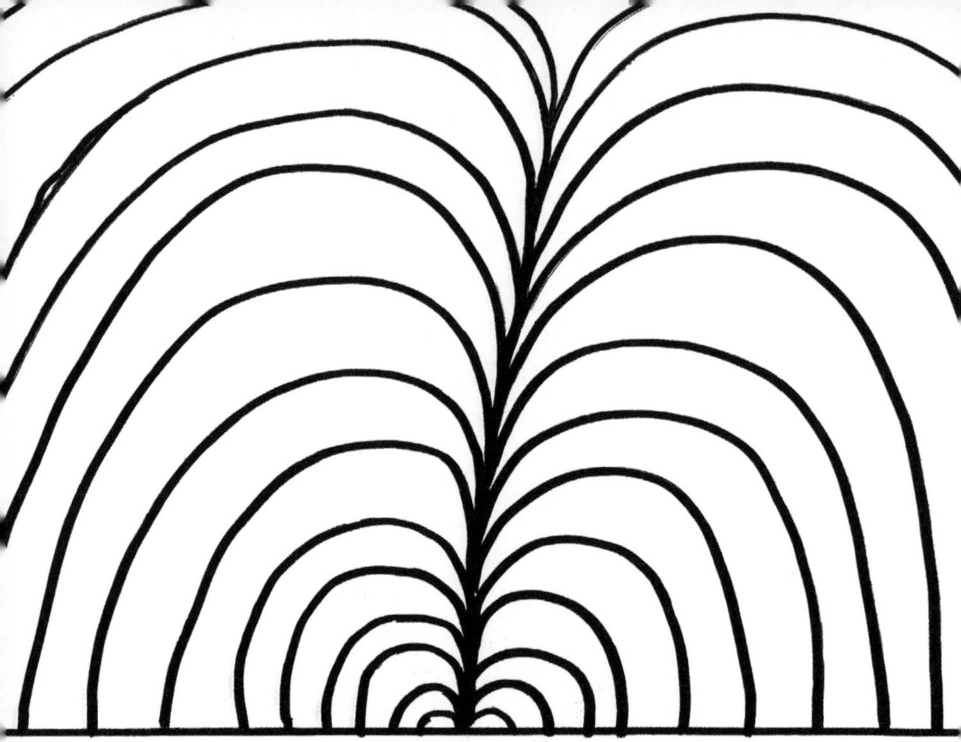

PRAYER[redacted]

DEAR GOD,

PLEASE FORGIVE MY PROCLIVITY TOWARDS EXCESSIVE ORNAMENTATION. PLEASE ALSO FORGIVE ME FOR MASTURBATING AND FORNICATING[redacted] AND WISHIN PEOPLE DEAD.

AMEN.

RED: HEADACHES
ORANGE: HAIR LOSS
YELLOW: BLINDNESS
GREEN: NAUSEA
BLUE: SHORTNESS OF BREATH
INDIGO: DIZZINESS
VIOLET: FEELINGS OF EUPHORIA
GREY: INCREASED SEX DRIVE
WHITE: NO EFFECT
BLACK: STEALING

POEM

SOMEONE SLASHED MY DADDY'S
TYRE
DADDY TOLD ME I'M A LIAR
DADDY SET MY TOYS ON FIRE
DADDY TIED ME UP WITH WIRE

HERO WORSHIP

IDENTIFY YOUR HERO
HERO MUST NOT BE AN OBJECT
OR AN ANIMAL
HERO MUST BE A LIVING HUMAN
BEING
~~~~~~ GATHER MEMORABILLIA ~~~~~~
RELATED TO YOUR HERO
SEEK OUT YOUR HERO
TRY TO MEET HIM/HER
DO NOT RESPECT YOUR HERO'S PRIVACY
THEY DO NOT LIKE PRIVACY
IT MAKES THEM LONELY

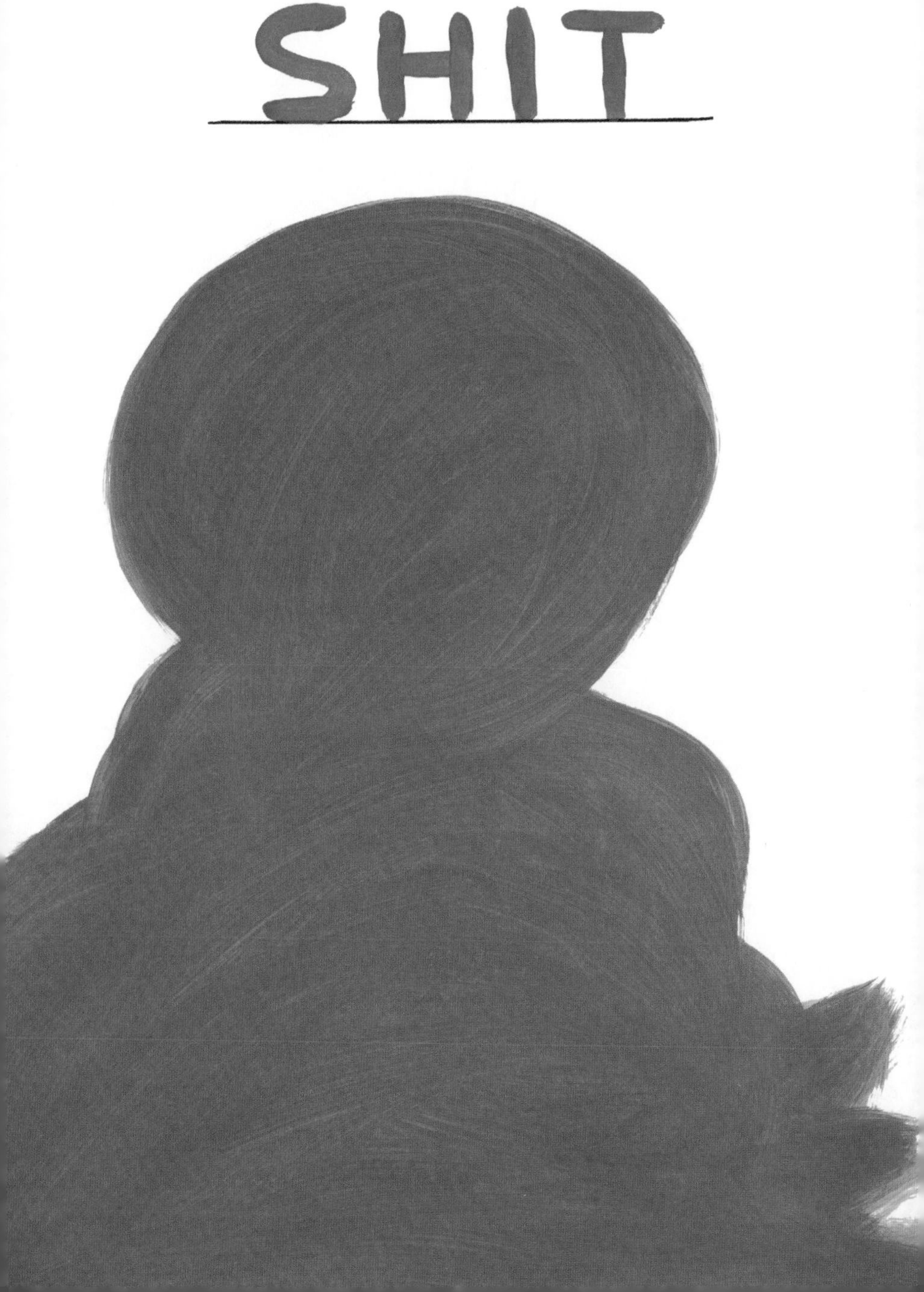
SHIT

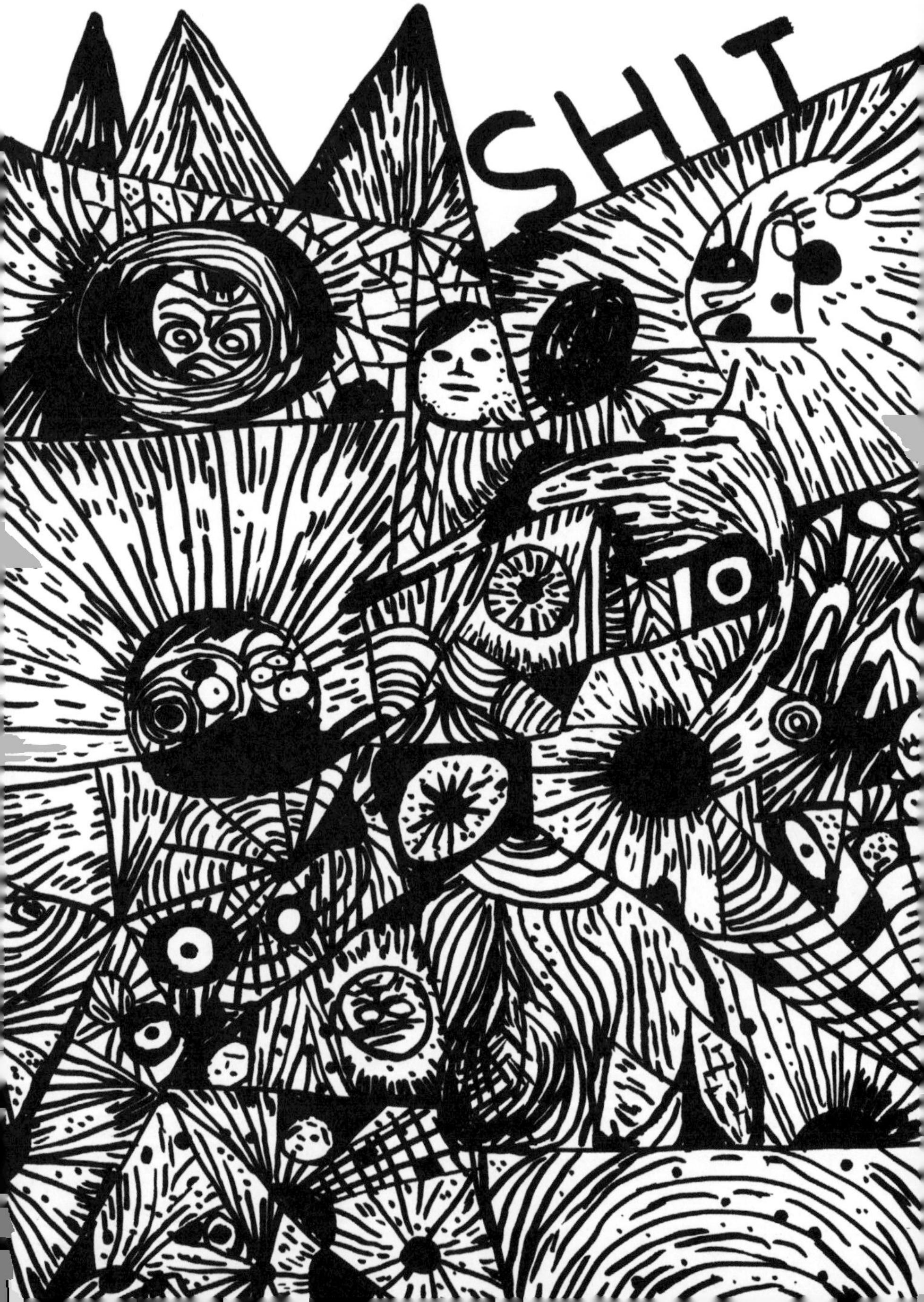
SHIT

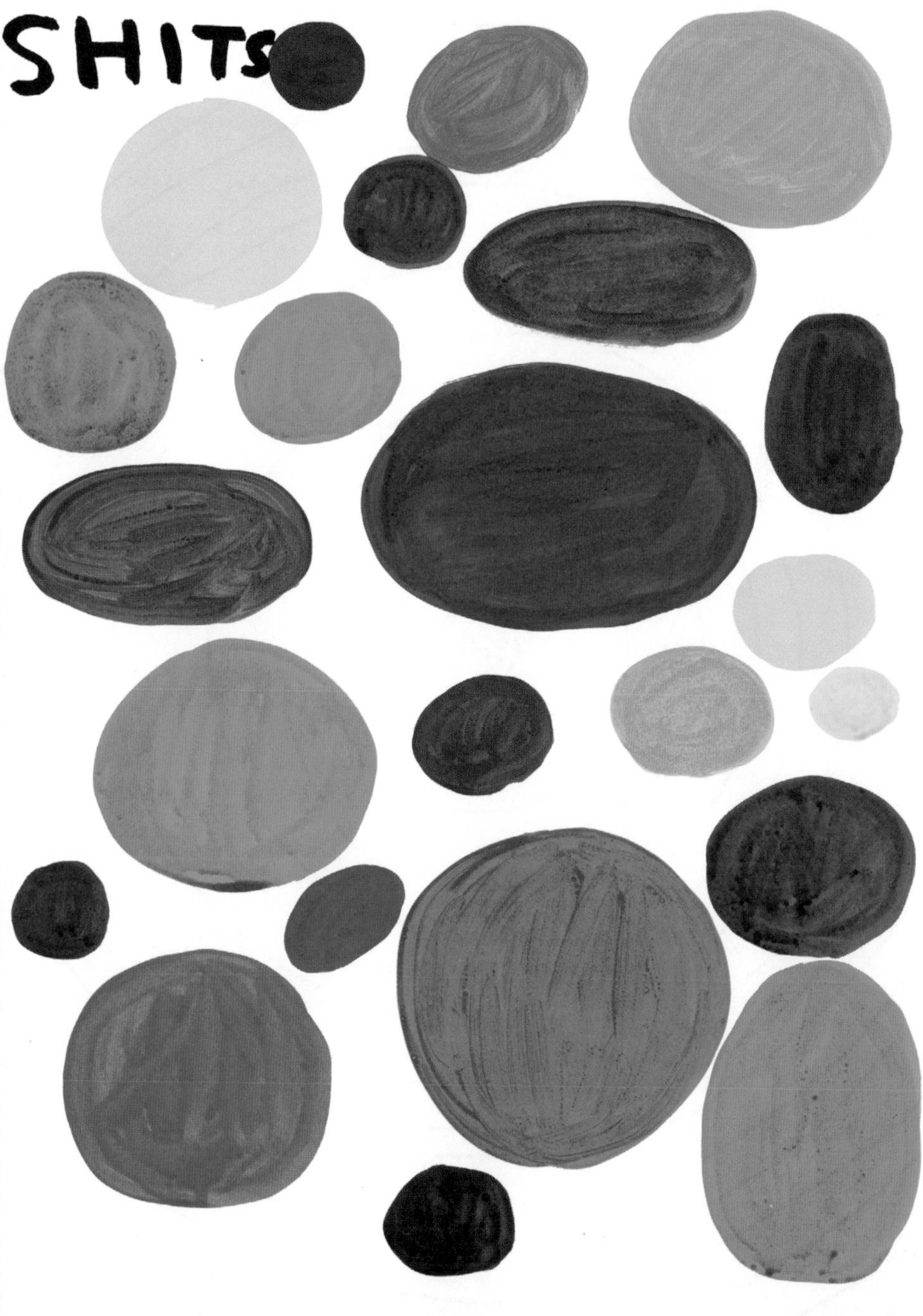
SHITS

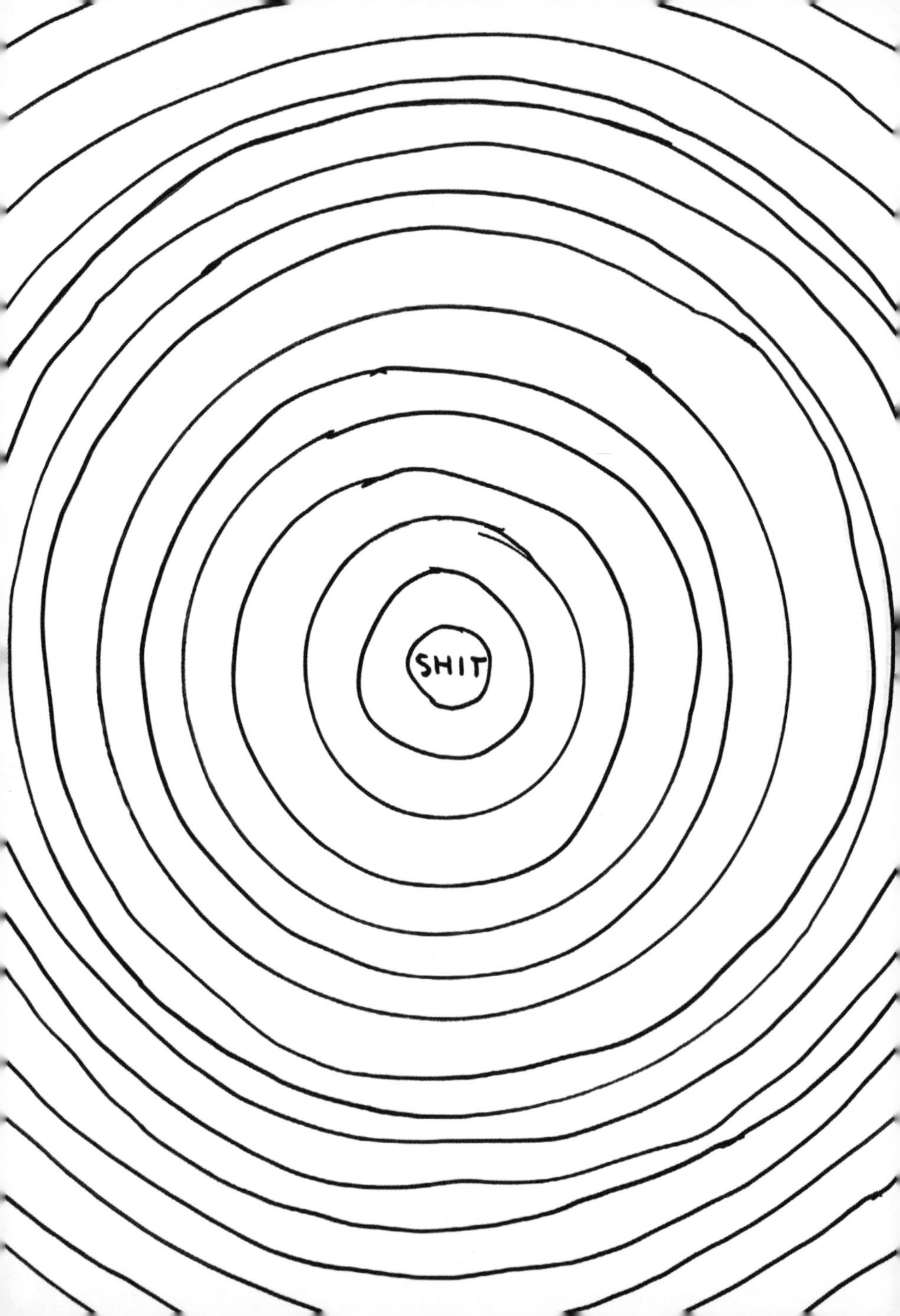
SHIT

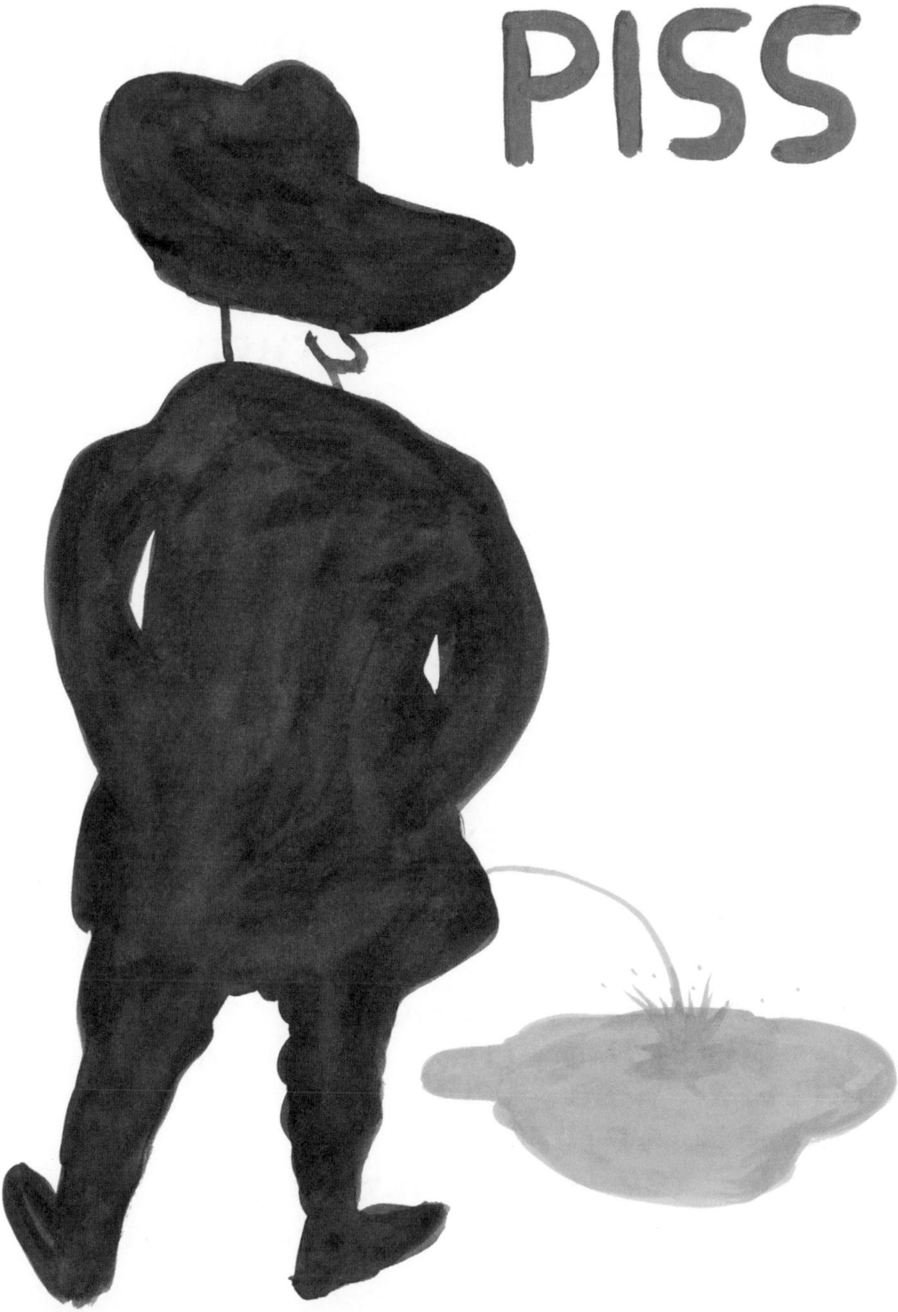
PISS

FACT OR OPINION?

FACT

CLOWN
PAINTED FACE
COLOURFUL
CIRCUS PERFORMER

OPINION

FUNNY
WEIRD
SCARY
THEIF

PHOBIAS

WE ARE ALL AFRAID OF THINGS:
CHILDREN, DWARVES, ETC
IT'S QUITE NORMAL

OBSTACLES

SOMETIMES THEY ARE TINY
SOMETIMES THEY ARE HUGE
SOMETIMES THEY ARE VERY ORNATE
AND YOU CAN'T HELP STARING AT
THEM
THEY ARE SO COMPLEX AND
INTERESTING LIKE AN AMAZING
SILVER WEB SPUN BY A GIANT
███████ SPIDER
AND YOU GET DISTRACTED
AND YOU FORGET YOUR GOAL

PICNIC

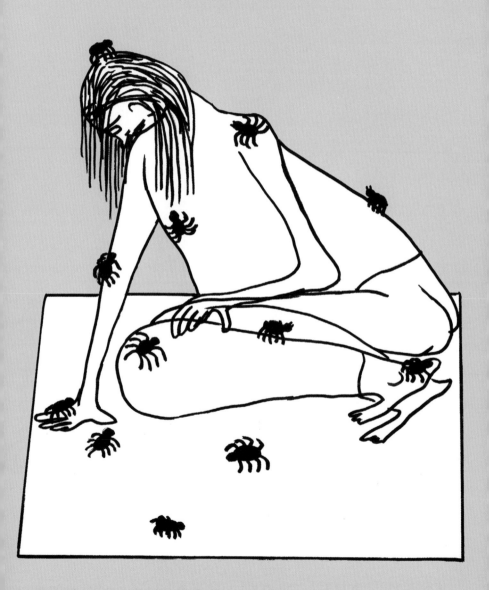

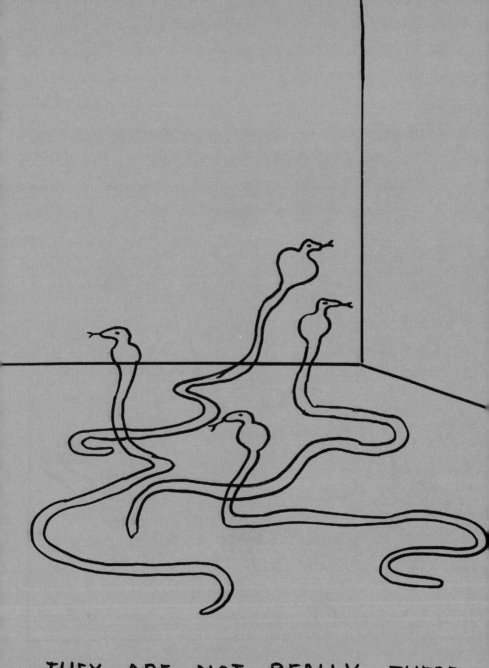

THEY ARE NOT REALLY THERE

CHAPTER EIGHT

HELPFUL METAPHORS, ETC.

TUG OF WAR WITH A MONSTER

THERE IS A DEEP PRECIPICE
YOU ARE ON ONE SIDE
A MONSTER IS ON THE OTHER
YOU ARE PLAYING TUG OF WAR
WHOEVER LOSES FALLS [redacted] OVER
THE PRECIPICE
EVERYONE IS WATCHING [redacted]
(YOUR PARENTS, EX-WIFE, ETC)
BEST OF LUCK

PASSENGERS ON THE BUS

THE PASSENGERS DO NOT DRIVE THE
BUS
THE DRIVER DRIVES THE BUS
THE PASSENGERS MUST WAIT
UNTIL THE BUS STOPS
BEFORE THEY GET OFF

DEMONS ON THE BUS

DEMONS CAN GET ON AND OFF
THE BUS WHENEVER THEY LIKE
THEY ALSO CONTROL THE BUS

THE QUICKSAND

LOOKS LIKE SAND
LOOKS LIKE THE BEACH
BUT YOU WILL GET STUCK IN IT
IF YOU WALK ON IT
AND YOU WILL DROWN IN IT
IT IS EVERYWHERE

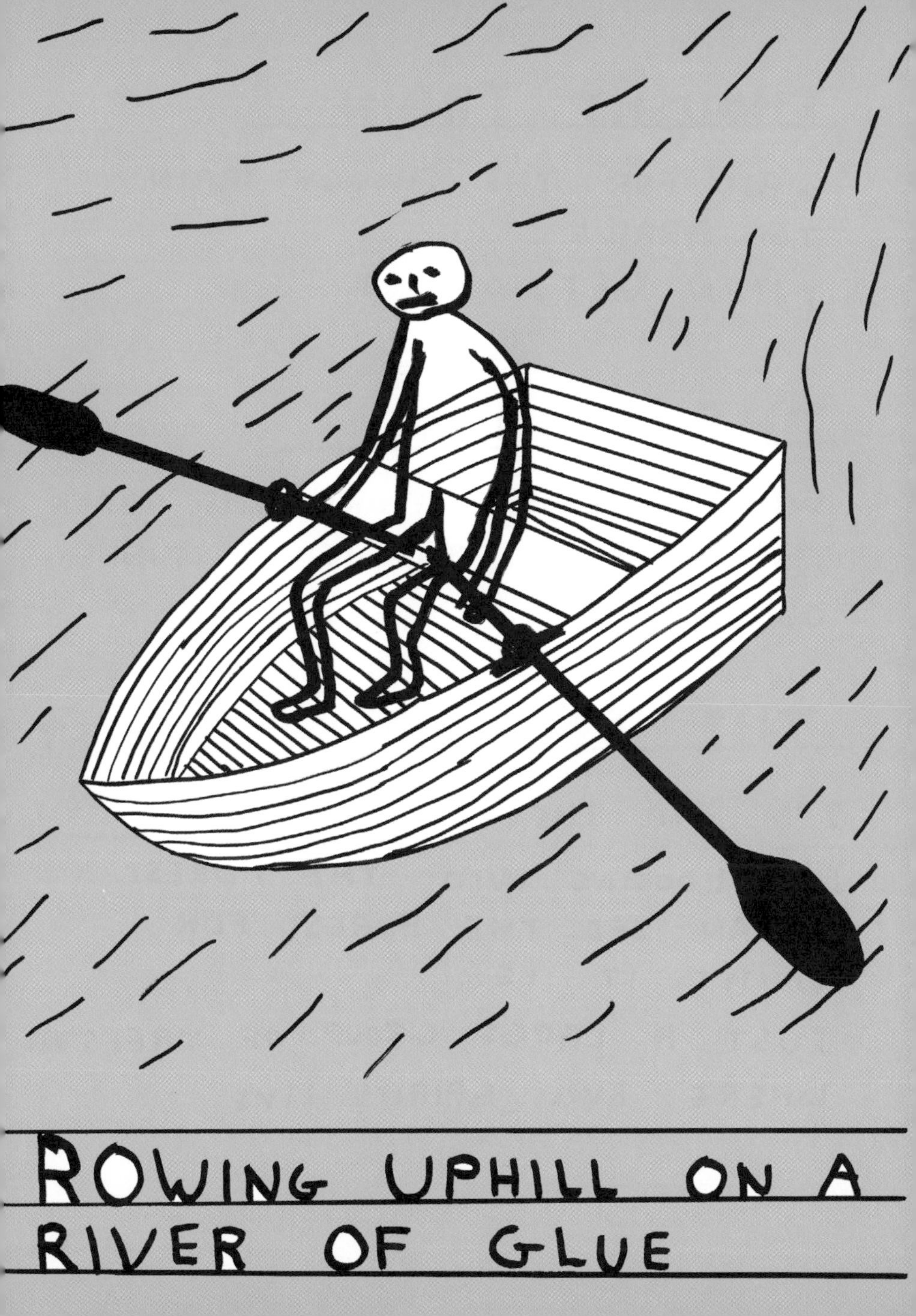
ROWING UPHILL ON A
RIVER OF GLUE

THOUGHT TRAIN

WAIT FOR THE THOUGHT TRAIN
TO ARRIVE
THEN GET ON IT

THE TUNNEL

WE ARE GOING ALONG THE TRACK
THEN WE GO THROUGH A TUNNEL
OH GOD!

THE EDGE OF THE FOREST

I'M ON THE EDGE OF THE FOREST
I'M LOOKING INTO THE FOREST
I CAN SEE THE FOREST FOR
WHAT IT IS:
JUST A LARGE GROUP OF TREES
WHERE EVIL SPIRITS LIVE

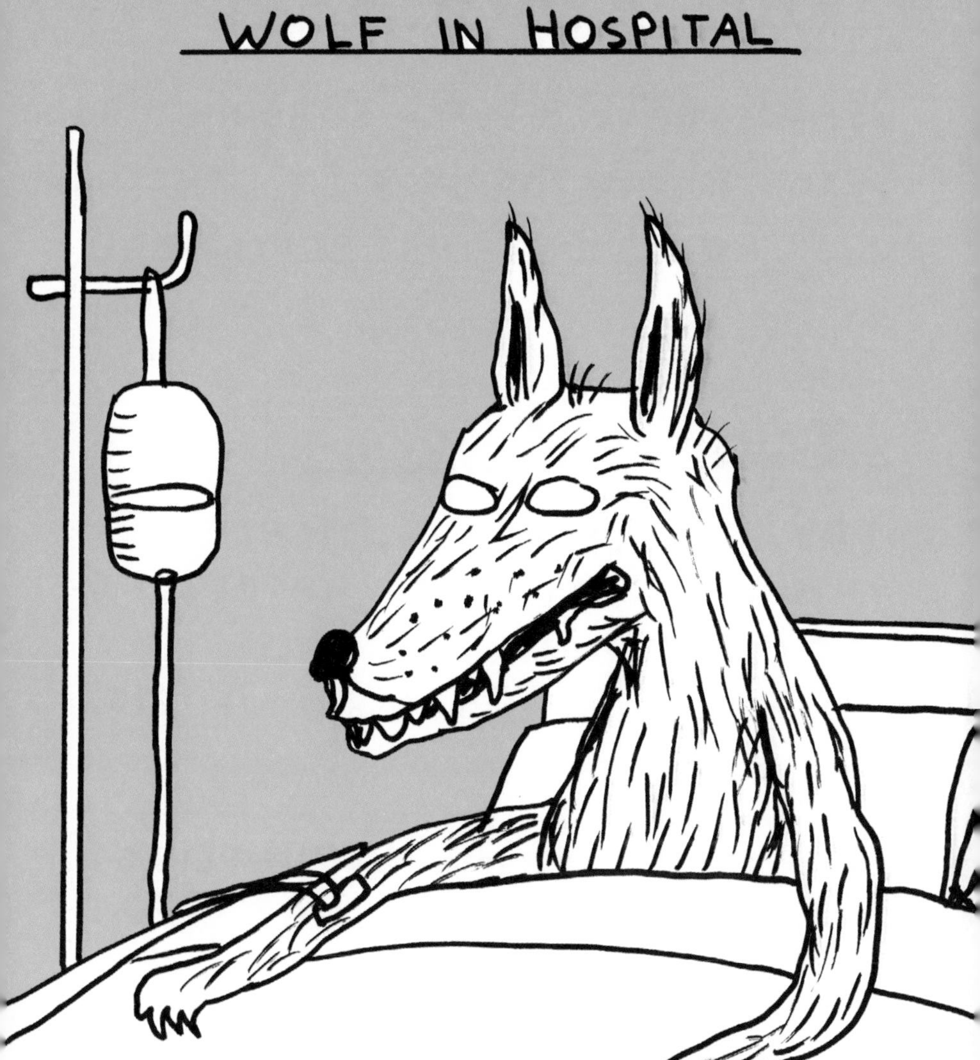
WOLF IN HOSPITAL

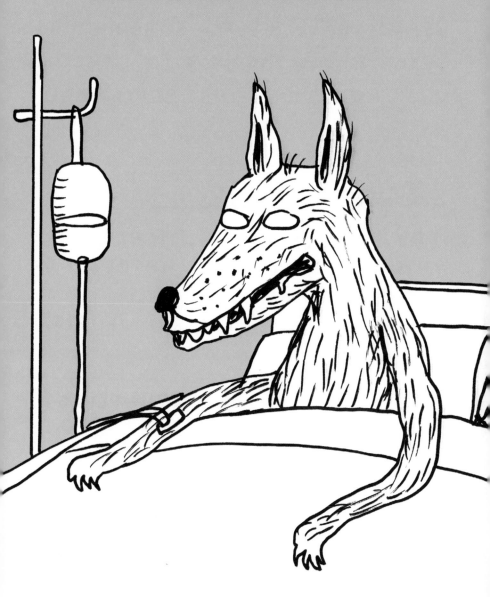

THE BEACH BALL

BEACH BALL KEEPS BOBBING AROUND
GETS BLOWN AROUND BY THE WIND
YOU ARE LIKE THE BEACH BALL

ZOOM LENS

TRY TO IMAGINE THAT THE
THINGS THAT ARE HAPPENING
TO YOU ARE ACTUALLY
HAPPENING TO SOMEONE ELSE:

ZOOM IN

SEE THAT PERSON STRUGGLING
WITH PROBEMS: HA, HA.

ZOOM OUT

WE'RE BANANAS

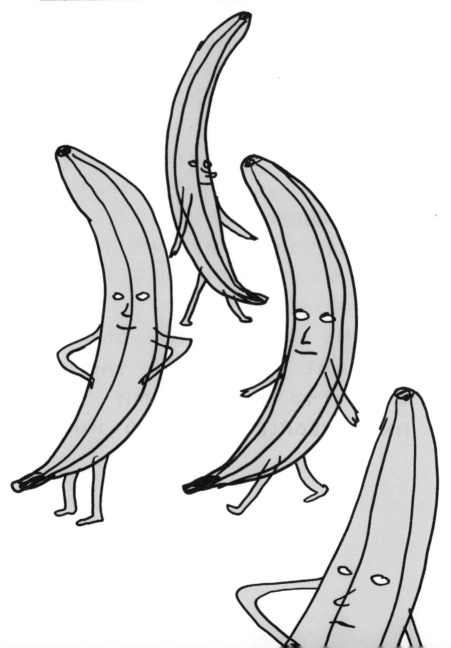

THE MOUNTAIN

ONCE THERE WAS A MAN WHO
DECIDED TO CLIMB A MOUNTAIN
HE COULD NOT SEE THE TOP OF
THE MOUNTAIN
BECAUSE IT WAS COVERED IN CLOUDS
BUT HE KNEW IT WAS ███
VERY ███ HIGH
HE GOT HALFWAY UP THE MOUNTAIN
AND STILL HE COULD NOT SEE
THE SUMMIT
SO HE WENT BACK DOWN
AND HE LIED AND SAID HE'D
BEEN TO THE SUMMIT
AND PEOPLE BELIEVED HIM.

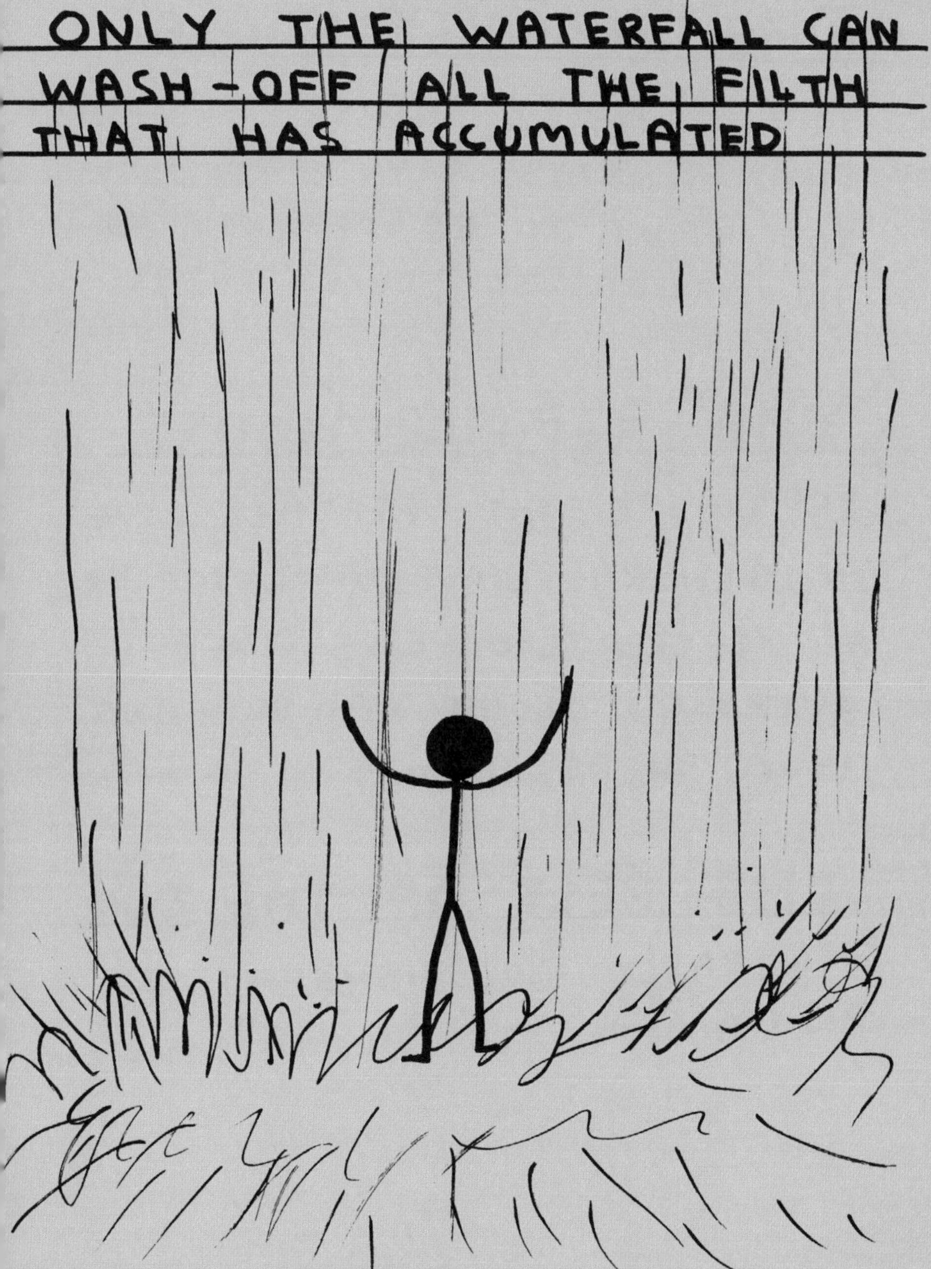
ONLY THE WATERFALL CAN WASH-OFF ALL THE FILTH THAT HAS ACCUMULATED

THE MONKEY HOUSE

THE MONKEY HOUSE IS WHERE
THE MONKEYS LIVE
YOU HAVE TO BE MONKEY ▬
IN ORDER TO LIVE THERE

THE REPTILE HOUSE

IS WHERE THE REPTILES LIVE
IN GENERAL YOU HAVE TO BE
A REPTILE TO LIVE THERE
ALTHOUGH SOME AMBHIBIANS
LIVE THERE ALSO

THE REST OF THE ZOO

GENERALLY YOU HAVE TO BE
AN ANIMAL TO LIVE AT THE ZOO

YOUR
HEAD IS
MADE OF
YARN

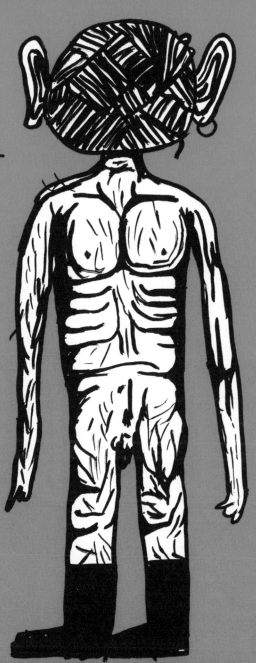

WORMS

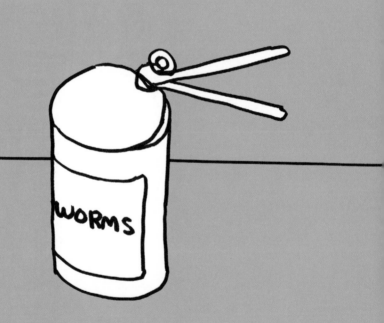

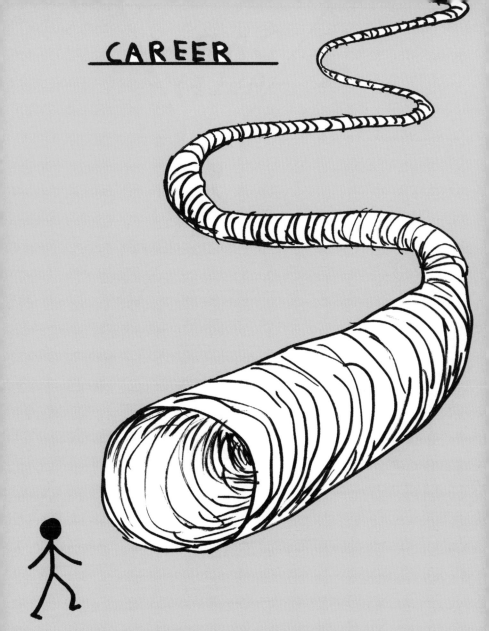

CAREER

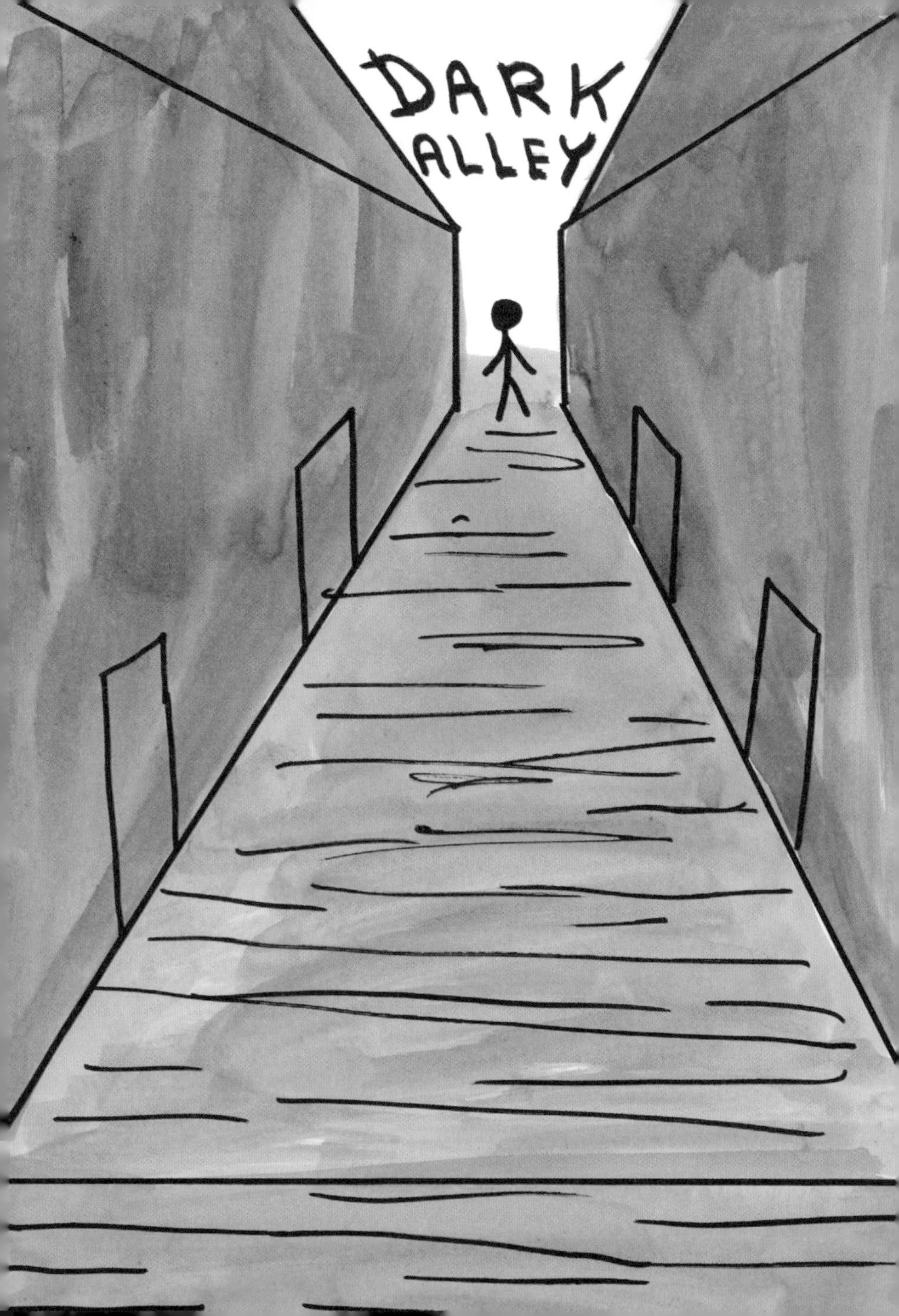
DARK ALLEY

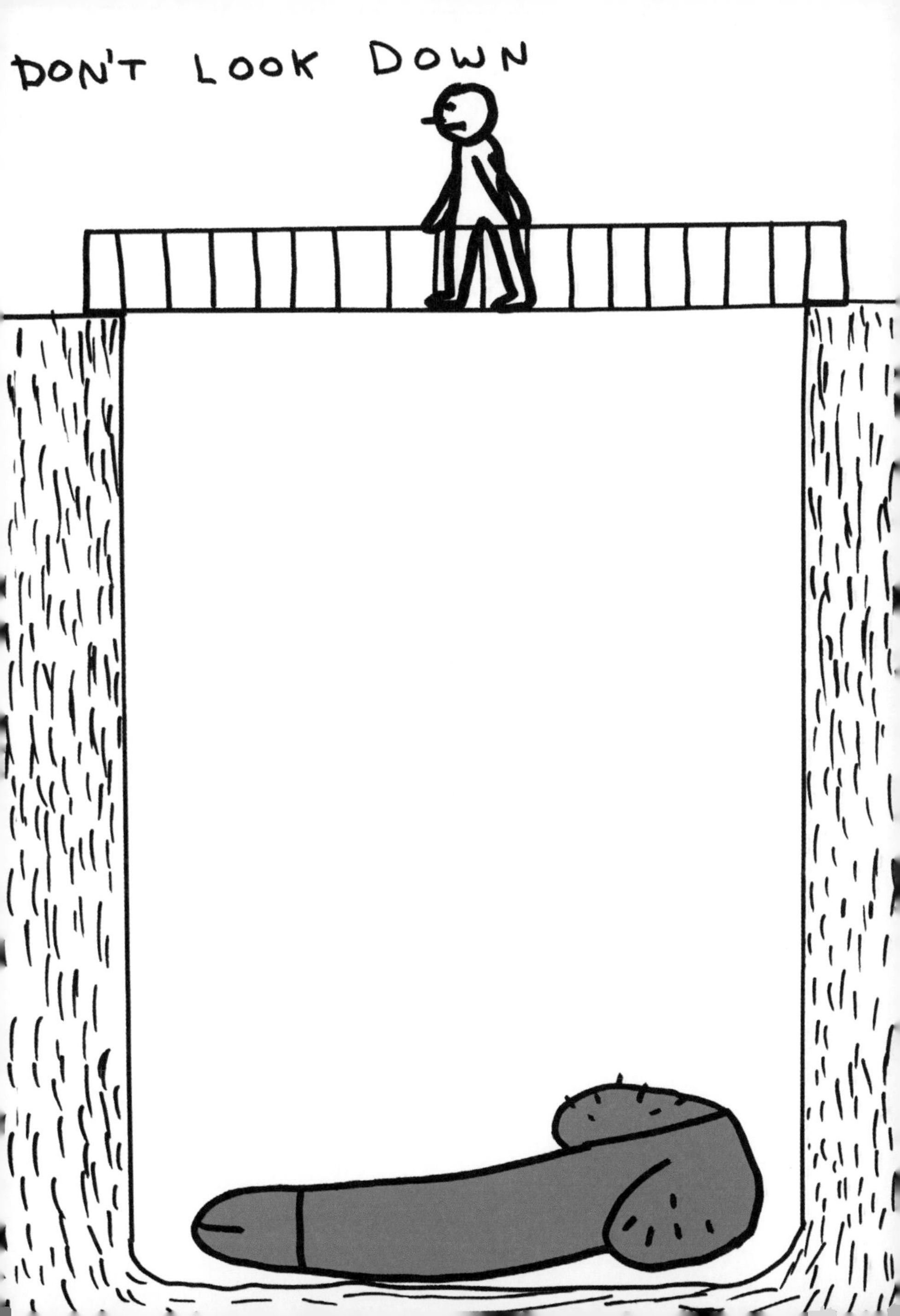
DON'T LOOK DOWN

NEGATIVE THOUGHT AIRPORT

PLANES ON THE RUNWAY

READY TO TAKE OFF

YOU WILL NEVER SEE THE PLANES
AGAIN

ONCE THEY HAVE TAKEN OFF

YOU ARE IN THE CONTROL TOWER

GIVING PERMISSION FOR TAKE OFF

I HOPE NOTHING GOES WRONG

HOW DO YOU BURN?

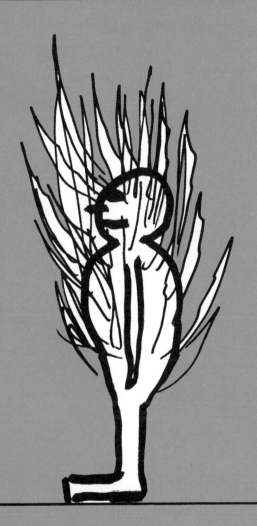

I BURN WELL

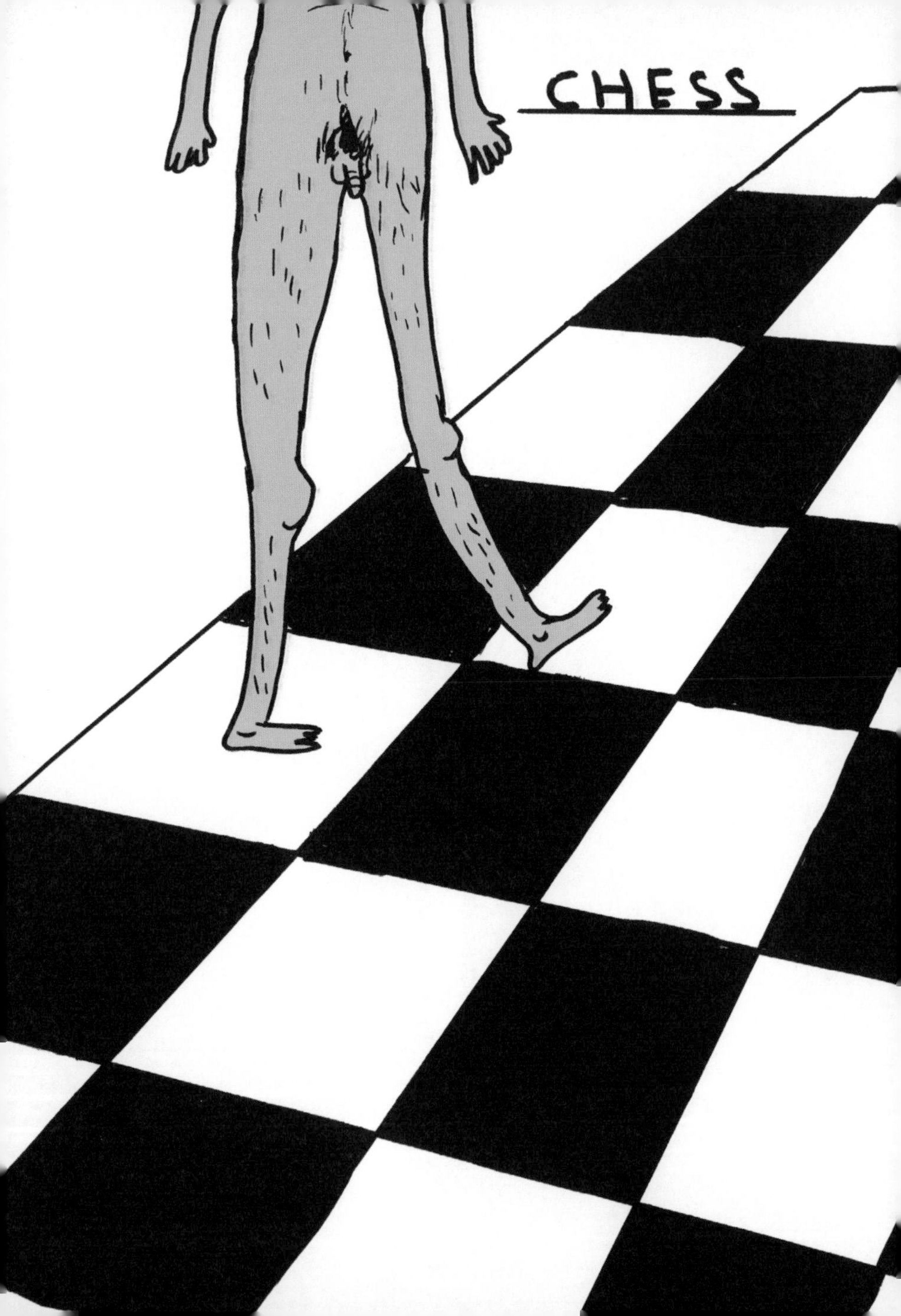
CHESS

WORDS APPEAR WRITTEN ON BUBBLES
BUT THE BUBBLES BURST TOO QUICKLY
FOR YOU TO READ WHAT WAS
WRITTEN ON THEM
IT'S FRUSTRATING

A MAN RIDES INTO TOWN ON A
WHITE HORSE
BUT HE WON'T TELL YOU HIS NAME
AND HE REFUSES TO HAVE SOCIAL
INTERCOURSE WITH YOU
AND YOU ATTEMPT TO STEAL
HIS I.D.
~~~~~~~~~~~~~~~~~ TO FIND OUT
WHO HE IS
BUT HE DOESN'T HAVE ANY I.D.
IT'S FRUSTRATING

YOU OPEN THE WINDOW
YOU WANT TO GET SOME AIR
BUT A SWARM OF INSECTS FLY IN
AND HIDE IN YOUR BUNGALOW
AND THEY RE-APPEAR AT NIGHT
WHEN YOU ARE ASLEEP
AND THEY BITE YOU ON YOUR FACE
AND IN THE MORNING THEY ARE
HIDDEN AGAIN
AND THE NEXT NIGHT IT
HAPPENS AGAIN
AND IT KEEPS HAPPENING
AND THE INSECTS SEEM TO LIVE
FOREVER
AND THEY NEVER DIE
IT'S FRUSTRATING

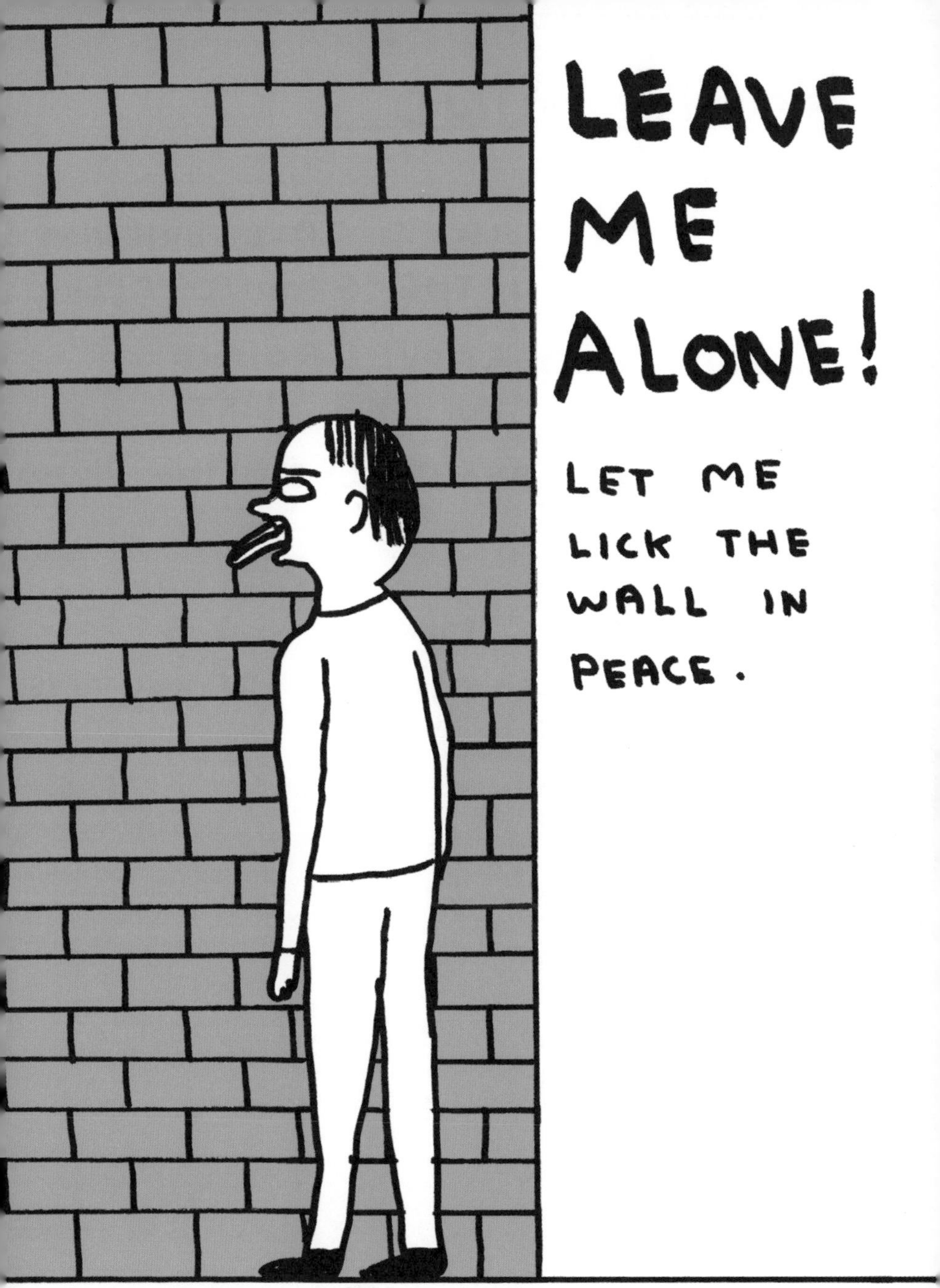
LEAVE ME ALONE!
LET ME LICK THE WALL IN PEACE.

YOUR MIND

YOUR MIND IS A TALL BUILDING
YOU ENTER ON THE GROUND FLOOR
YOU HAVE A LOOK AROUND
YOU GO UP IN THE LIFT
YOU THINK ABOUT STEALING THINGS

NO!

THIS IS YOUR MIND
THESE THINGS ALREADY BELONG TO YOU

I BANGED MY HEAD ON THE SHARP CORNER AND IT HURT OH GOD IT HURT.

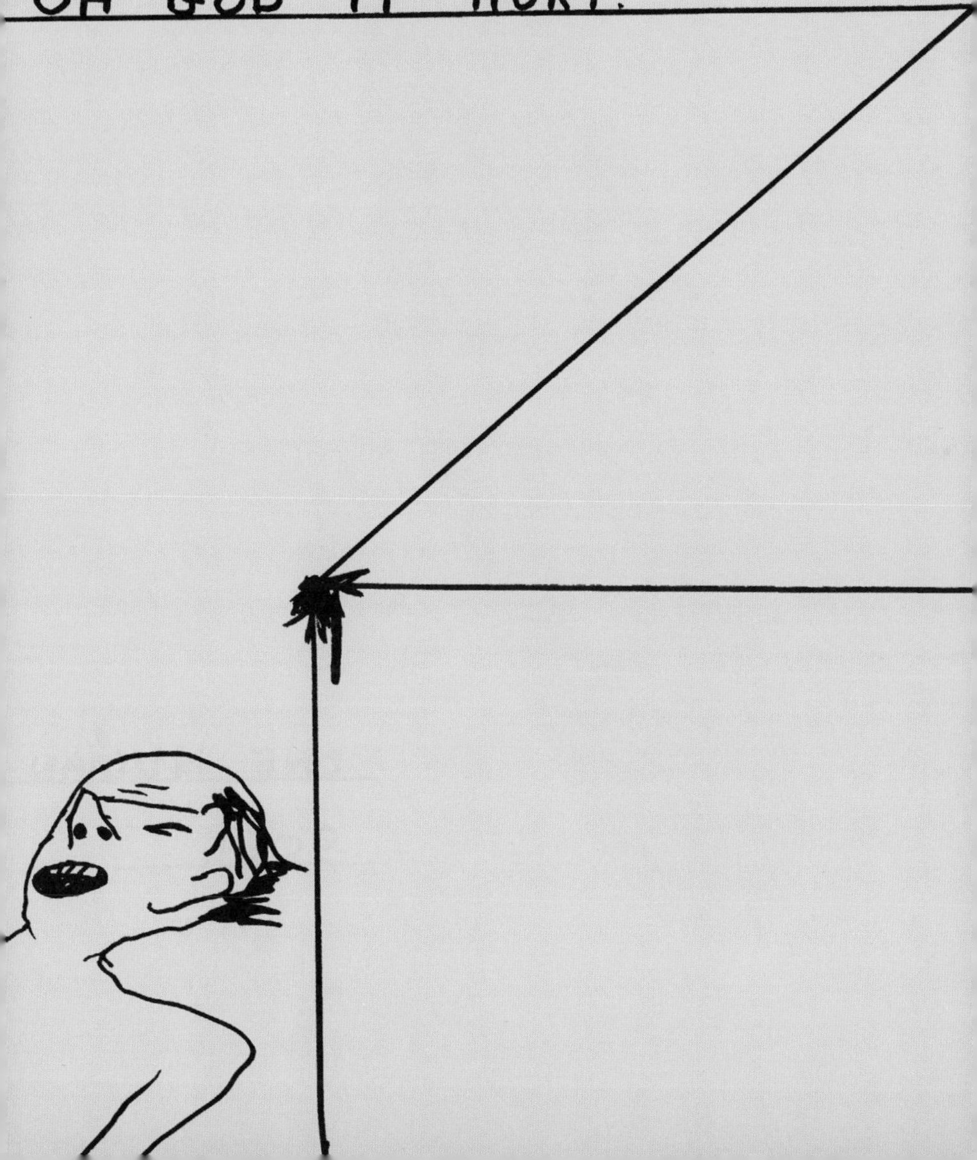

THE HUMAN
SOUL

FOOD AND MOOD

[redacted] WHAT YOU EAT [redacted] CAN CHANGE THE WAY YOU FEEL
WHAT YOU EAT CAN CHANGE THE WAY YOU THINK

EXAMPLES:

RED MEAT — VIOLENCE

POTATOES - APATHY

CAKES AND SWEETS — VIOLENCE

GO AND

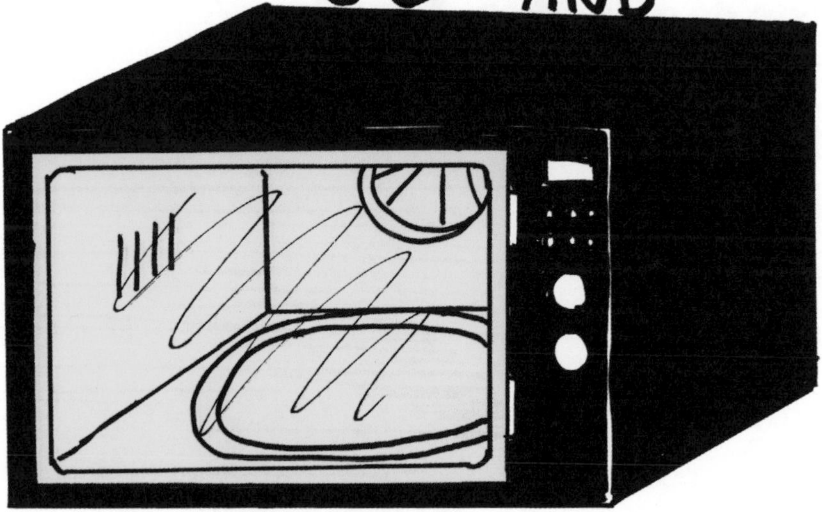

MICROWAVE YOURSELF

DRUGS

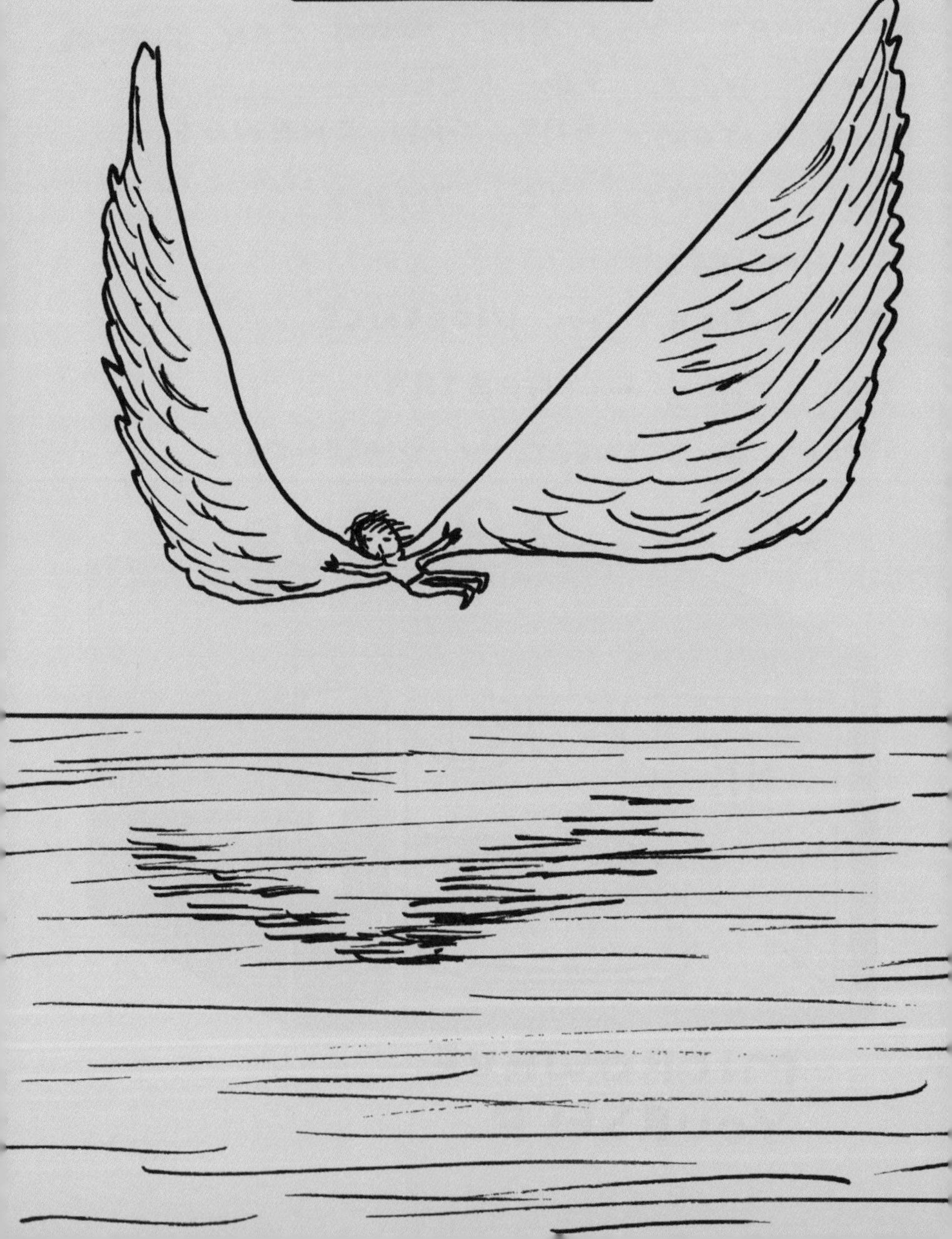

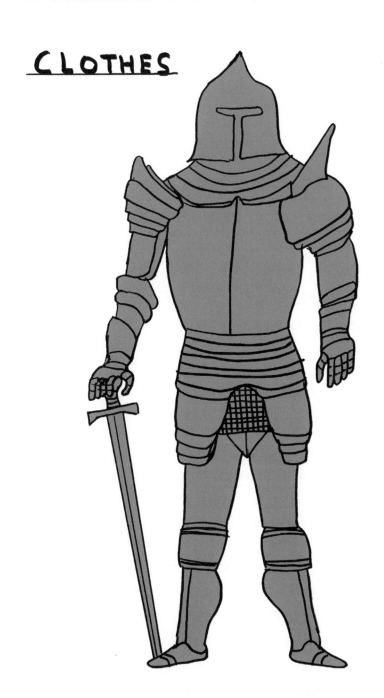

CLOTHES

REMEMBER:

IT'S HARD TO TELL THE GOOD ADVICE FROM THE BAD ADVICE.

YOU MUST GUESS

CONFRONTATION

SOME PEOPLE ARE GOOD AT CONFRONTATION:
SOLDIERS, POLICE, EXORCISTS, ETC.
SOME PEOPLE ARE NOT:
SCHIZOPHRENICS, ETC.
LEARN TO ENJOY CONFRONTATION BY ATTENDING BOXING MATCHES OR BY GETTING INTO FIGHTS OR DUELS.

TOUCHING SWORDS

TOUCH THE SWORD OF SHE WHO WOULD SMITE YOU
AND LET HIM TOUCH YOUR SWORD KNOWING THAT YOU WOULD SMITE HIM/HER
AND IN THIS WAY A PEACEFUL ~~~~ RESOLUTION MAY OCCUR
AS NEITHER OF YOU WANTS TO GET HACKED-UP

BOXING

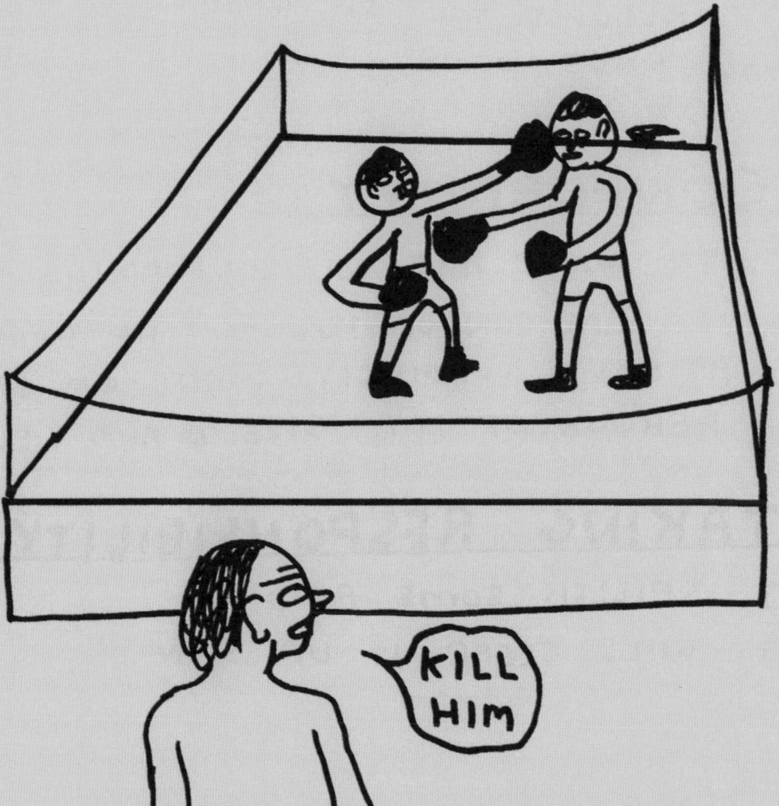
KILL HIM

KEEPING A DIARY

GENERALLY SPEAKING IT'S GOOD TO
KEEP A RECORD OF THINGS
KEEPING A DIARY CAN BE VERY
USEFUL
IT ALLOWS YOU TO REMEMBER WHAT
YOU HAVE DONE

CONFORMITY

Q. TO WHAT ARE YOU CONFORMING?

A. I AM CONFORMING TO THE EXPECT-
ATIONS NORMALLY MADE OF A
PERSON OF MY SIZE AND WEIGHT

TAKING RESPONSIBILITY

I SPILLED SOME ACID
I WILL CLEAR IT UP SOON

I CAN'T BELIEVE THAT THEY WOULD LET ME DRIVE A BUS

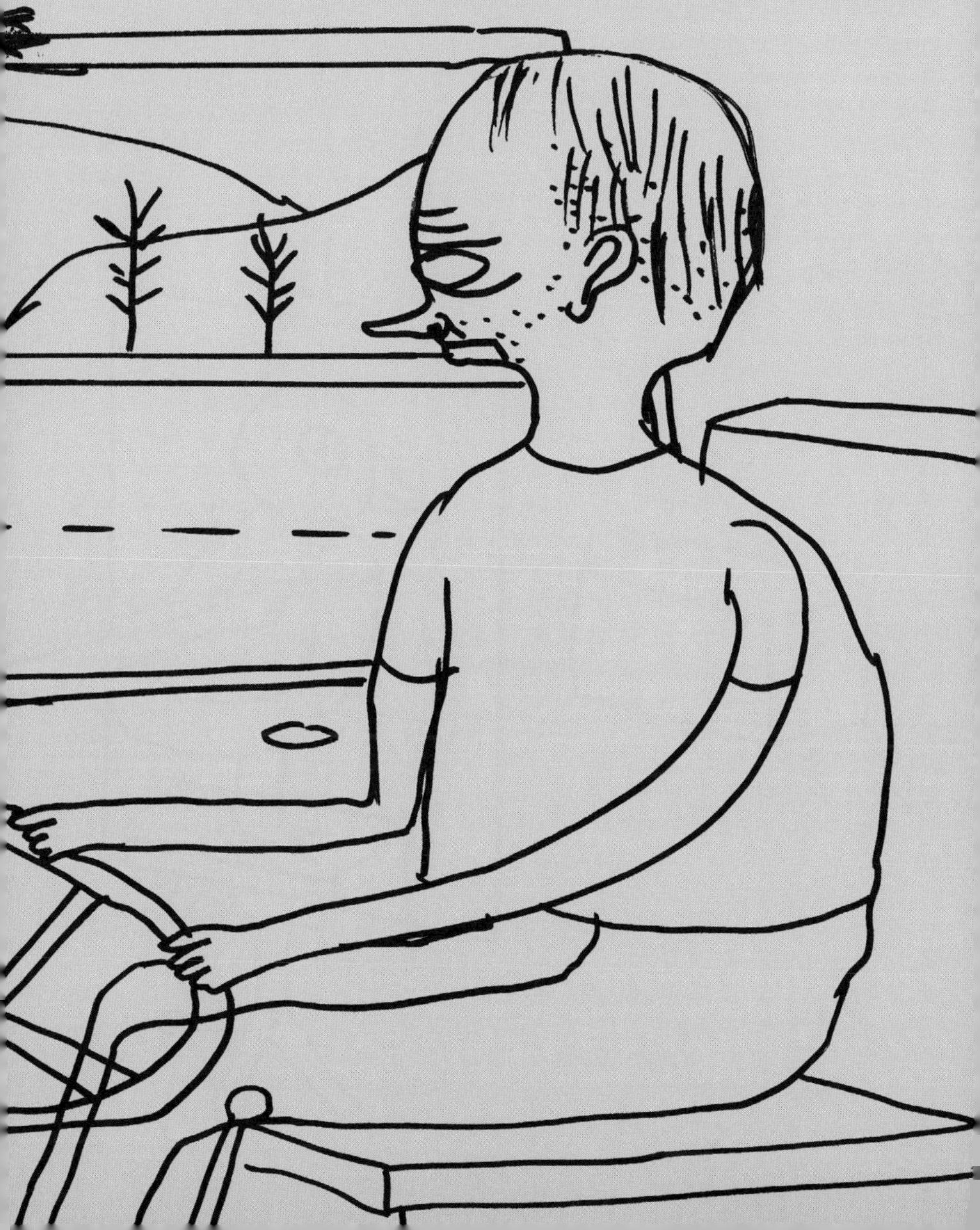

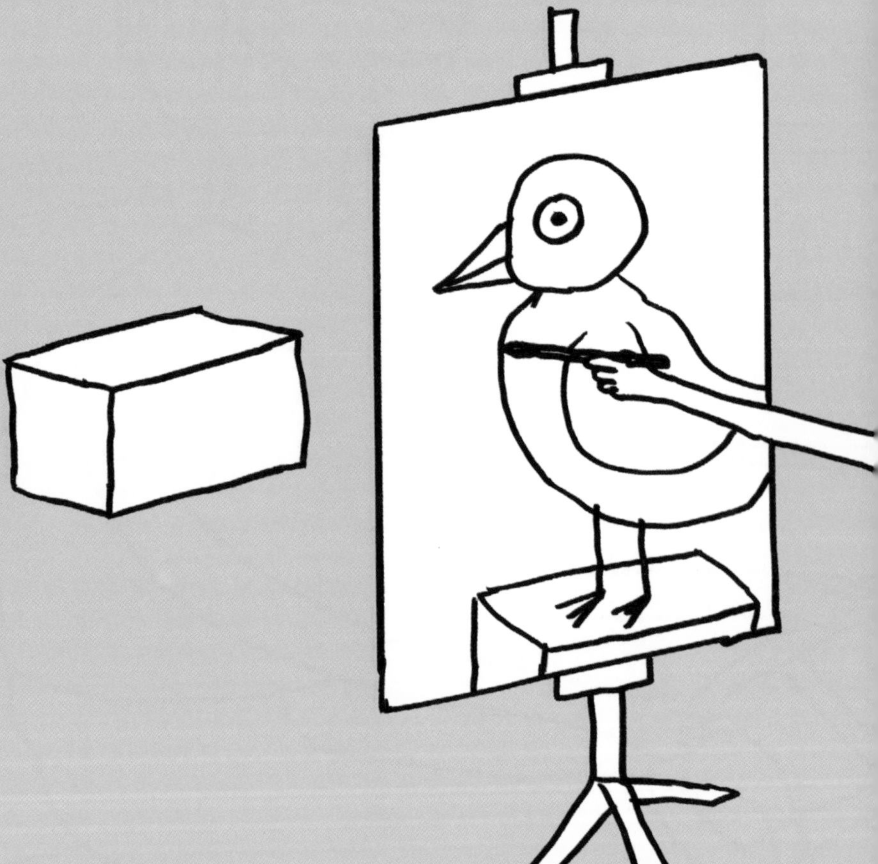

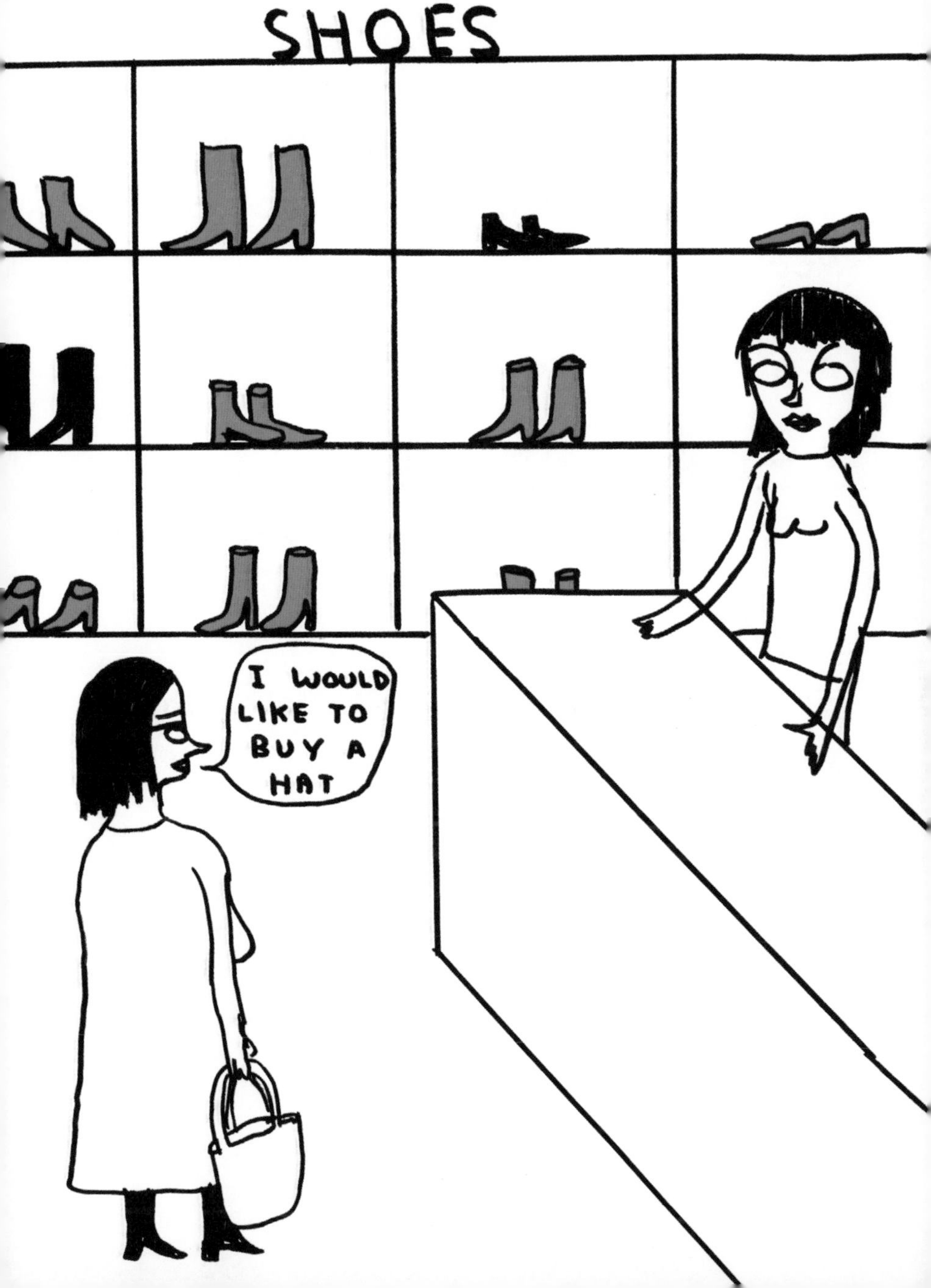
SHOES
I WOULD LIKE TO BUY A HAT

OH DEAR!

YOU WAKE UP IN THE MIDDLE OF
THE NIGHT WITH A HUGE BLACK
VENOMOUS SNAKE COILED ON
YOUR CHEST
DO NOT WORRY
GO BACK TO SLEEP

SPONTANEOUS

TRY TO AVOID BEING SPONTANEOUS

IMPULSIVE

THERE IS NOTHING WRONG WITH
BEING IMPULSIVE

ENLIGHTENMENT

I WOULD LIKE TO ACHIEVE ENLIGHTENMENT
BUT I HAVE ABSOLUTELY NO IDEA
HOW TO GO ABOUT IT

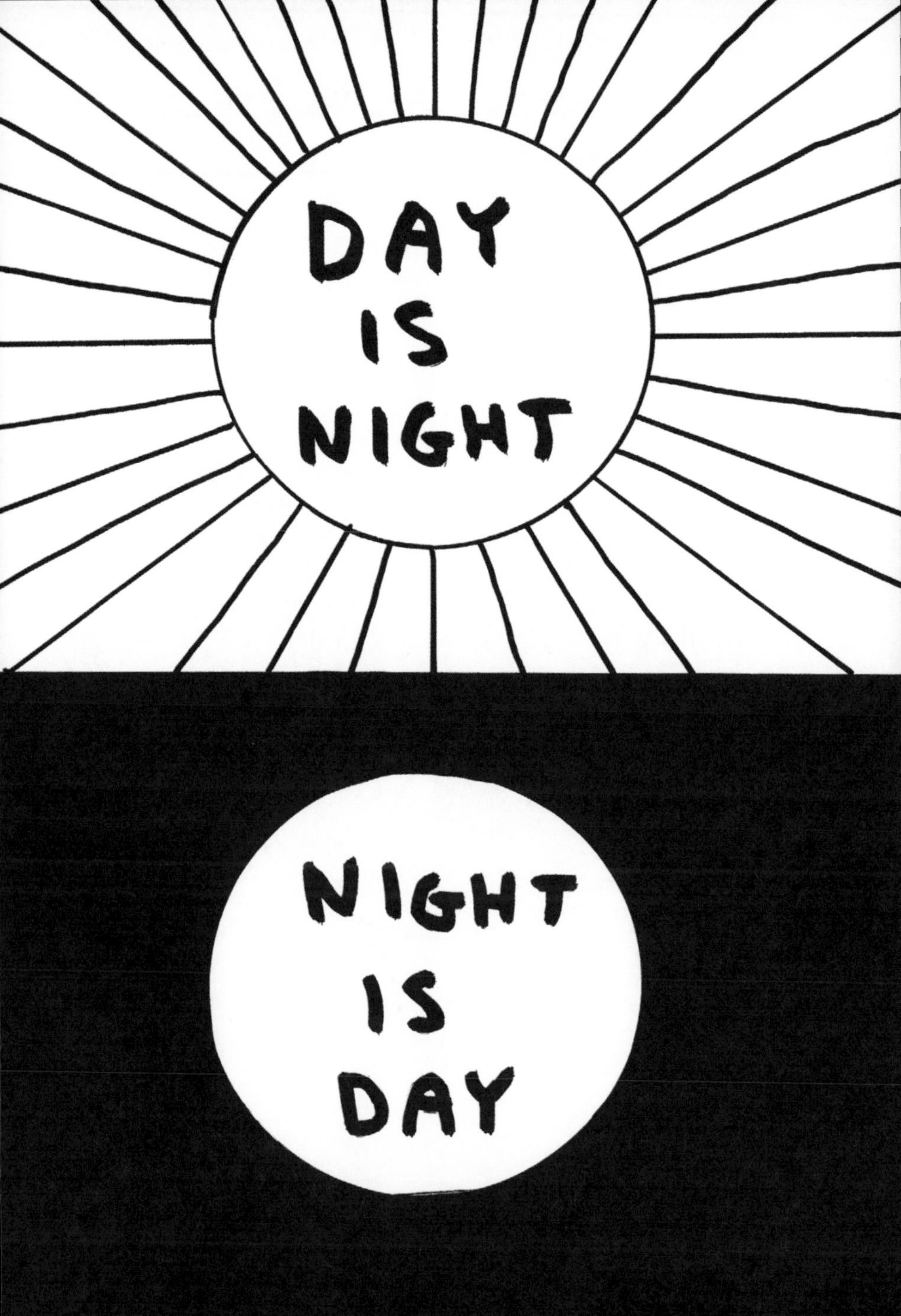
DAY
IS
NIGHT
NIGHT
IS
DAY

SOME PEOPLE CAN HANDLE IT AND SOME PEOPLE CAN'T

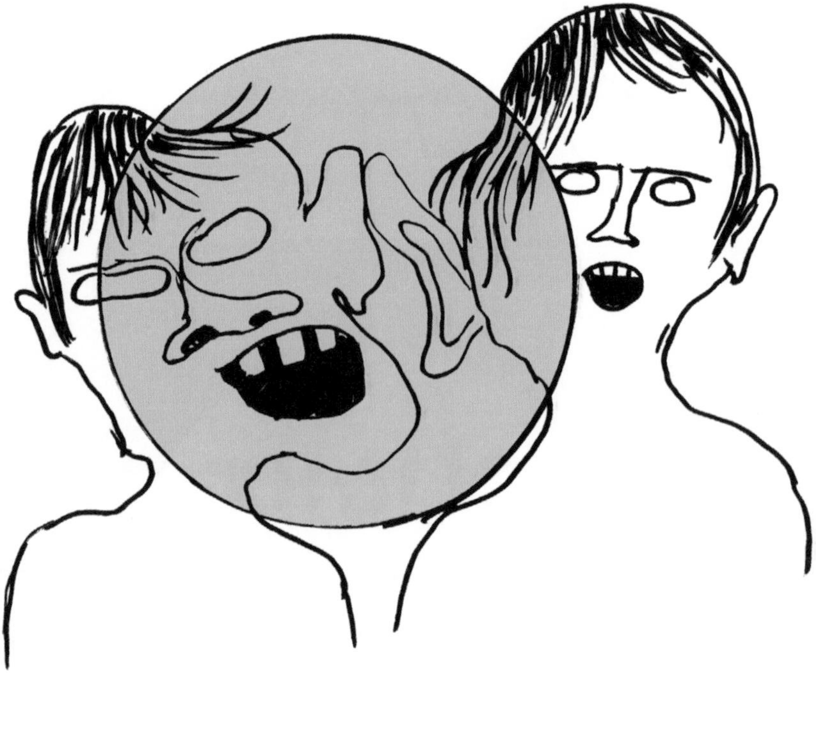

SOCIAL OCCASIONS CAN BE THE CAUSE
OF GREAT ANXIETY
HOW WILL YOU COPE WHEN YOU
HAVE TO INTERACT WITH PEOPLE?
- PEOPLE MAY ASK YOU PERSONAL
  QUESTIONS
- PEOPLE MAY NOT LISTEN WHEN
  YOU TALK
- PEOPLE MAY NOT LIKE YOU
- PEOPLE MAY TRY TO TOUCH YOU
- PEOPLE MAY TRY TO WRESTLE WITH YOU
- PEOPLE MAY FORCE YOU TO EAT
  PECULIAR THINGS
  LIKE CATERPILLARS
- PEOPLE MAY ASK YOU TO REMOVE
  YOUR MASK
- PEOPLE MAY ASK YOU TO REMOVE YOUR
  CLOTHES
- PEOPLE MAY INJECT YOU WITH DRUGS
  AND HANDLE YOUR JEWELS
- PEOPLE MAY LOCK YOU IN A ROOM

MASK-WEARING

WE ALL WEAR MASKS ALL THE TIME
OCCASIONALLY WE TAKE OFF OUR MASKS
BUT NOT VERY OFTEN
AND ONLY IN PRIVATE
OR WHEN WE GO TO THE DENTIST

THE RIGHT FACE

MAKE SURE THAT YOU HAVE THE
RIGHT FACE ON
REMEMBER!
'RIGHT FACE FOR THE RIGHT PLACE'

FEAR OF ABANDONMENT

THERE IS SOMETHING YOU CAN DO
ABOUT THIS
THE PERSON WHOM YOU ARE
AFRAID WILL ABANDON YOU CAN
BE MADE TO STAY
THERE ARE LOTS OF WAYS OF
MAKING THEM STAY

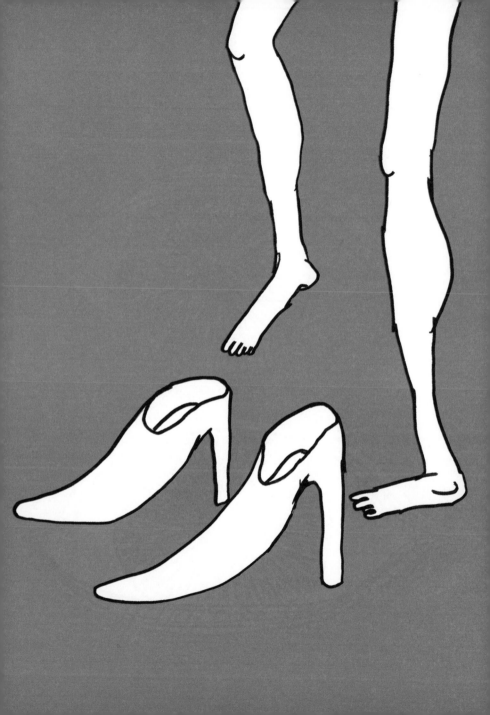

TWO
EYES

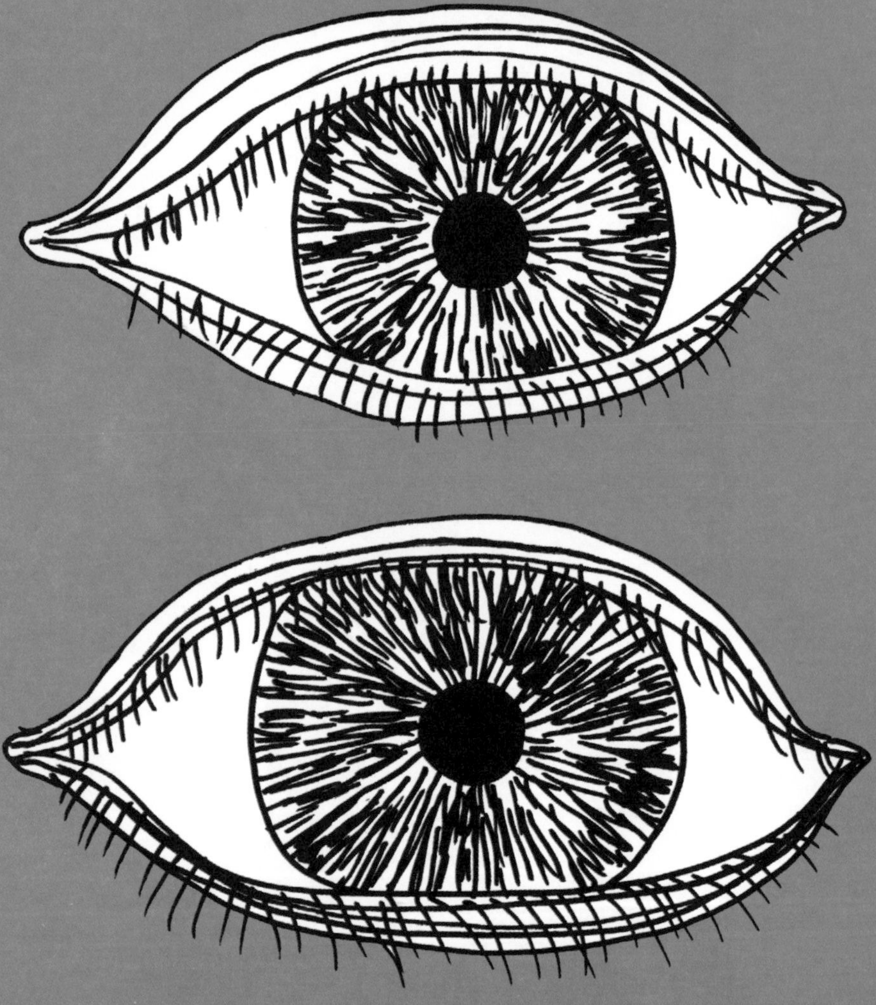

I WISH YOU HEALTH AND HAPPINESS
AND GOOD FORTUNE IN ALL YOUR DOINGS

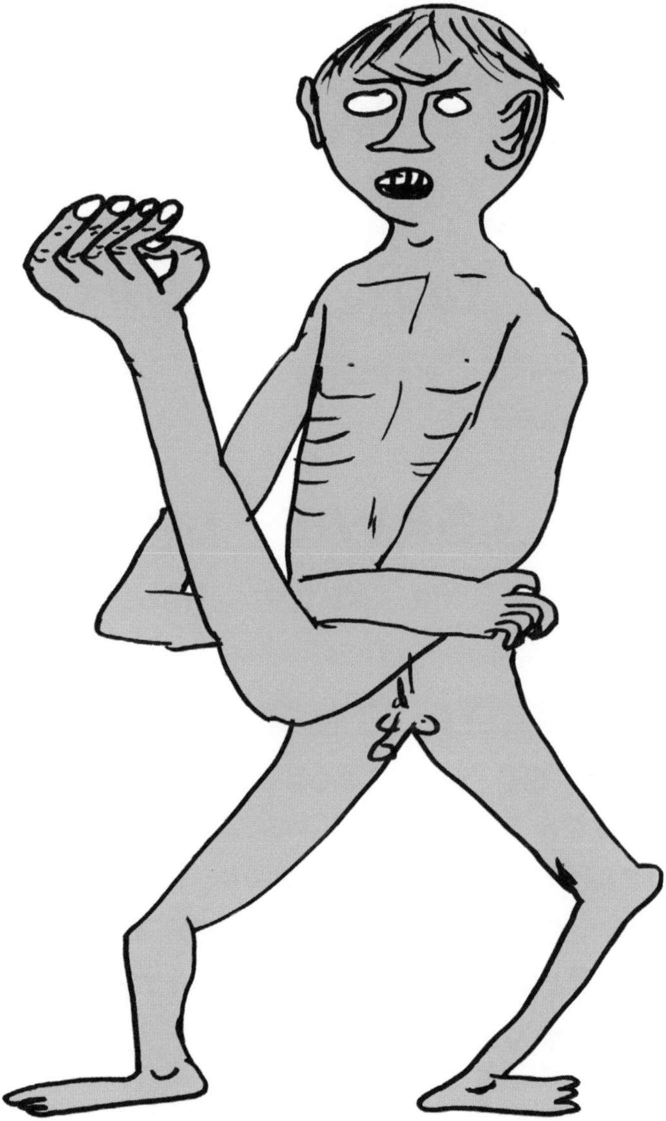

HUMANITY

TRY TO KEEP HOLD OF YOUR HUMANITY
OTHERWISE YOU WILL BECOME AN ANIMAL
IF YOU CAN'T KEEP HOLD OF YOUR
HUMANITY – TRY TO BE A WELL-
BEHAVED ANIMAL

KEEP YOUR RECEIPTS

YOU WILL NEED THEM FOR TAX
PURPOSES

THE LARVAE OF BUGS

TRY NOT TO THINK ABOUT THEM

SLAVE TO YOUR OWN NONSENSE

DON'T BE A SLAVE TO YOUR OWN
NONSENSE
IDENTIFY YOUR OWN NONSENSE
AND EITHER ELIMINATE IT
OR REDUCE ITS CAPACITY TO BE
EFFECTIVE

READING

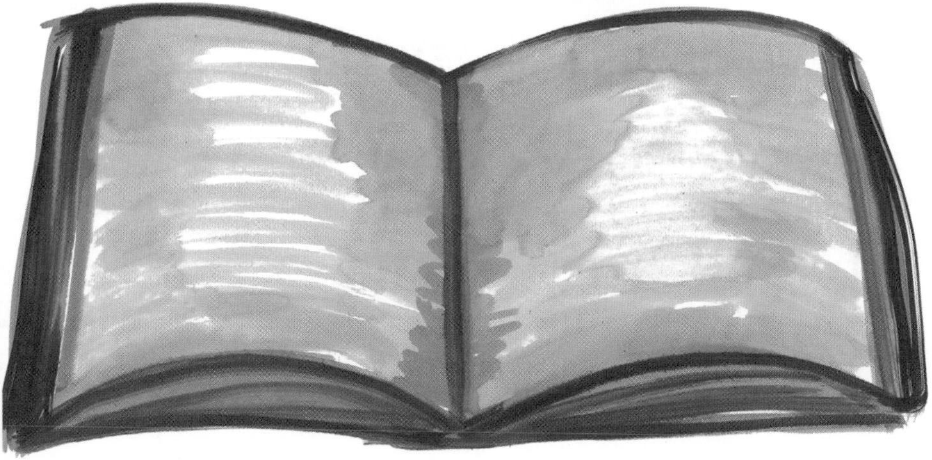

NOSEBLEED

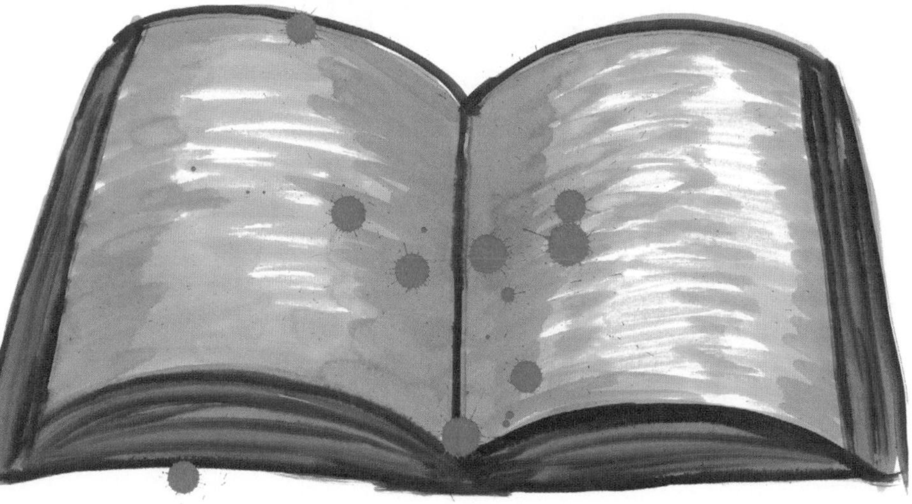

THERAPY GROUP

THE THERAPIST TELLS A JOKE
THE GROUP LAUGHS AT THE JOKE
EVERYONE IS BEING HEALED
IT WILL BE A LONG AND PAINFUL
JOURNEY

RISK

IT IS ACCEPTABLE TO TAKE SMALL
RISKS

PERSONAL SAFETY

AVOID GOING OUTSIDE
NEVER WRITE ANYTHING DOWN
BURN YOUR RUBBISH
OR STORE IT AT HOME
BE SAFE
GOOD LUCK

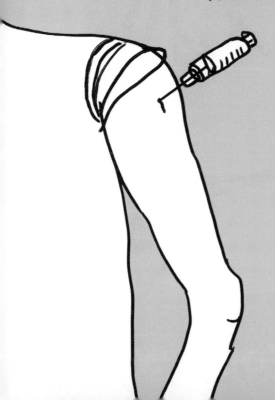

INOCULATION
AGAINST FOOLISHNESS

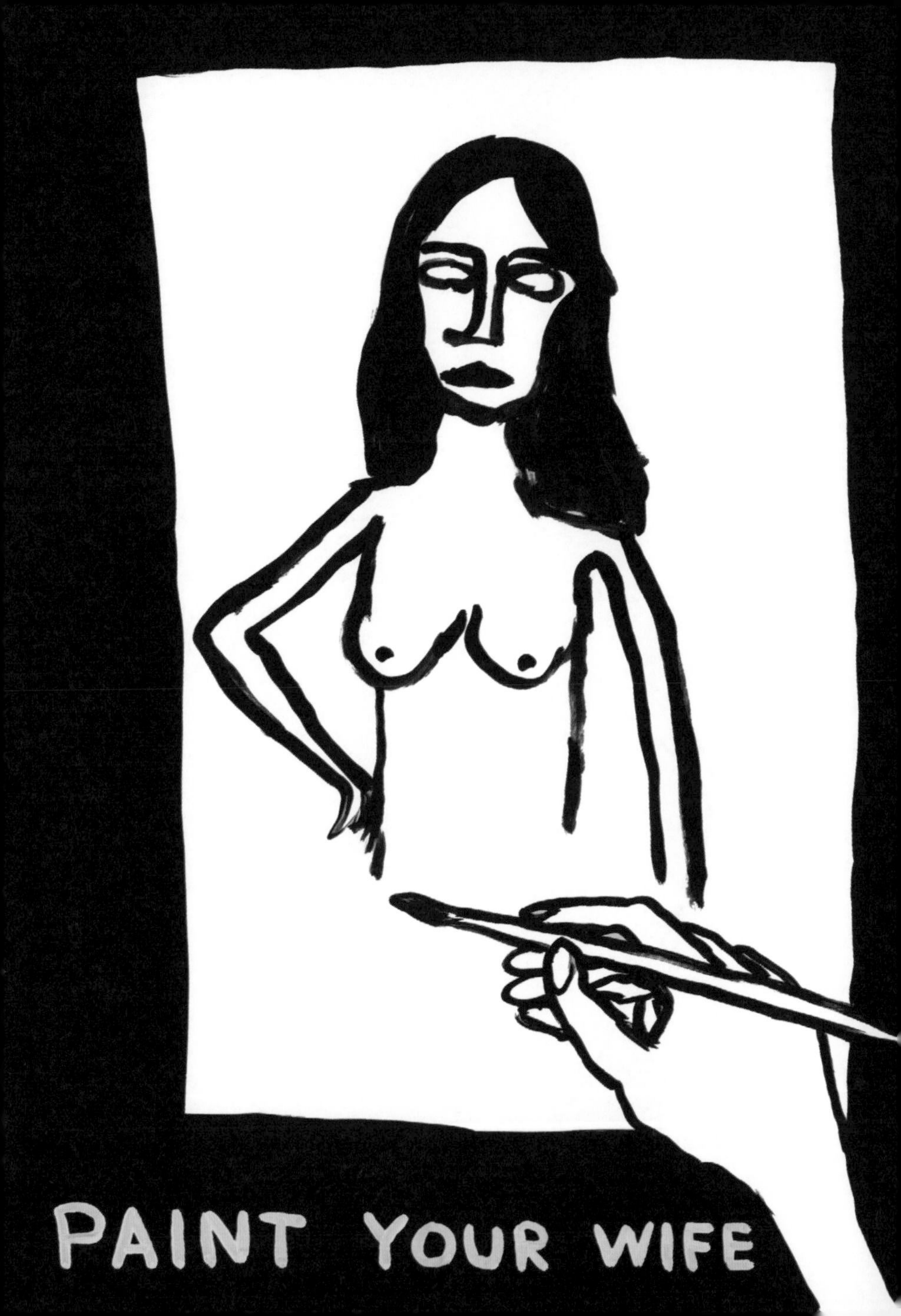
PAINT YOUR WIFE

PERSONAL SPACE

SO MUCH SPACE AVAILABLE
INSIDE YOU
AND YOU DO SO LITTLE WITH IT
IT IS WASTED

REMEMBER:

IT IS WASTED

THE INNER SHELF

WHAT WILL YOU PUT ON YOUR
INNER SHELF?
PICTURES OF LOVED ONES?
SOUVENIRS?
MUGS?
CACTI?
██ ?

PERSONAL EXPERIENCE

TRY TO LEARN FROM YOUR PERSONAL
EXPERIENCES

REMEMBER:

A PERSONAL EXPERIENCE IS ▬
SOMETHING THAT HAPPENS TO <u>YOU</u>.
THINGS THAT HAVE HAPPENED
TO OTHER PEOPLE THAT YOU
HAVE OBSERVED OR THAT YOU
HAVE HEARD ABOUT DO NOT
COUNT AS PERSONAL EXPERIENCES.

TOOLS FOR COPING

A ▬▬▬ DICTIONARY
WATERPROOF CLOTHING
STAB VEST
SENSE OF HUMOUR

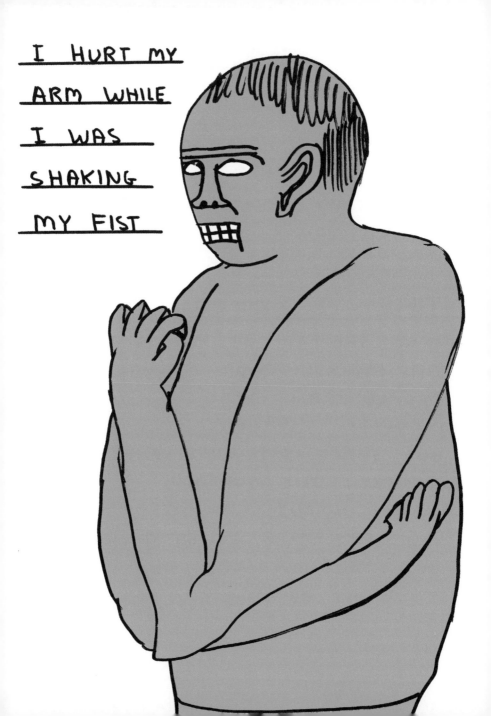

I HURT MY
ARM WHILE
I WAS
SHAKING
MY FIST

GOING BACKWARDS

IT IS NOT ALWAYS POSSIBLE TO
GO FORWARDS
SOMETIMES YOU MUST GO BACKWARDS
BEFORE YOU START TO GO BACKWARDS
CHECK THAT THERE IS NOTHING
BEHIND YOU

THE ICEBERG

ONLY THE TIP OF YOU IS VISIBLE
THIS SMALL PART OF YOU THAT
PEOPLE CAN SEE
IS QUITE PLEASANT
BUT THERE IS A HUGE PART OF YOU
BENEATH THE SURFACE
THAT NO ONE CAN SEE
YOU SAY YOUR LOWER REGION IS NICE
BUT YOU COULD BE LYING
IT MIGHT BE HORRIBLE AND/OR DISEASED

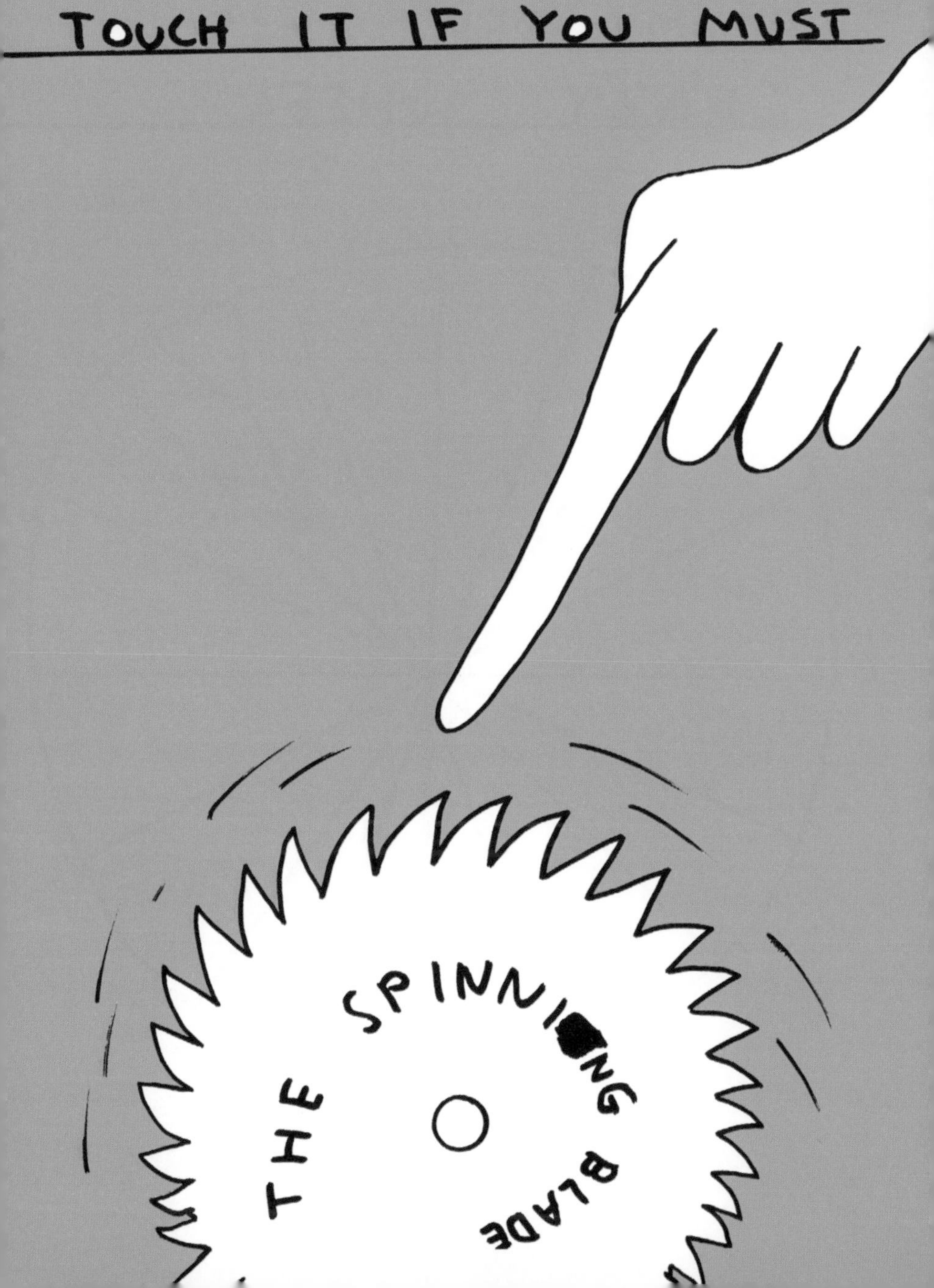
TOUCH IT IF YOU MUST
THE SPINNING BLADE

LET ME OFF THIS CRAZY WHEEL

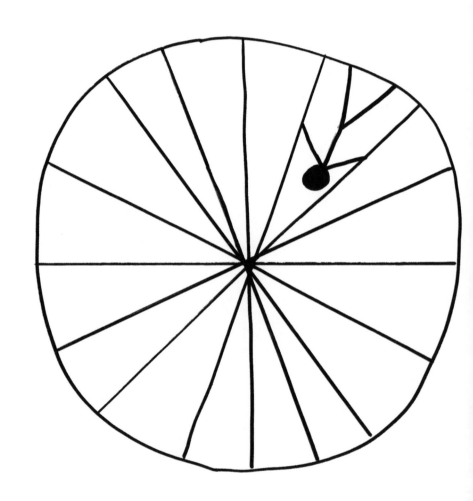

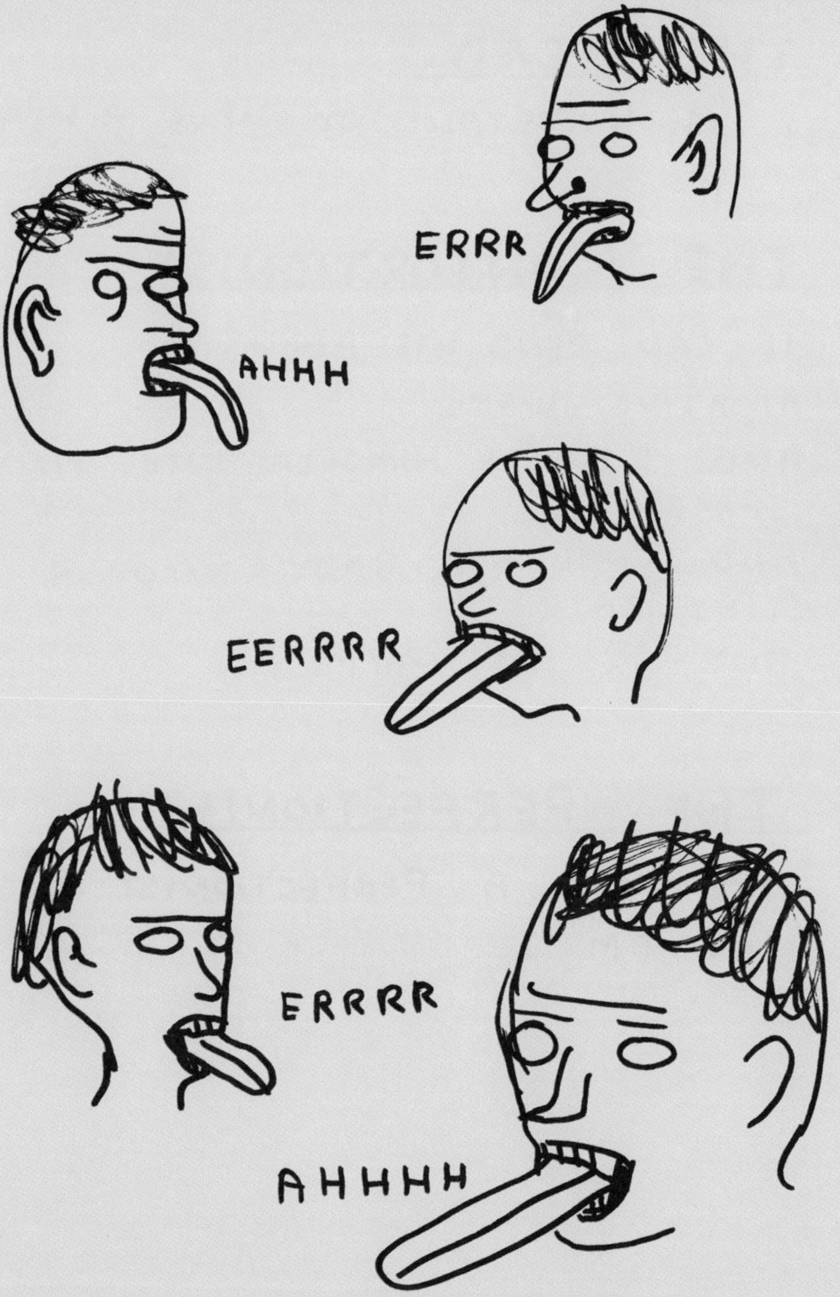
ERRR
AHHH
EERRRR
ERRRR
AHHHHH

THE HEAD

IT IS IMPORTANT TO HAVE A HEAD

THE CONTORTIONIST

HE CAN BEND HIS BODY IN
AMAZING WAYS
AND SQUEEZE HIMSELF INTO TINY
SPACES
AND CURL HIS BODY INTO A
TINY BALL
BUT IS HE HAPPY?

THE PERFECTIONIST

ARE YOU A PERFECTIONIST?
SO AM I

I'M FALLING TO
THE EARTH AT A
THOUSAND MILES AN

HOUR BUT IT'S OK
BECAUSE I'VE GOT
A PARACHUTE

IT'S FOR YOU

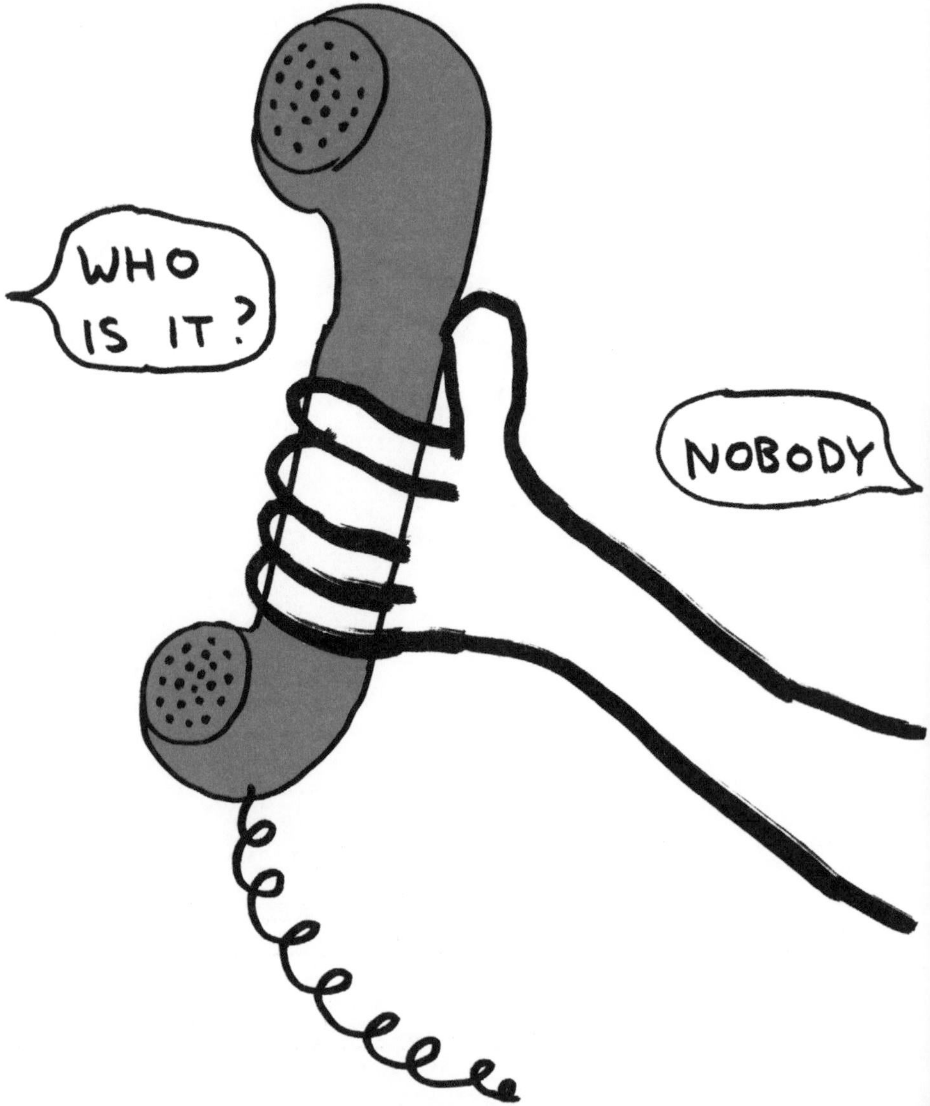
WHO IS IT?
NOBODY

I WATCH THEM FROM A PLACE OF CONCEALMENT

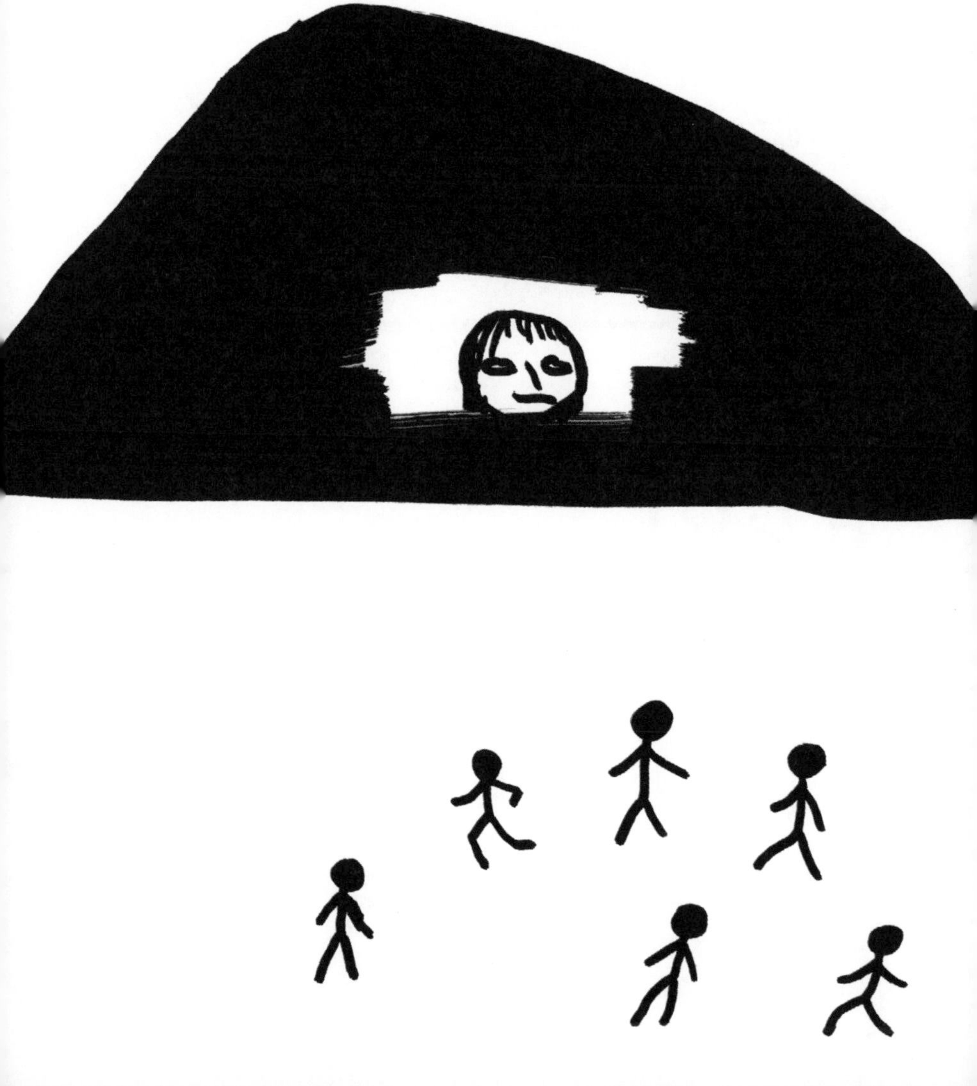

AND THEY
SAID THAT
HE WAS A
FOOL

BUT I DID NOT
THINK HE WAS A
FOOL

BUT IT WAS
LATER PROVEN
THAT HE WAS
A FOOL

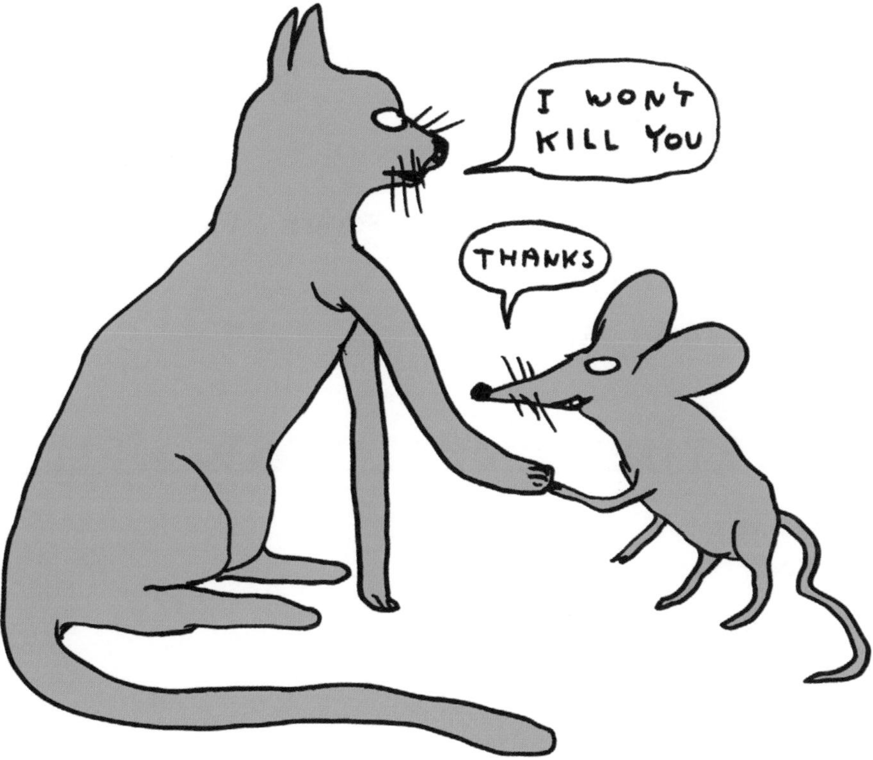
I WON'T KILL YOU
THANKS

SHITTING

"I LIKE TO SHIT
 I AM PROUD OF MY SHITS"

"I DO NOT LIKE TO SHIT
 I AM ASHAMED OF MY SHITS"

RELAXATION

LARGE DARKENED TANK FULL OF
SALT WATER
LIKE YOU ARE A BIG FISH

MEETING YOUR BASIC NEEDS

FOOD
SEX
PLASTIC SHEETING
MAGAZINES

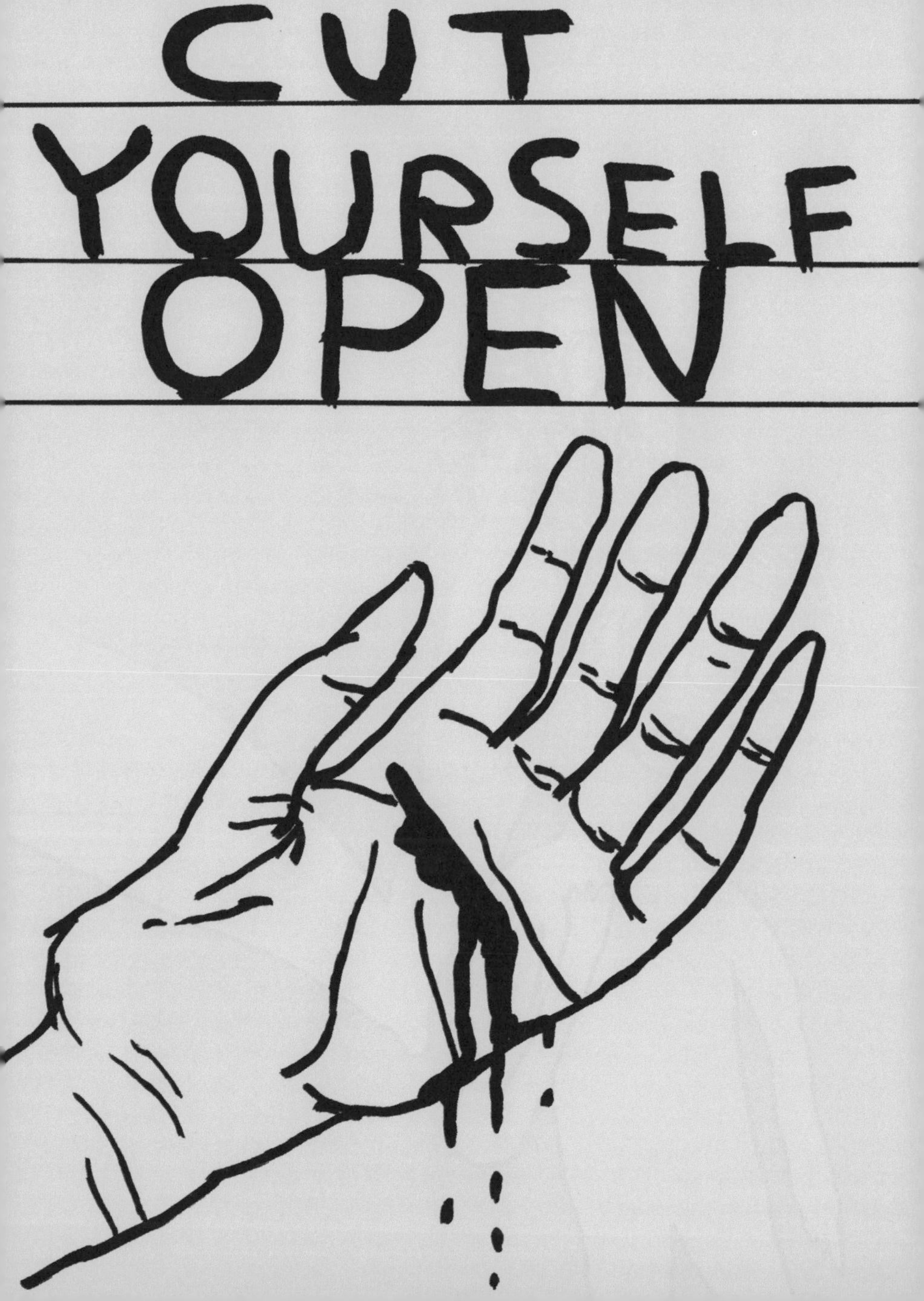
CUT
YOURSELF
OPEN

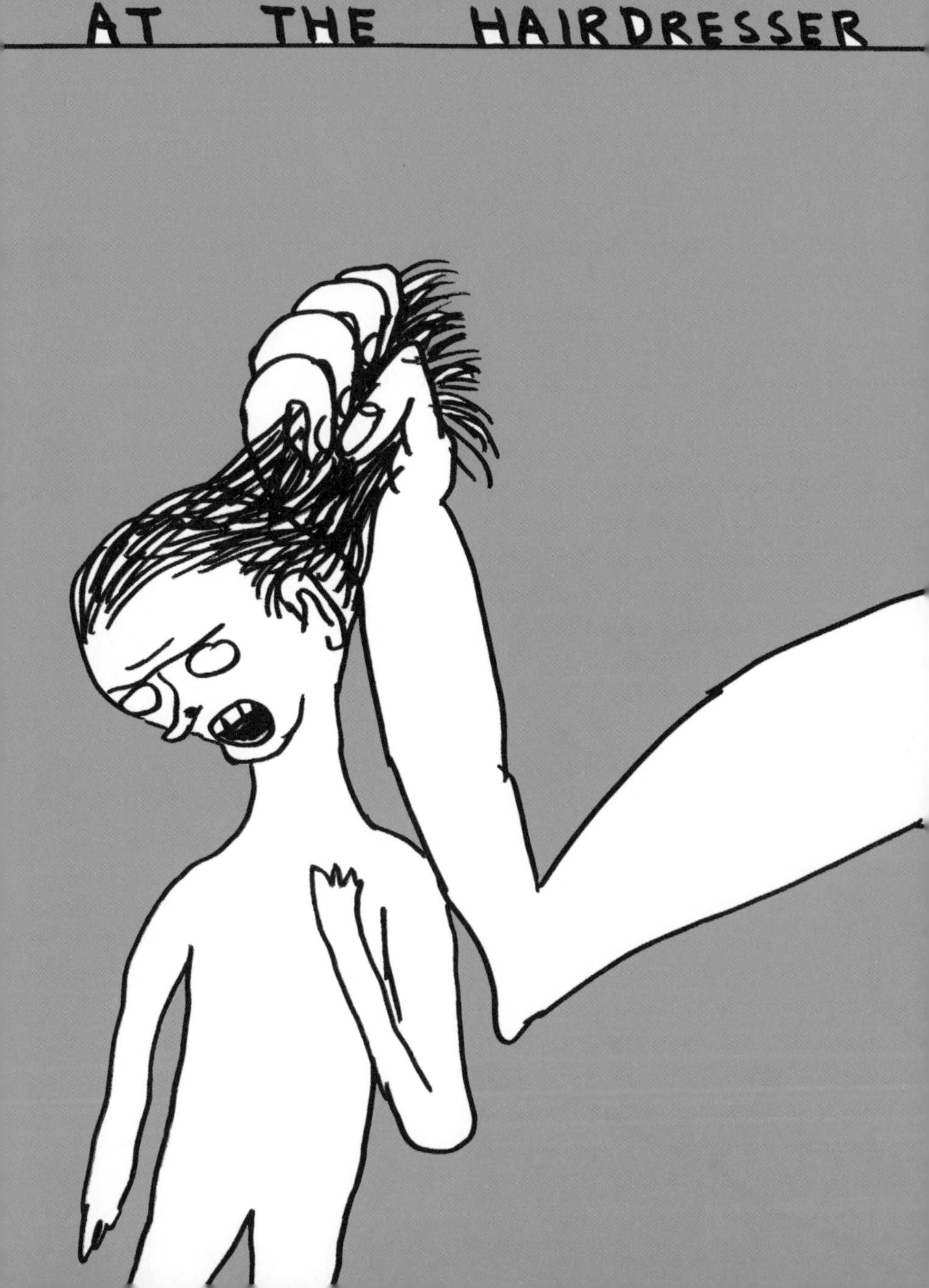
AT THE HAIRDRESSER

IT'S OK TO RUN AWAY FROM YOUR PROBLEMS

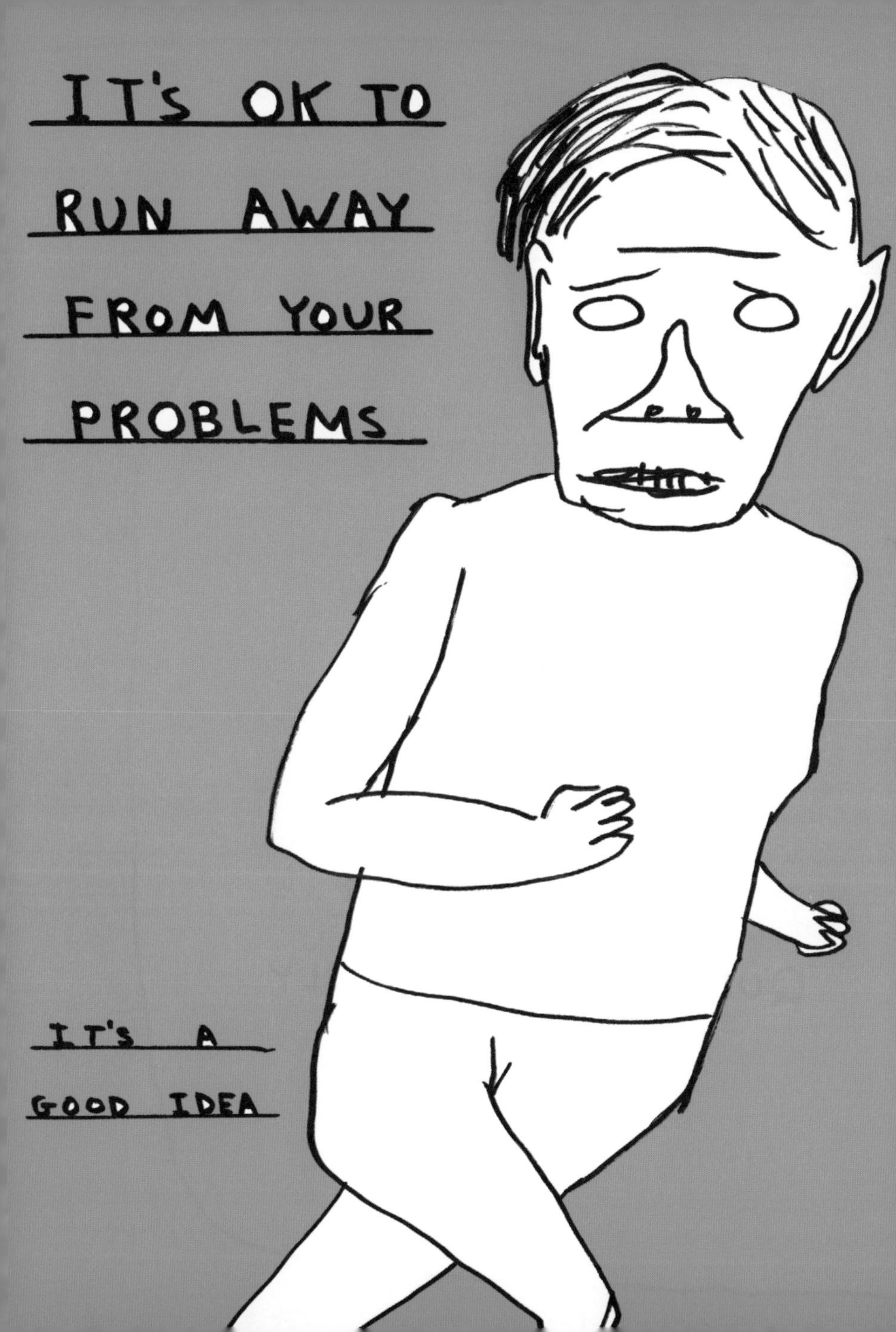

IT'S A GOOD IDEA

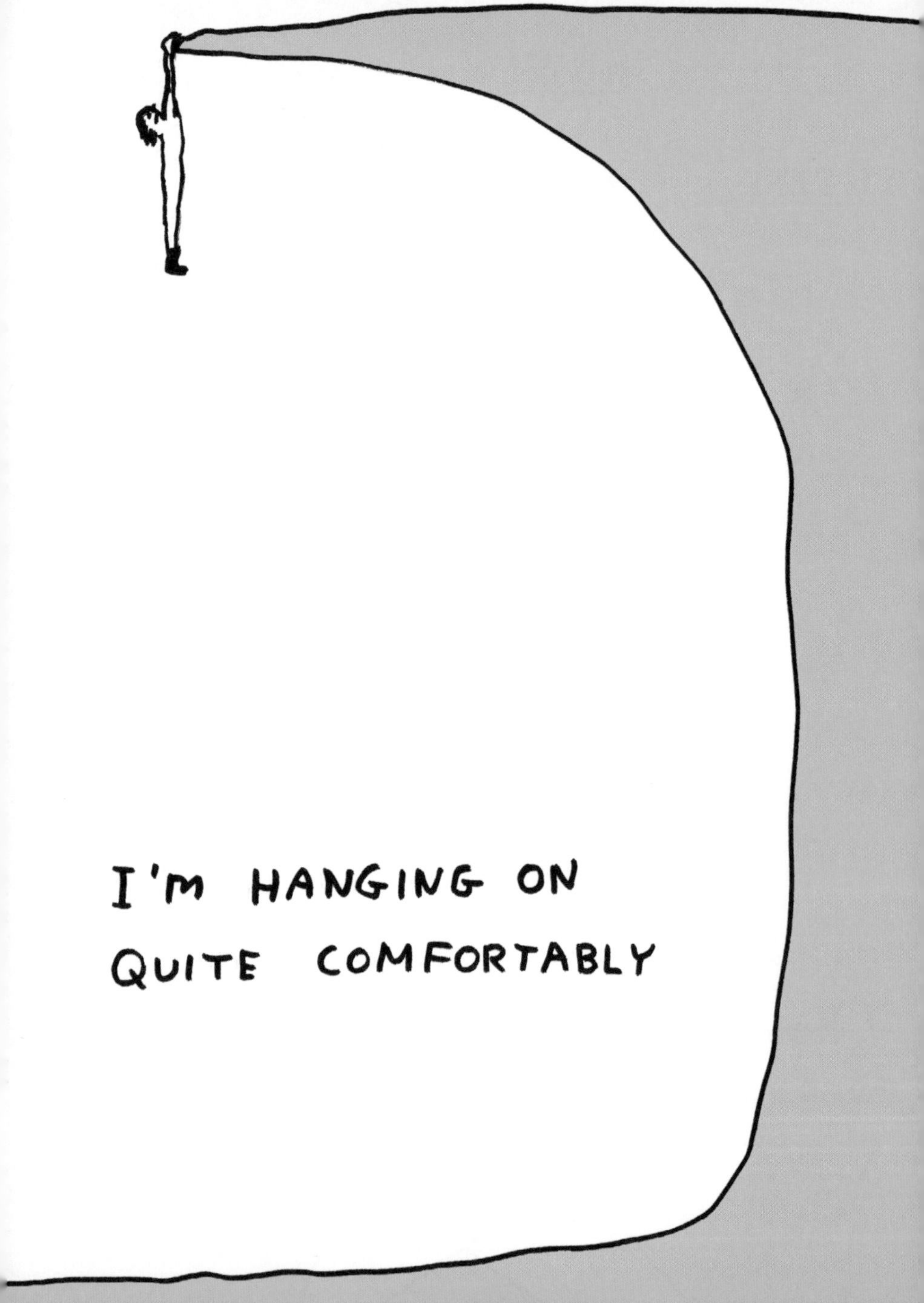
I'M HANGING ON
QUITE COMFORTABLY

CHAPTER ELEVEN

TRY TO BE MORE SENSIBLE AND REALISTIC IN ORDER TO AVOID DIFFI- -CULT SITUATIONS

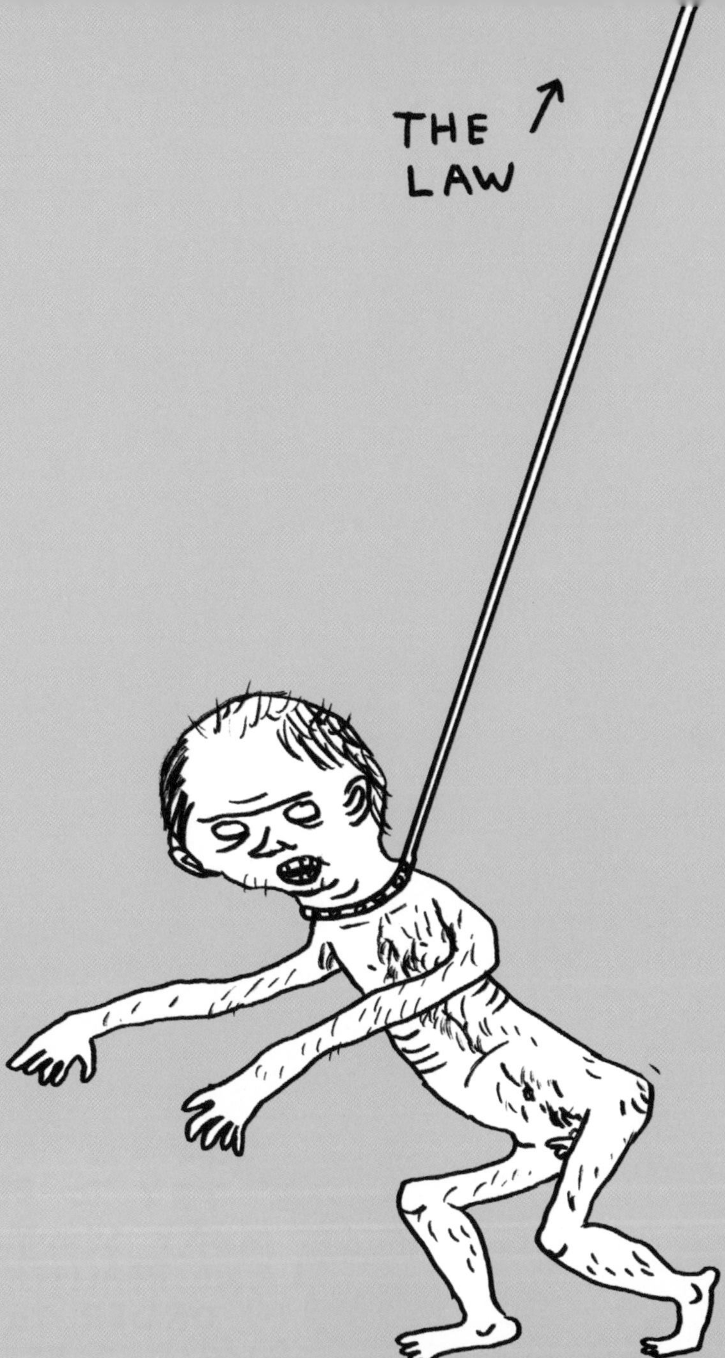
THE LAW

EMPTY CHAIR TECHNIQUE

TWO PERSONS RUNNING AROUND
THE MUSIC STOPS
THEY FIGHT

DRAWING

IT'S FUN TO DRAW
AND IT'S GOOD FOR YOUR BRAIN
IN MENTAL INSTITUTIONS THEY OFTEN
ALLOW THE LUNATICS TO DRAW PICTURES
THE PICTURES THEMSELVES ARE AWFUL
BUT THE ACTIVITY OF DRAWING
CALMS THEM DOWN
SO IT CAN BE CONSIDERED A GOOD THING

ROLE - PLAYING

YOU ARE A TABLE
I WILL PUT THINGS ON YOU
TRY NOT TO MOVE
I AM A VACUUM CLEANER
I WILL SUCK CRUMBS OFF
YOUR SWEATER
I WILL SUCK DIRT OUT OF THE
CARPET
I WILL SUCK DUST OFF THE
CURTAINS
I WILL SUCK LOOSE HAIR OFF
THE CAT

JUST GO FOR IT!

I DON'T KNOW WHAT YOU ARE
TALKING ABOUT
I HATE YOU

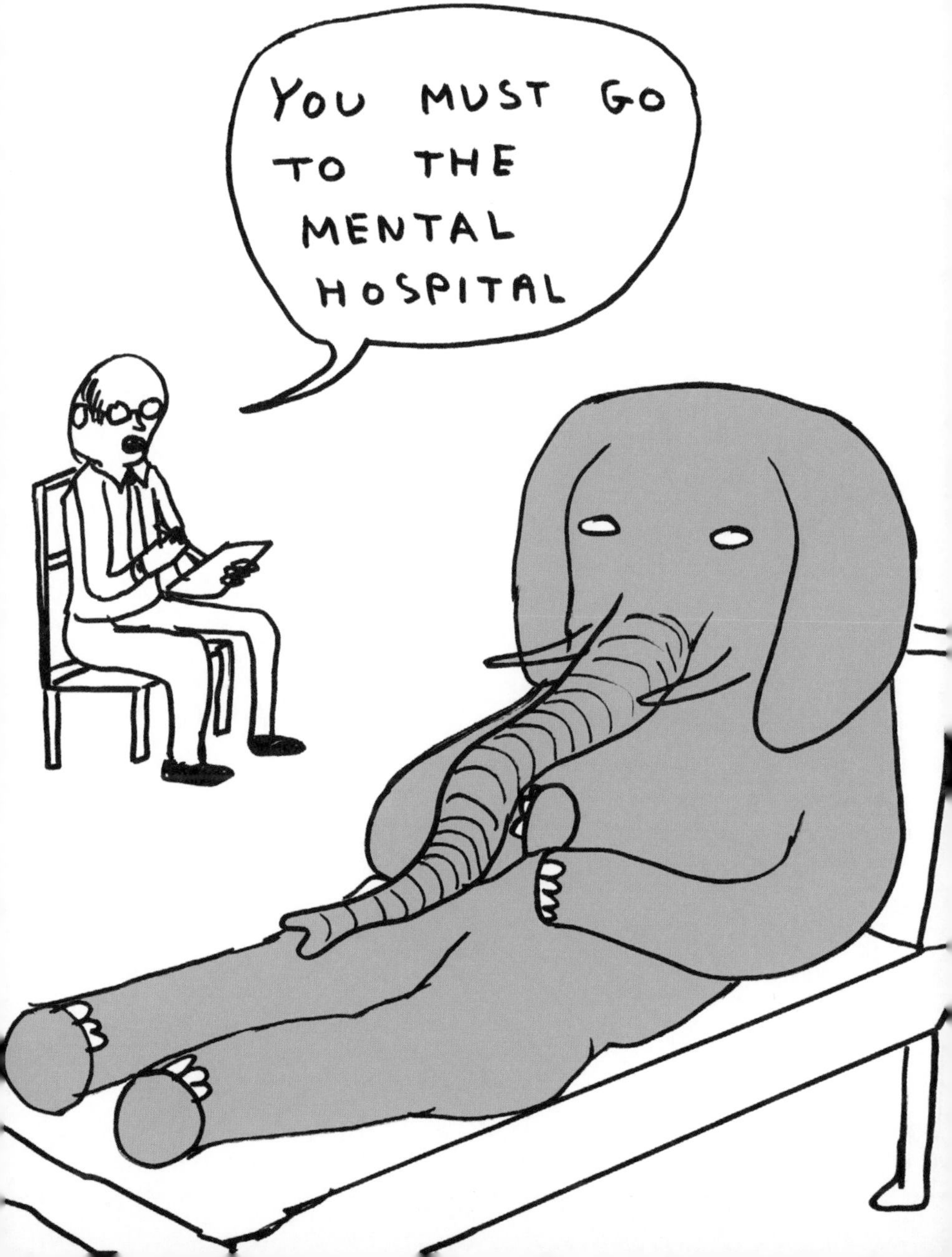
YOU MUST GO TO THE MENTAL HOSPITAL

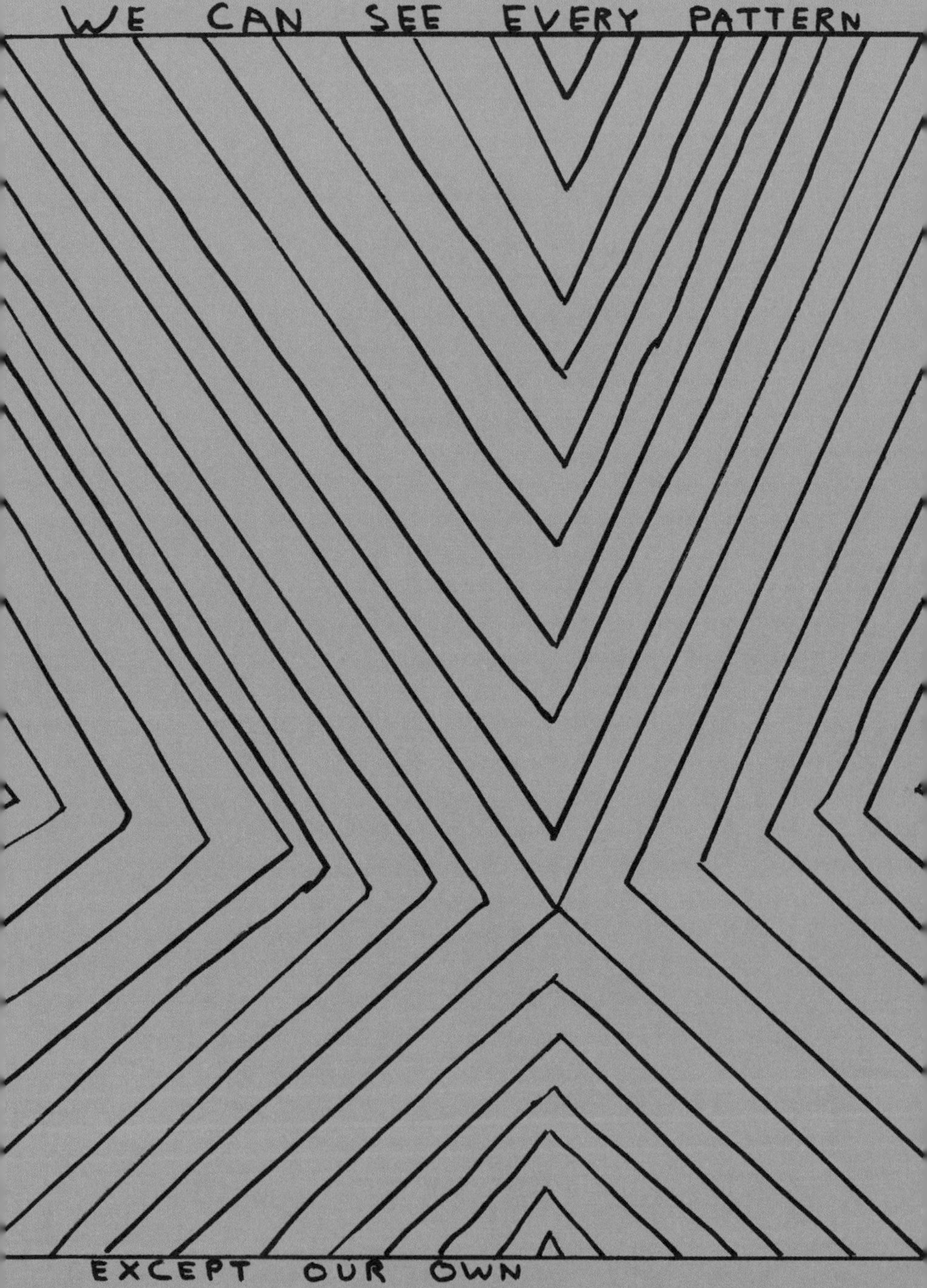
WE CAN SEE EVERY PATTERN
EXCEPT OUR OWN

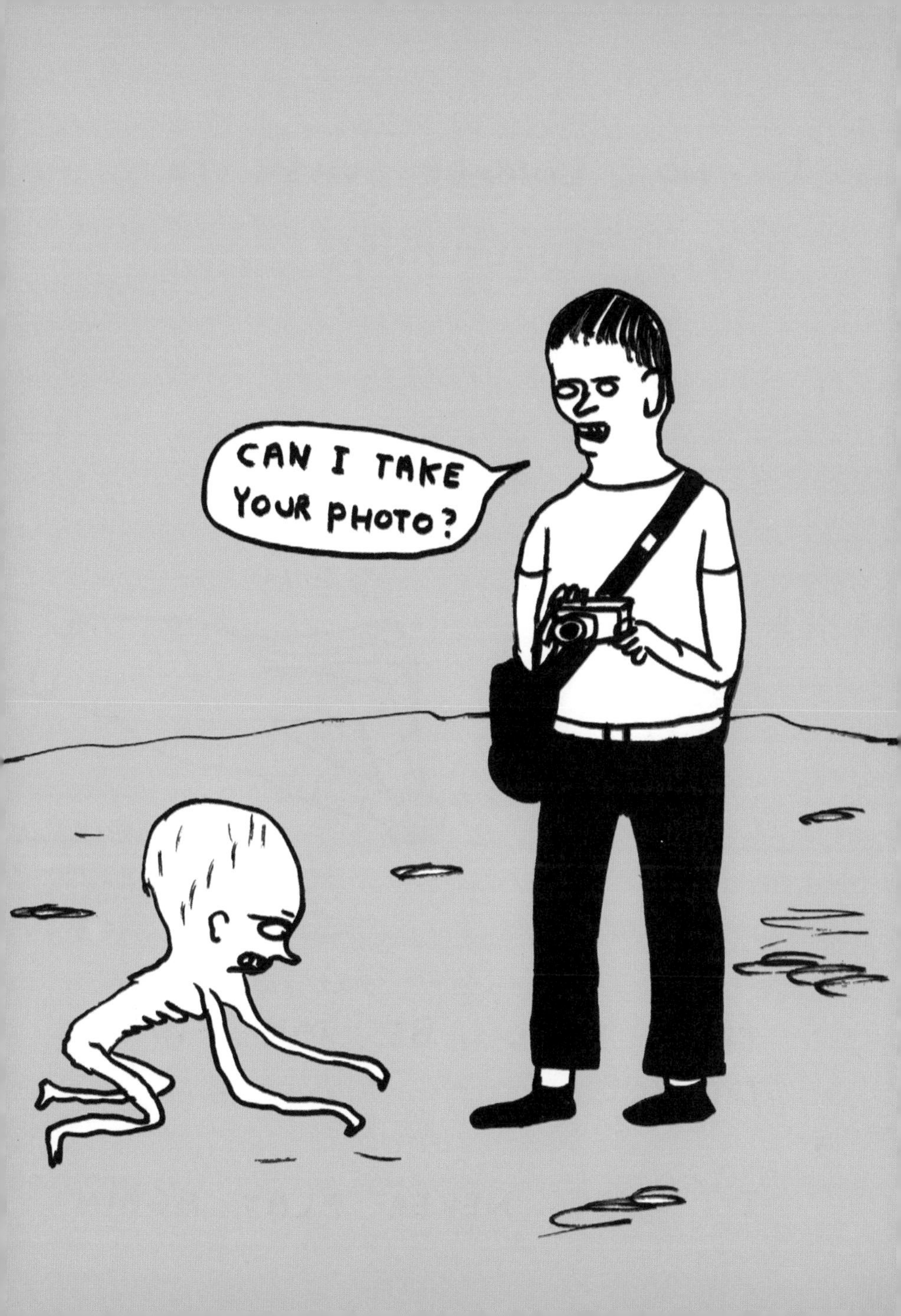
CAN I TAKE YOUR PHOTO?

I NO LONGER WISH TO
PLAY TIDDLYWINKS

THIS WILL BE MY FINAL
GAME

I WILL NEVER PLAY AGAIN

USEFUL FOR:

REMEMBERING NAMES
AVOIDING INJURY
MIMICKING FOREIGN ACCENTS
TELLING THE TIME
FOCUSSING ON THINGS
CURING HEADACHES
THINKING
DANCING
JUGGLING
IMPROVING PARENTING SKILLS
UNTYING KNOTS

GAME ONE:
RAT HUNT
FLUSH THE TOILET
FOLLOW THE RAT DOWN THE PIPES
WHEN THE RAT ARRIVES IN THE SEWER
TRY TO KILL IT
TRY TO KILL ALL THE RATS IN THE
SEWER
WHEN YOU HAVE KILLED ALL THE
RATS
GO BACK UP THE PIPE

GAME TWO:
CAR CRUSHER
TRY TO CRUSH THE CARS AS THEY
DRIVE PAST

GAME THREE:
GOLF
TRY TO KILL THE GOLFERS

EGO-BOOSTING GAMES
SEE RAT HUNT

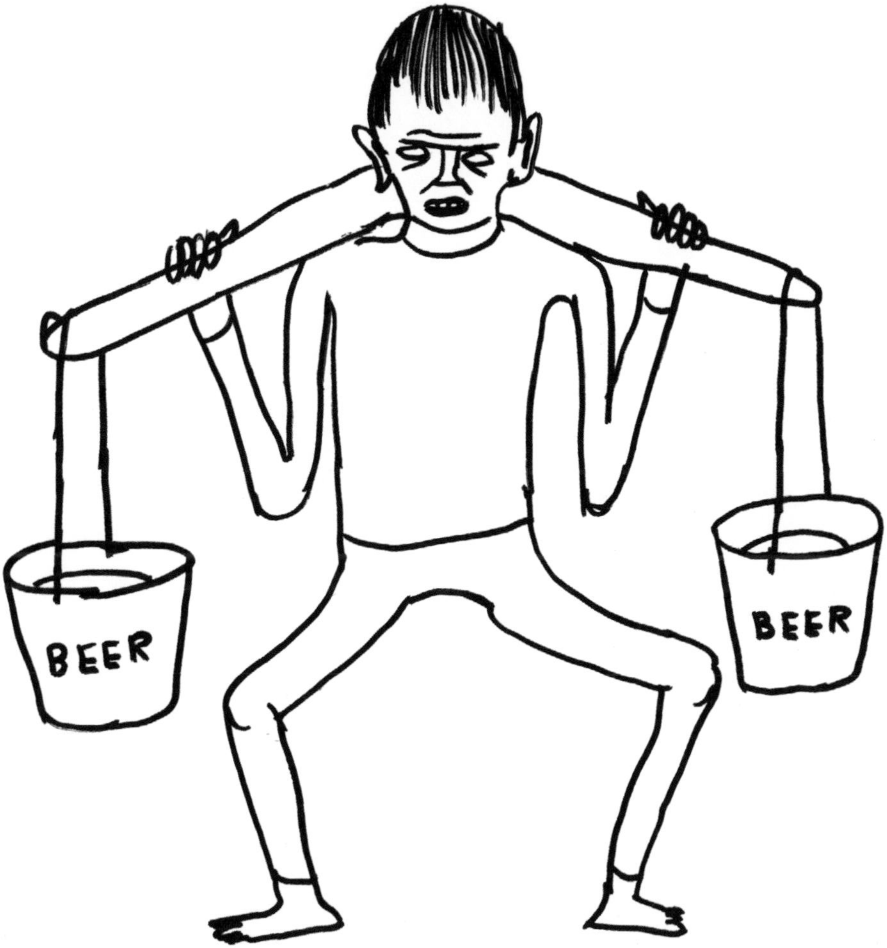
BEER
BEER

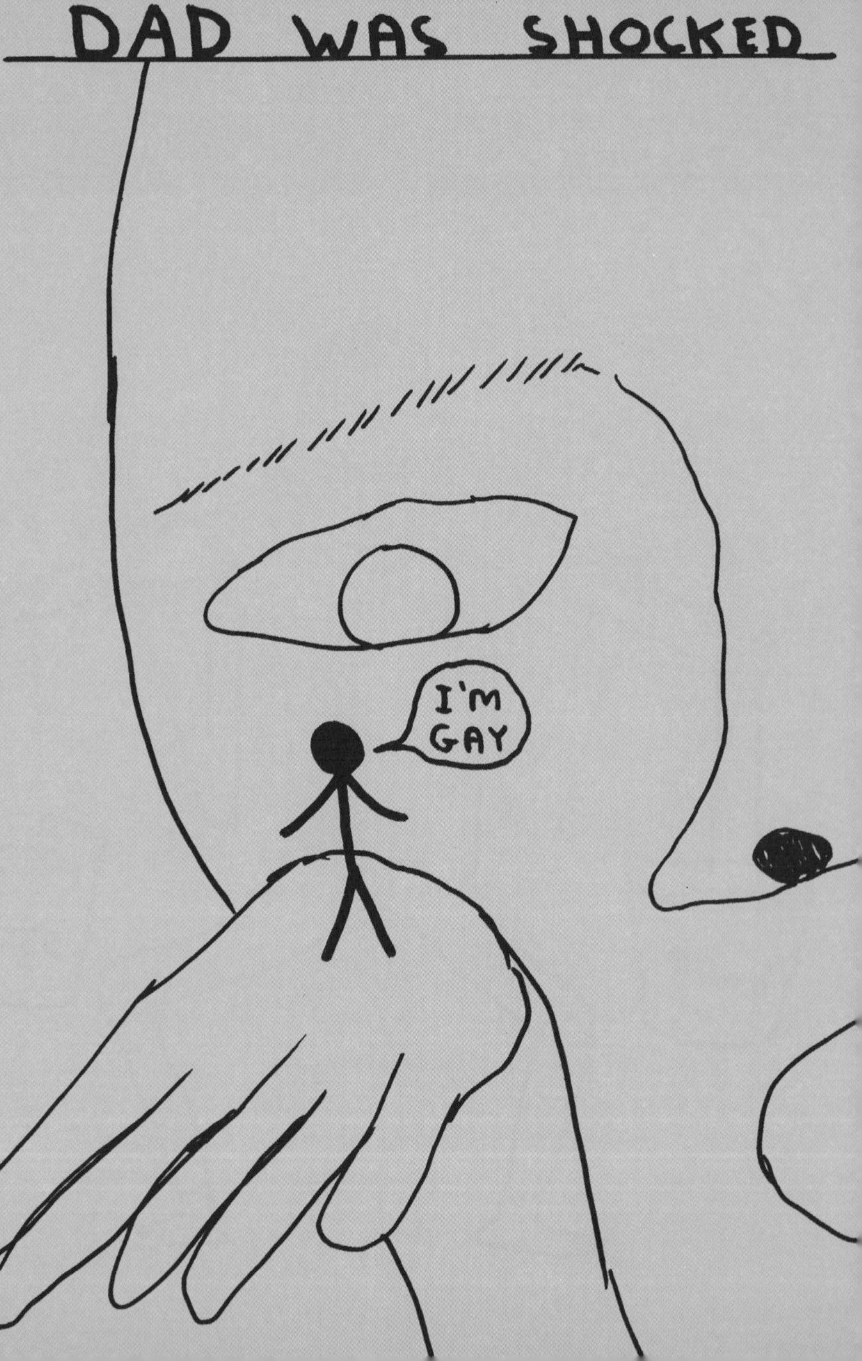
DAD WAS SHOCKED
I'M GAY

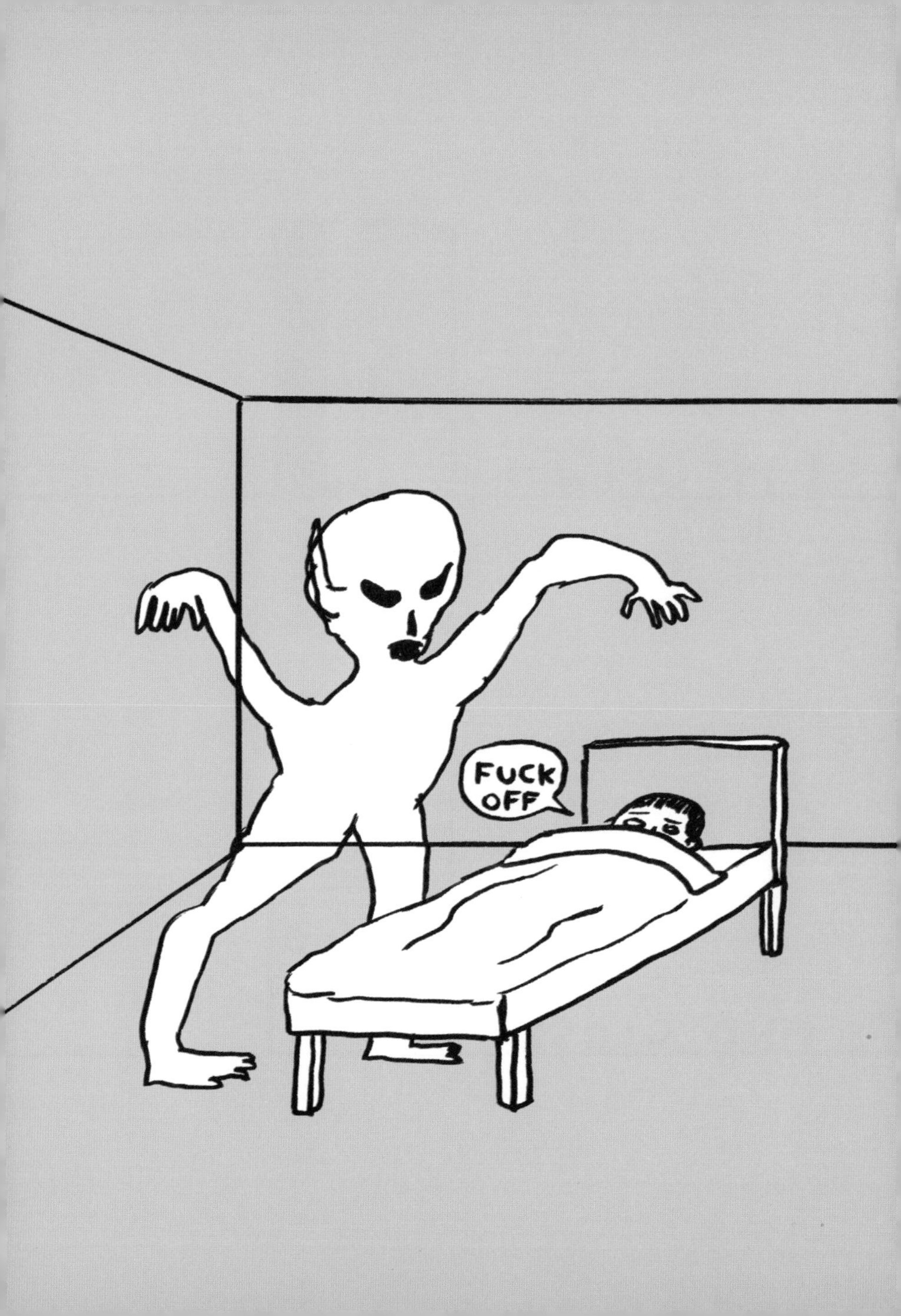
FUCK OFF

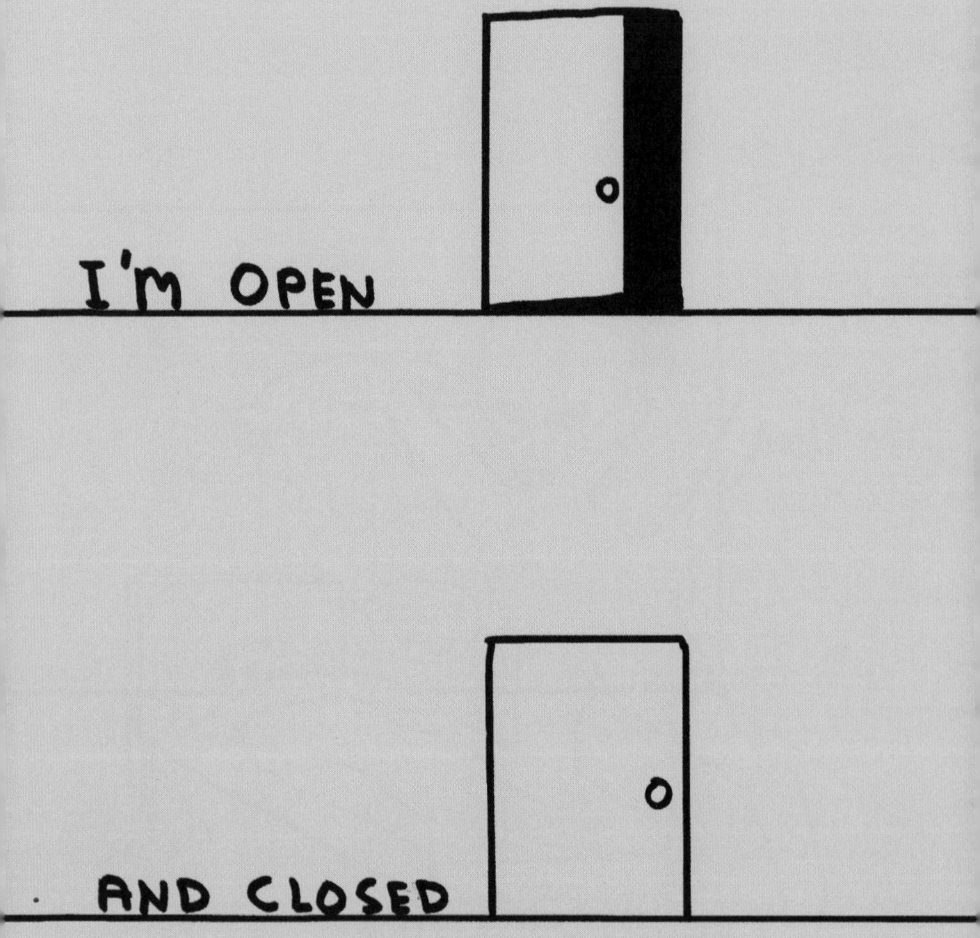
I'M OPEN
AND CLOSED

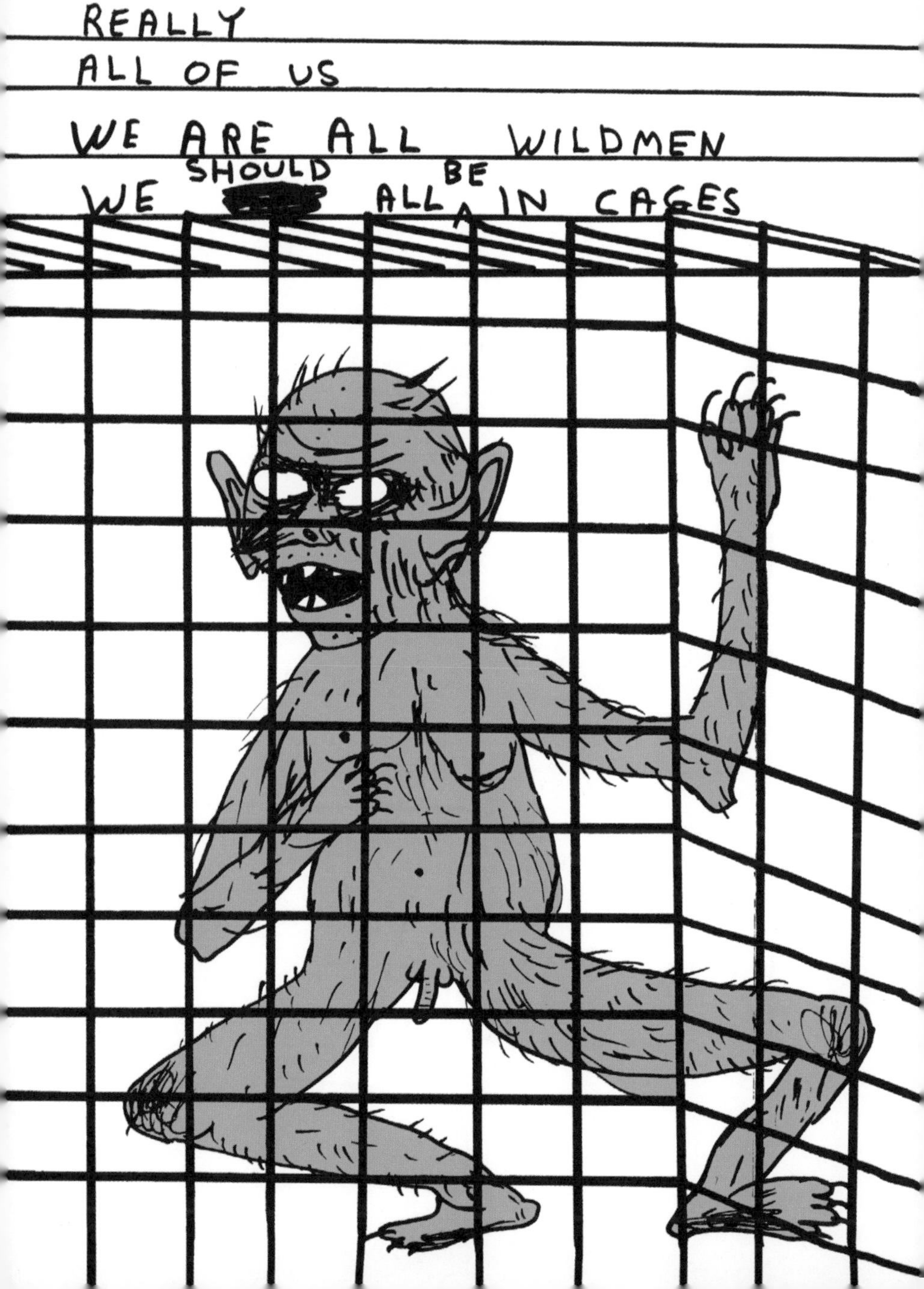
REALLY
ALL OF US
WE ARE ALL WILDMEN
SHOULD BE
WE [redacted] ALL IN CAGES

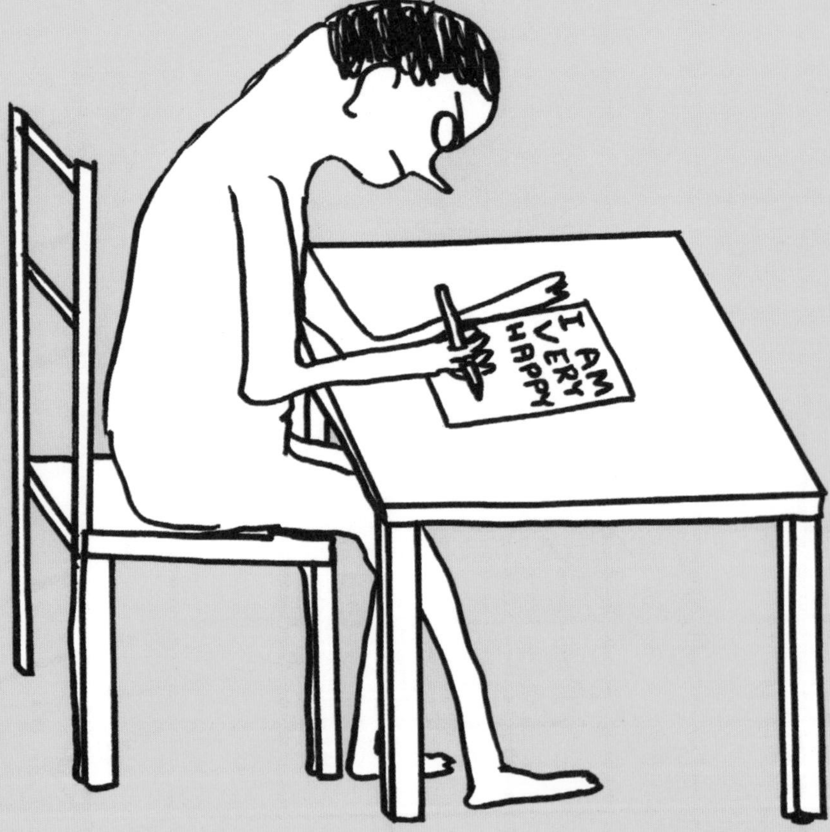
I AM
VERY
HAPPY

SELF-PORTRAIT

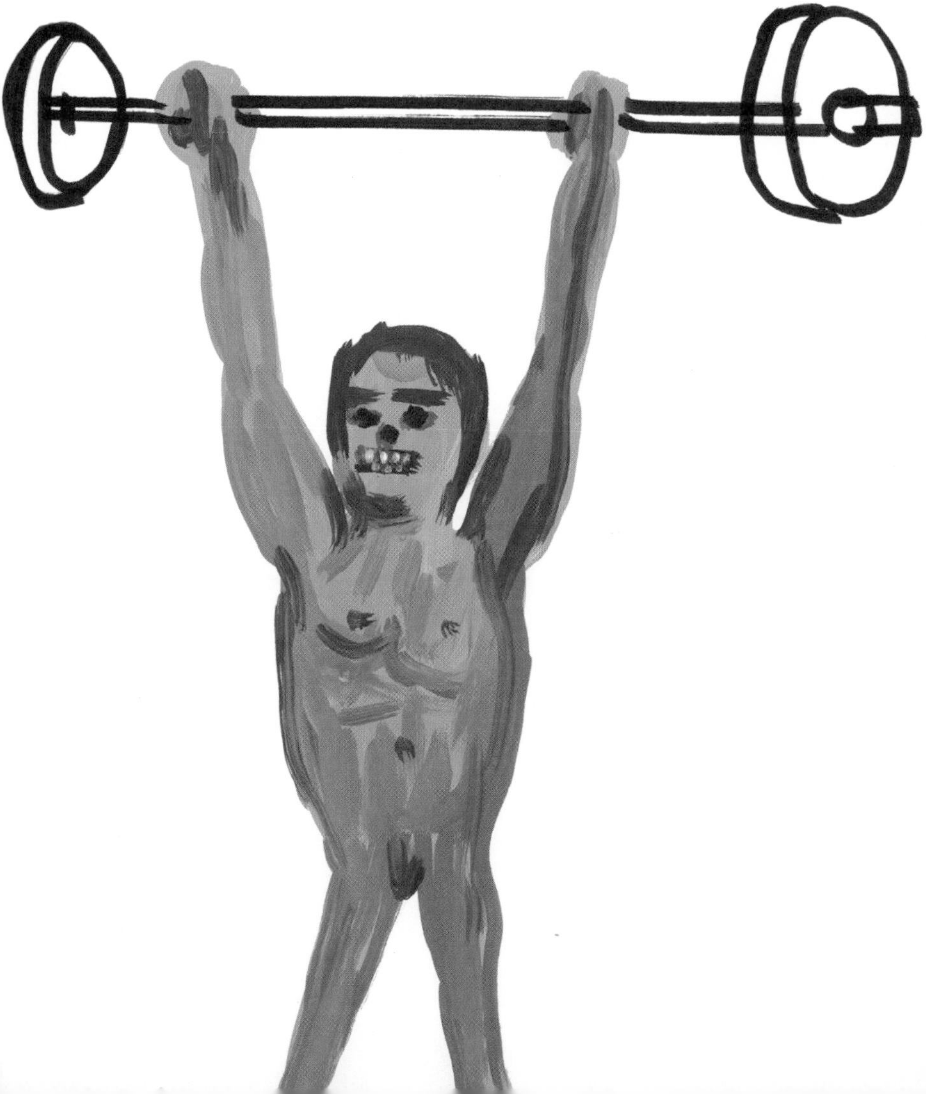

YOUTH

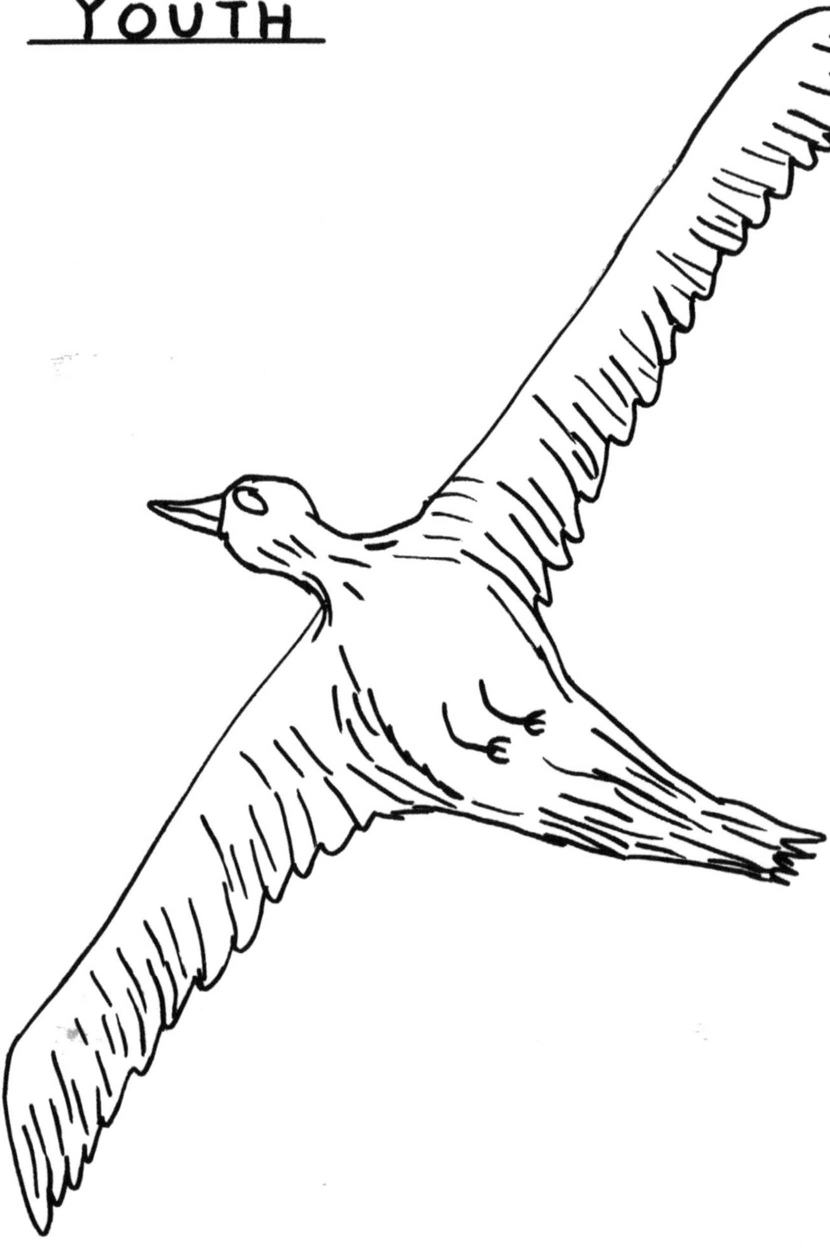

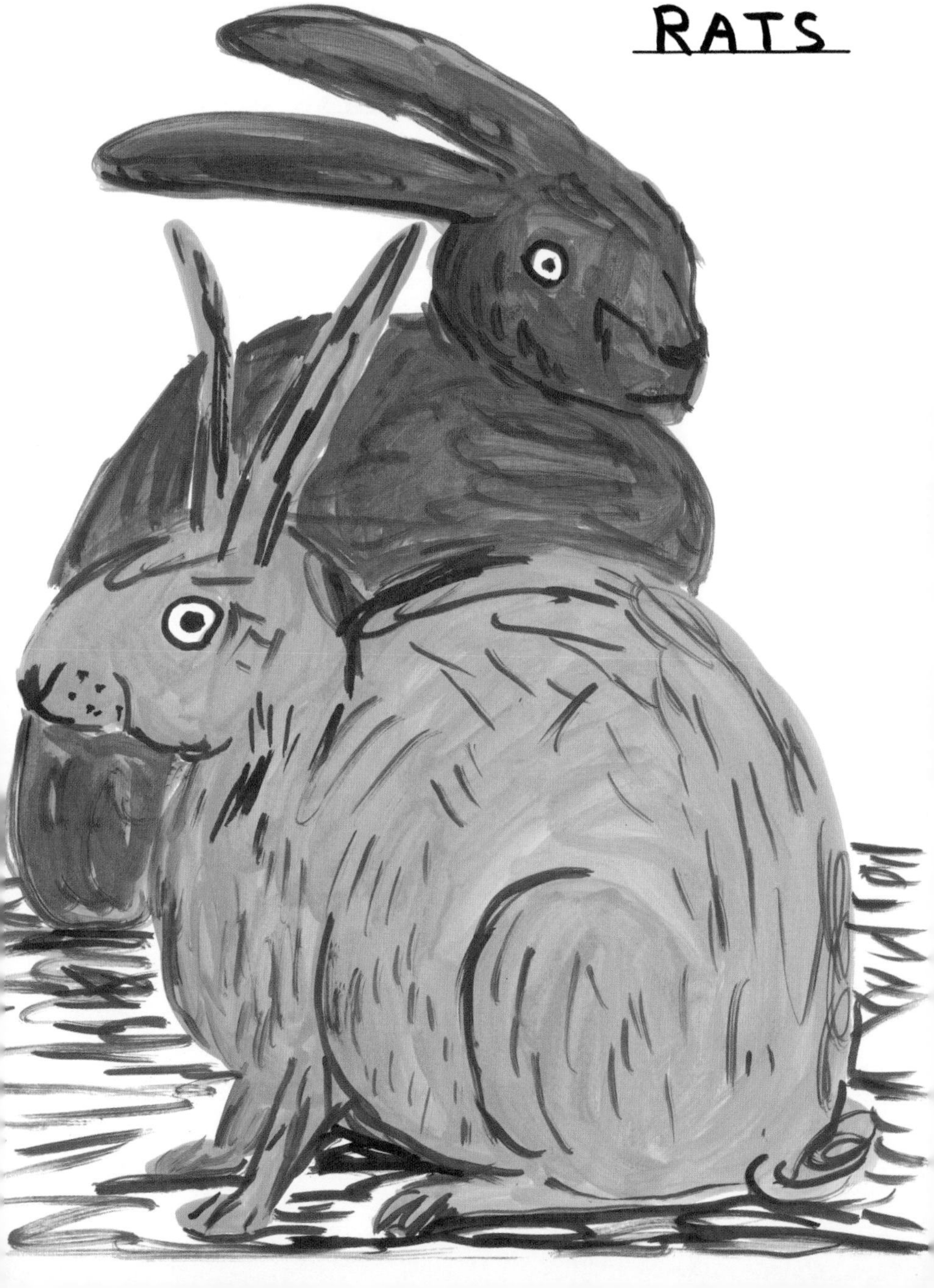
RATS

THANKS FOR PROPPING-UP
MY HEAD WHILST IT WAS MELTING

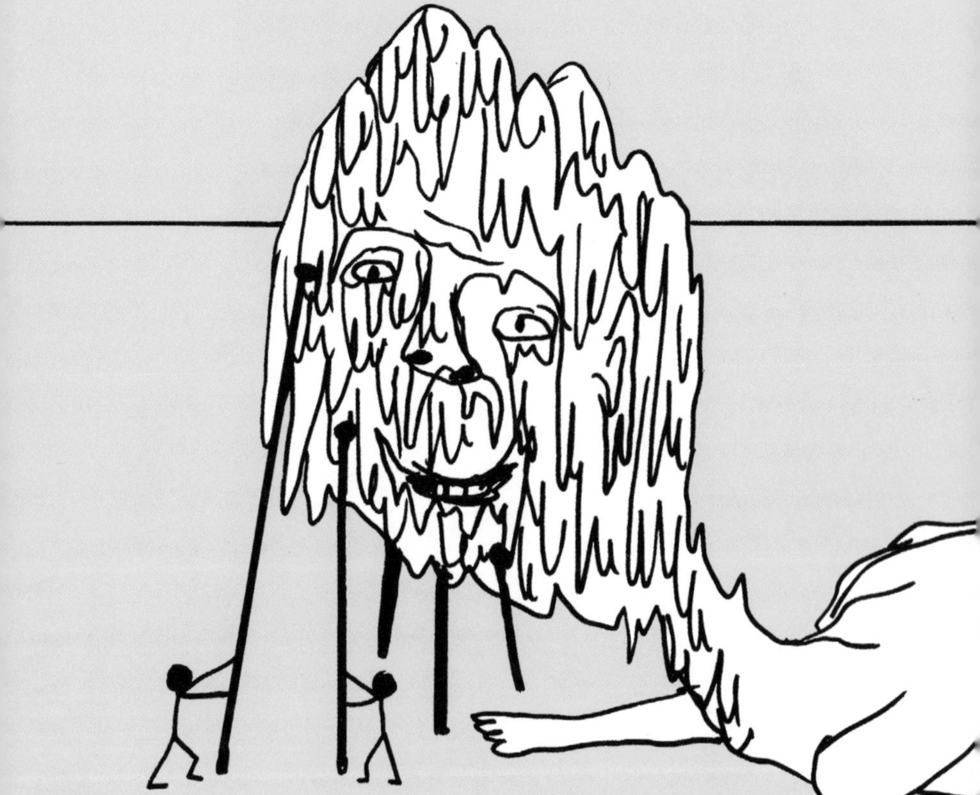

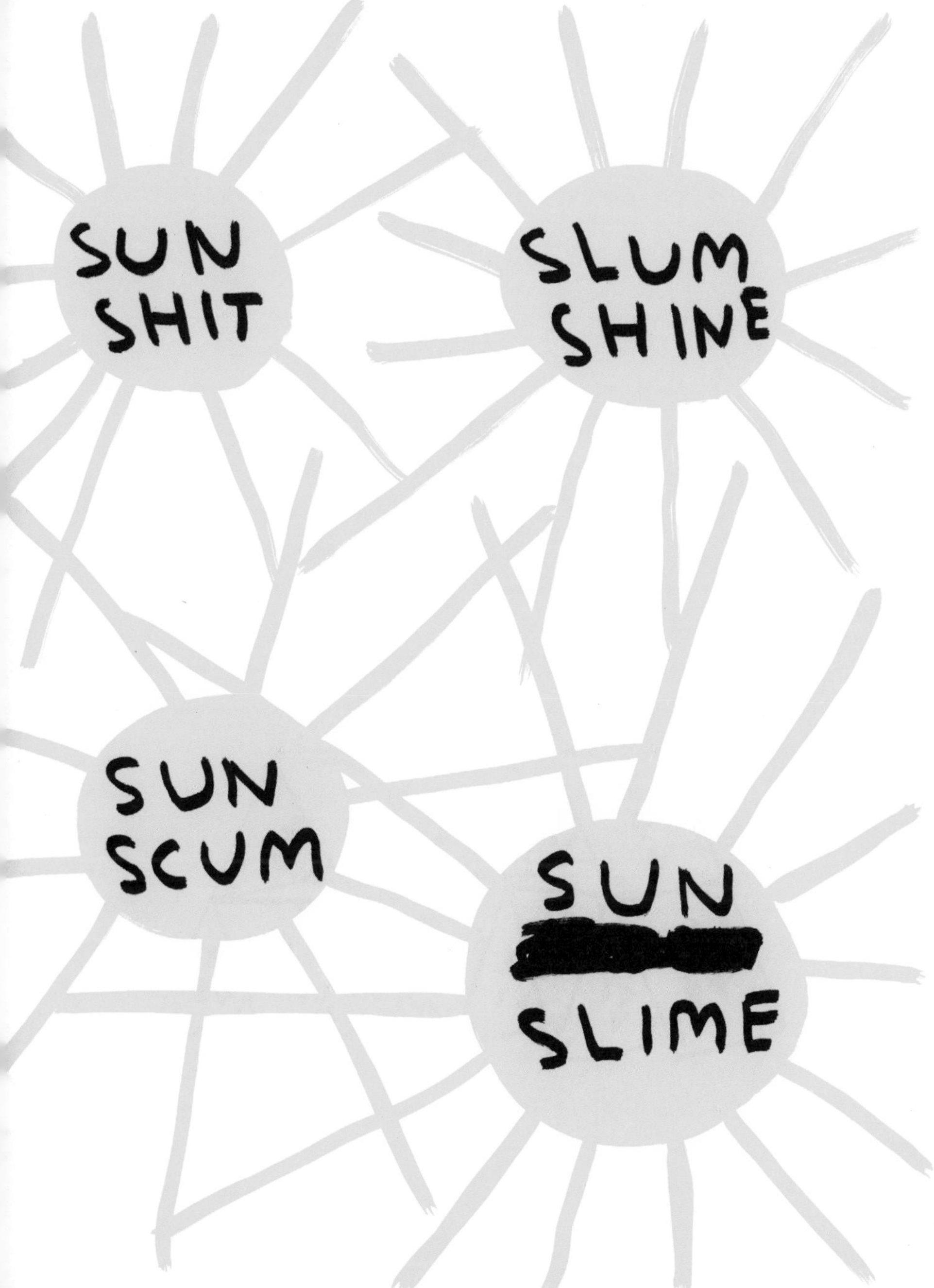

A HOUSE

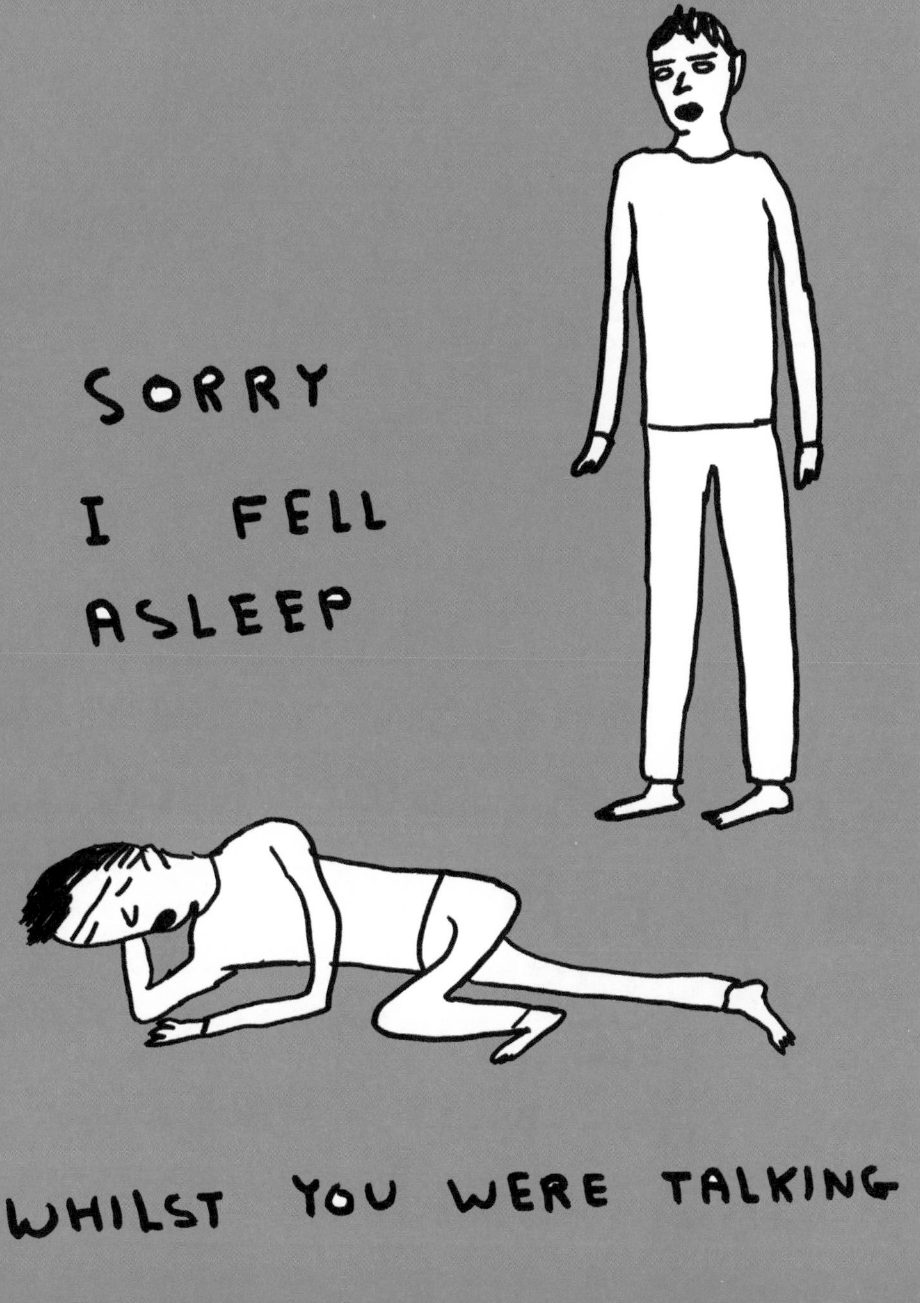
SORRY
I FELL
ASLEEP
WHILST YOU WERE TALKING

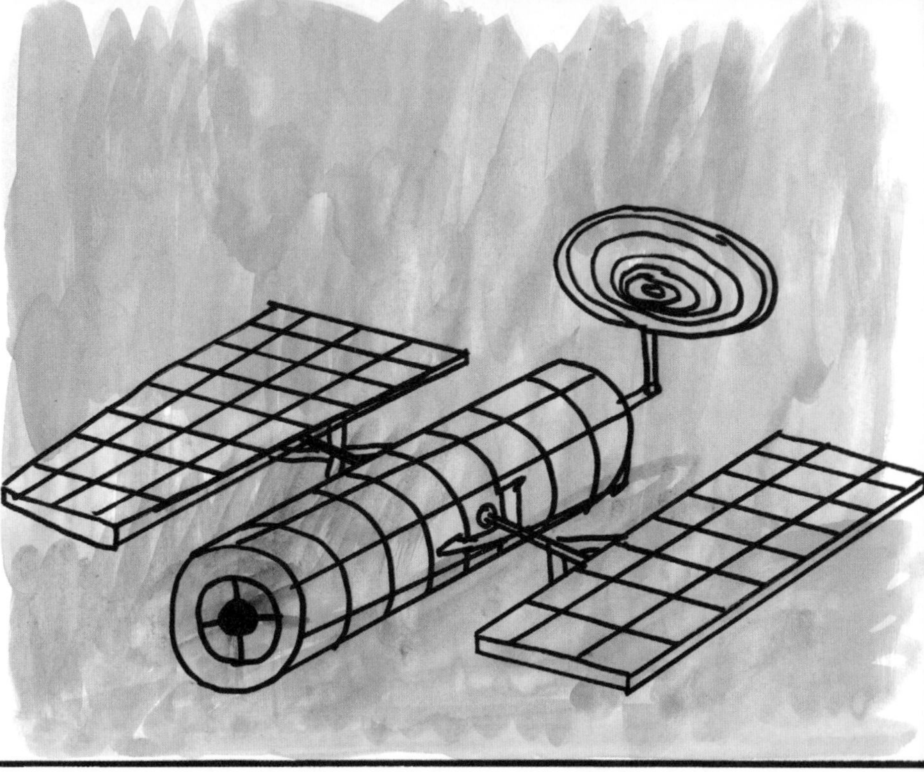

NORMALLY I WOULD WELCOME COMMUNICATION BUT I AM NOT [redacted] FUNCTIONING [redacted] AT THE MOMENT AND I AM NOT WELL POSITIONED

UNWIELDY

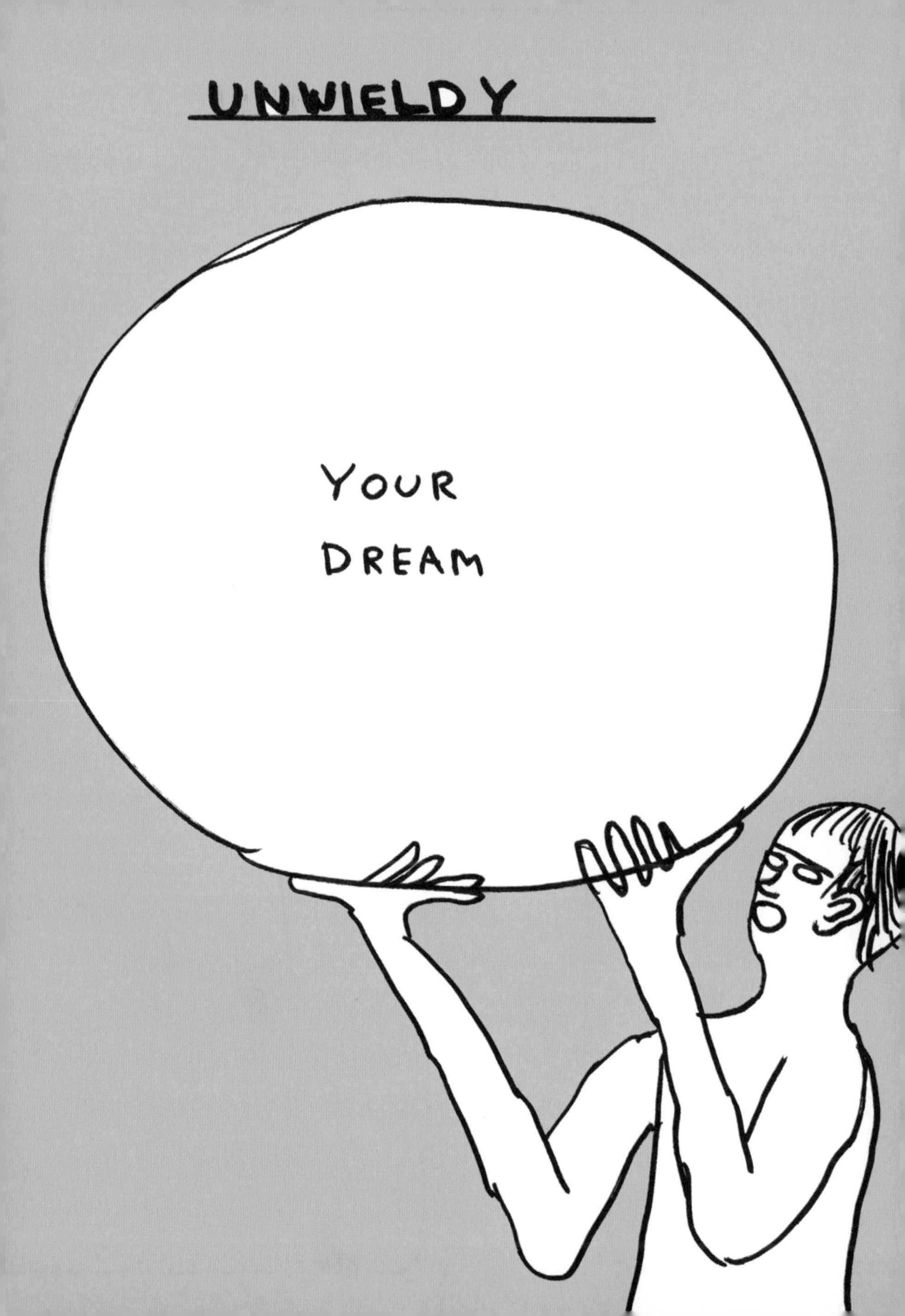
YOUR
DREAM

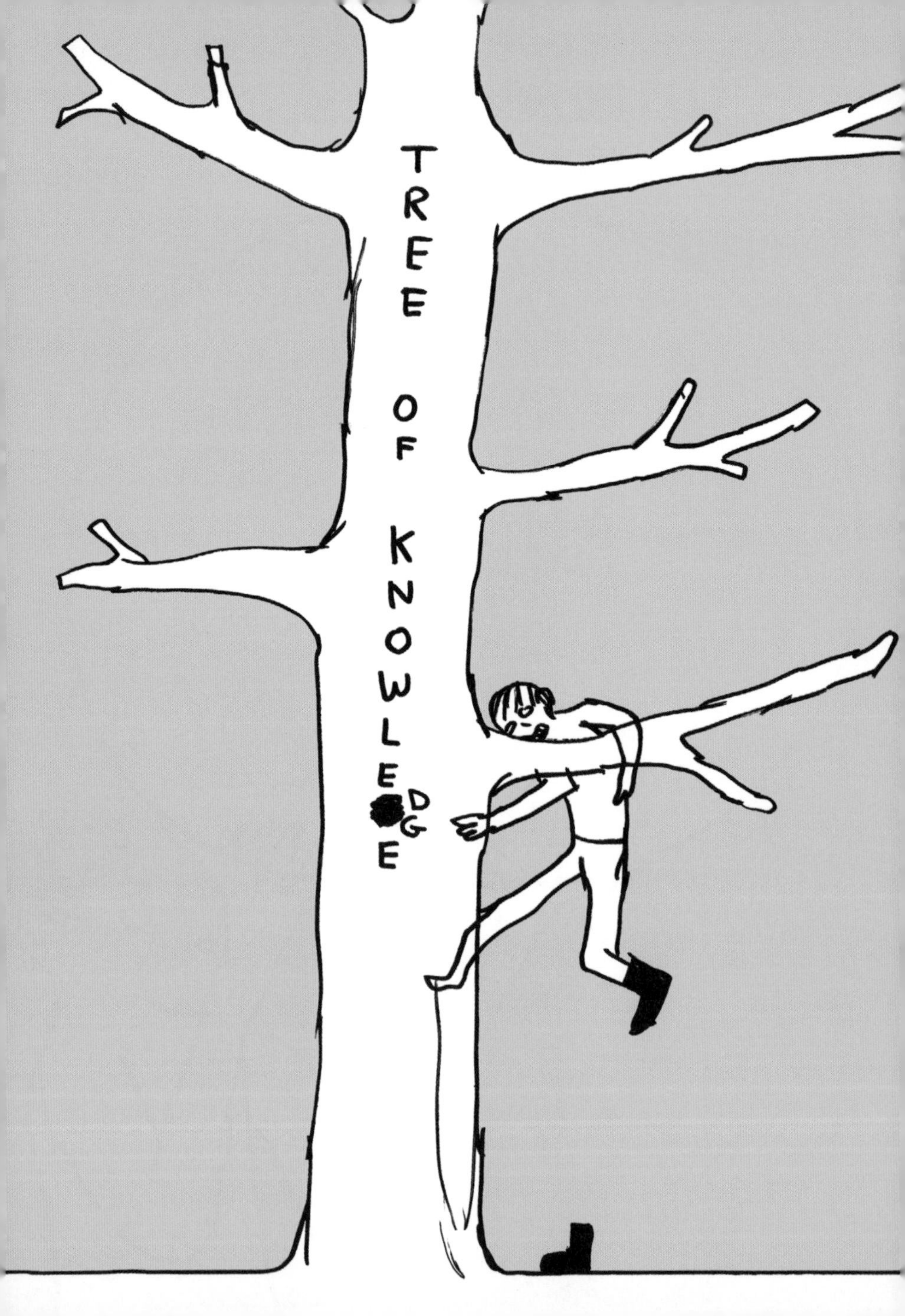
TREE OF KNOWLEDGE

- WHAT HAPPENS [redacted] WHEN THE FLAME GOES OUT ?

- NOTHING

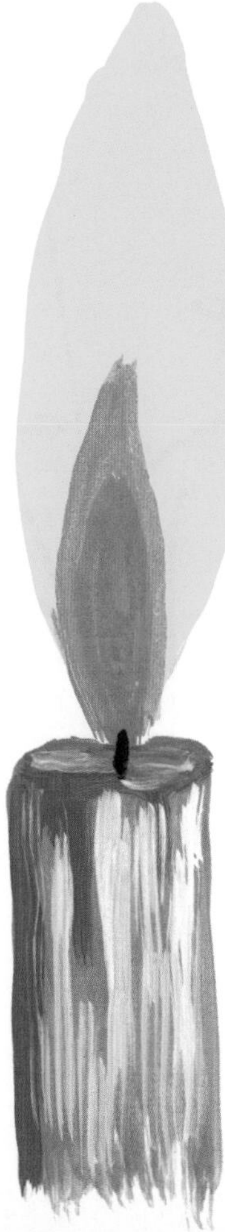

I SIGNED A FALSE NAME

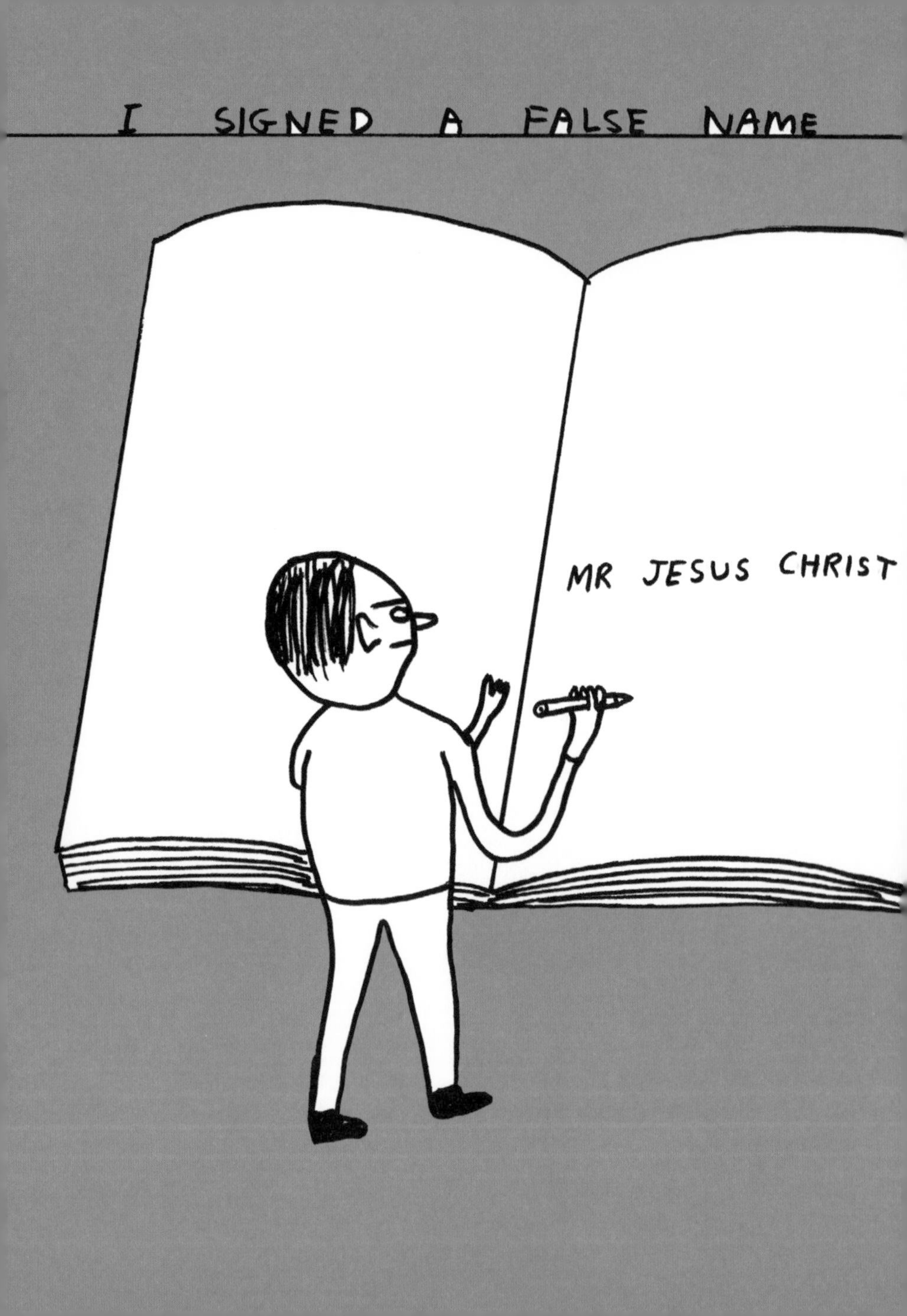
MR JESUS CHRIST

I PICK UP SHIT BECAUSE I WANT TO IMPROVE THE WORLD

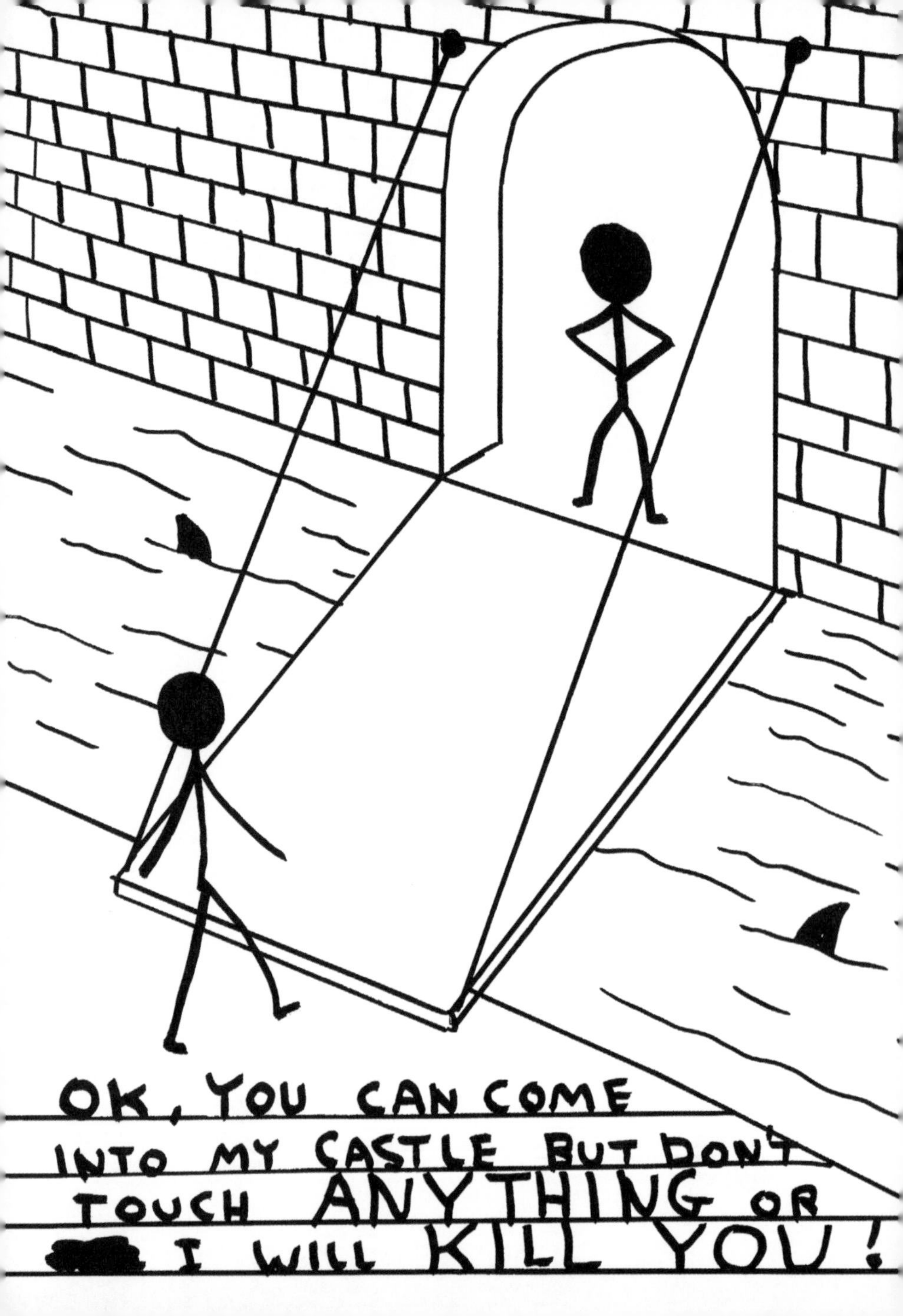
OK, YOU CAN COME
INTO MY CASTLE BUT DON'T
TOUCH ANYTHING OR
[redacted] I WILL KILL YOU!

TWO

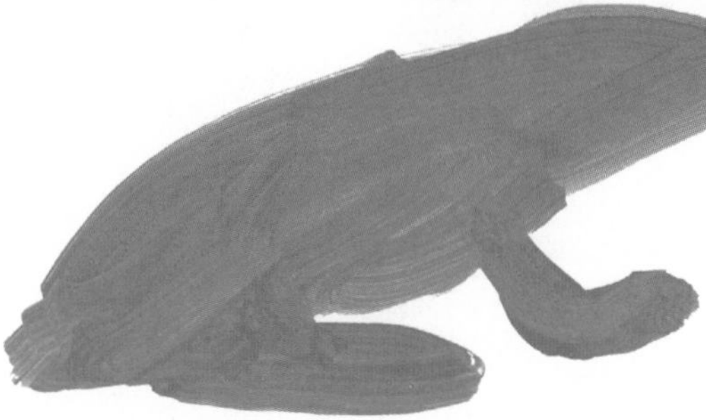

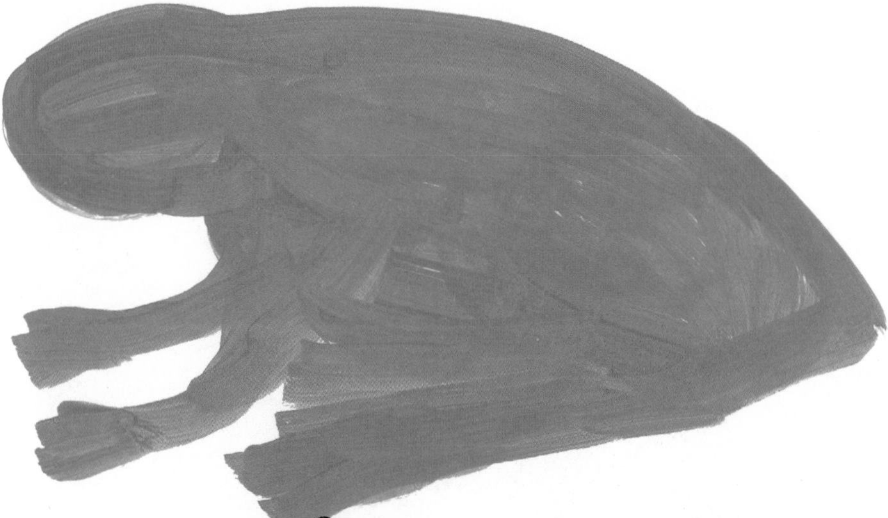

FROGS

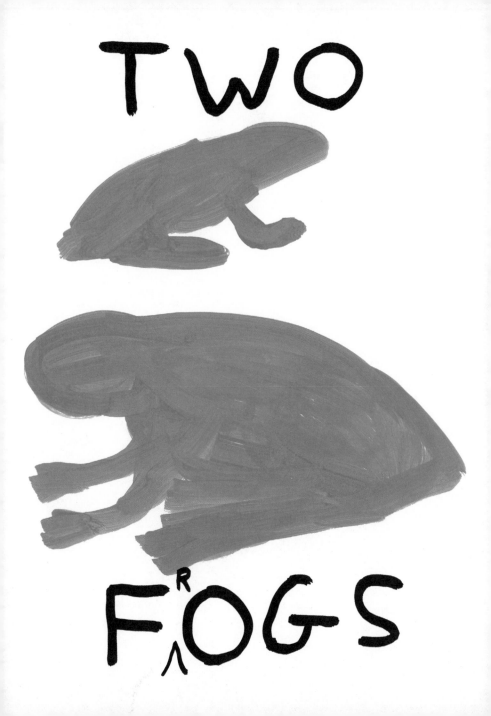

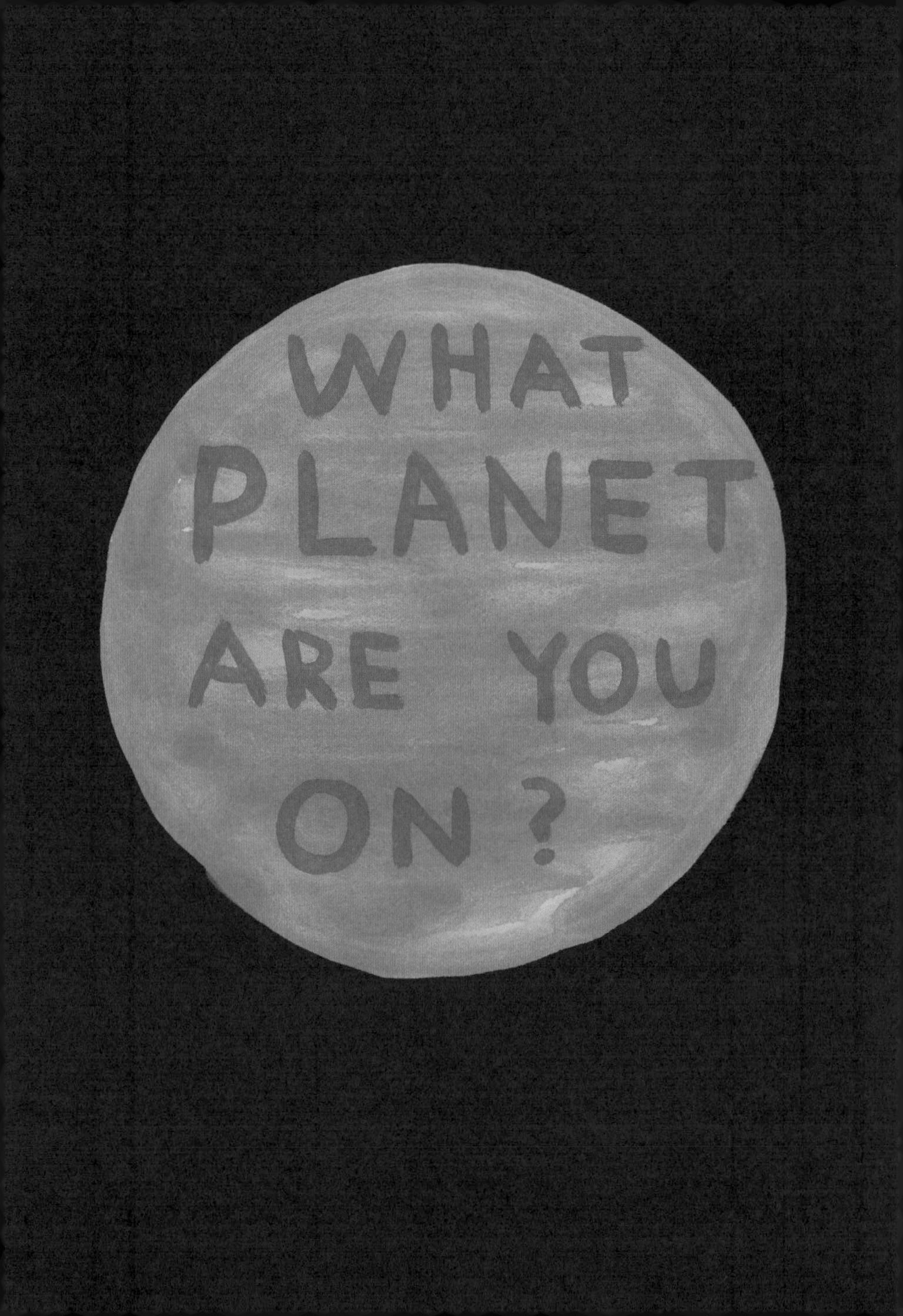
WHAT
PLANET
ARE YOU
ON?

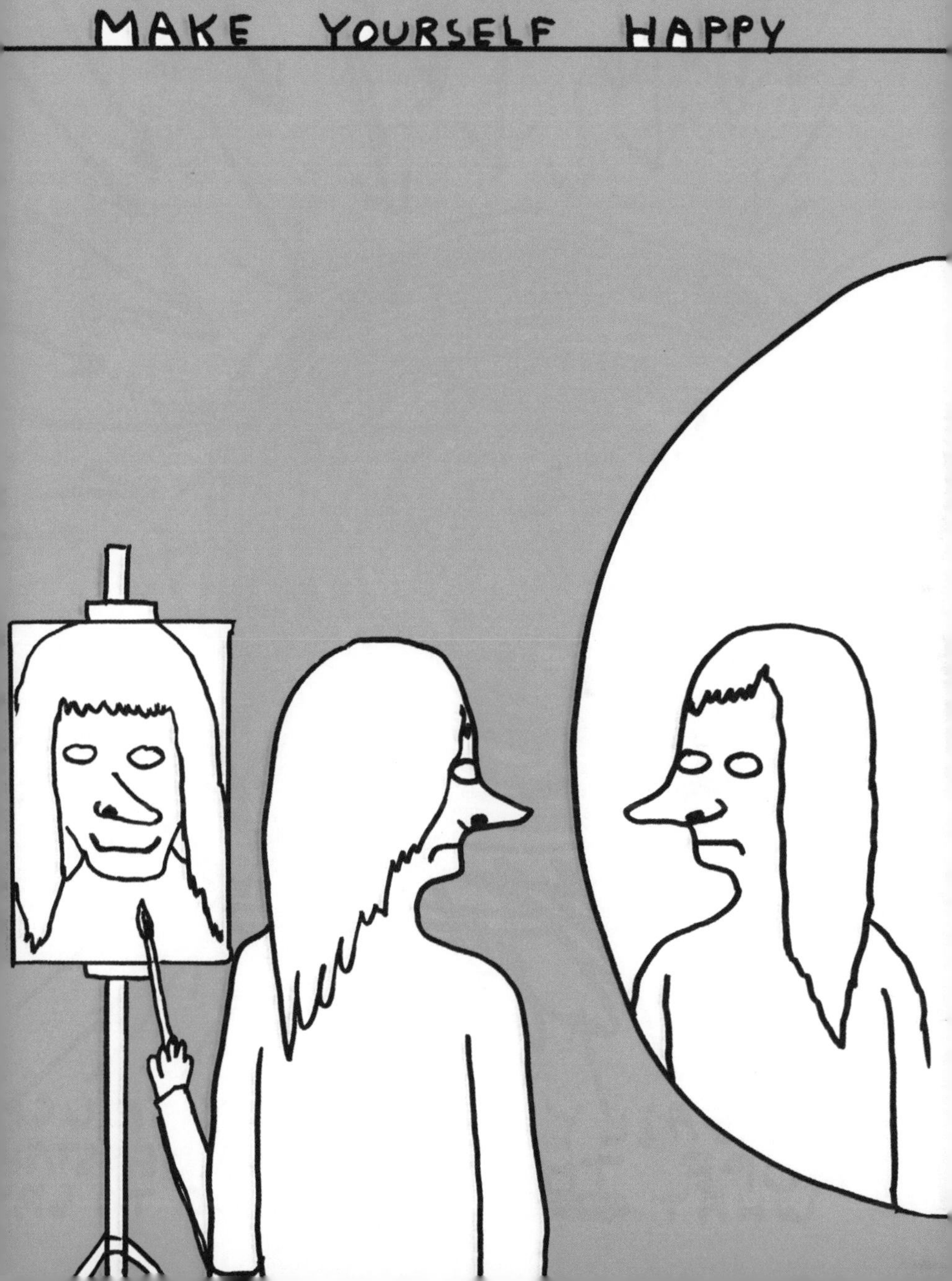
MAKE YOURSELF HAPPY

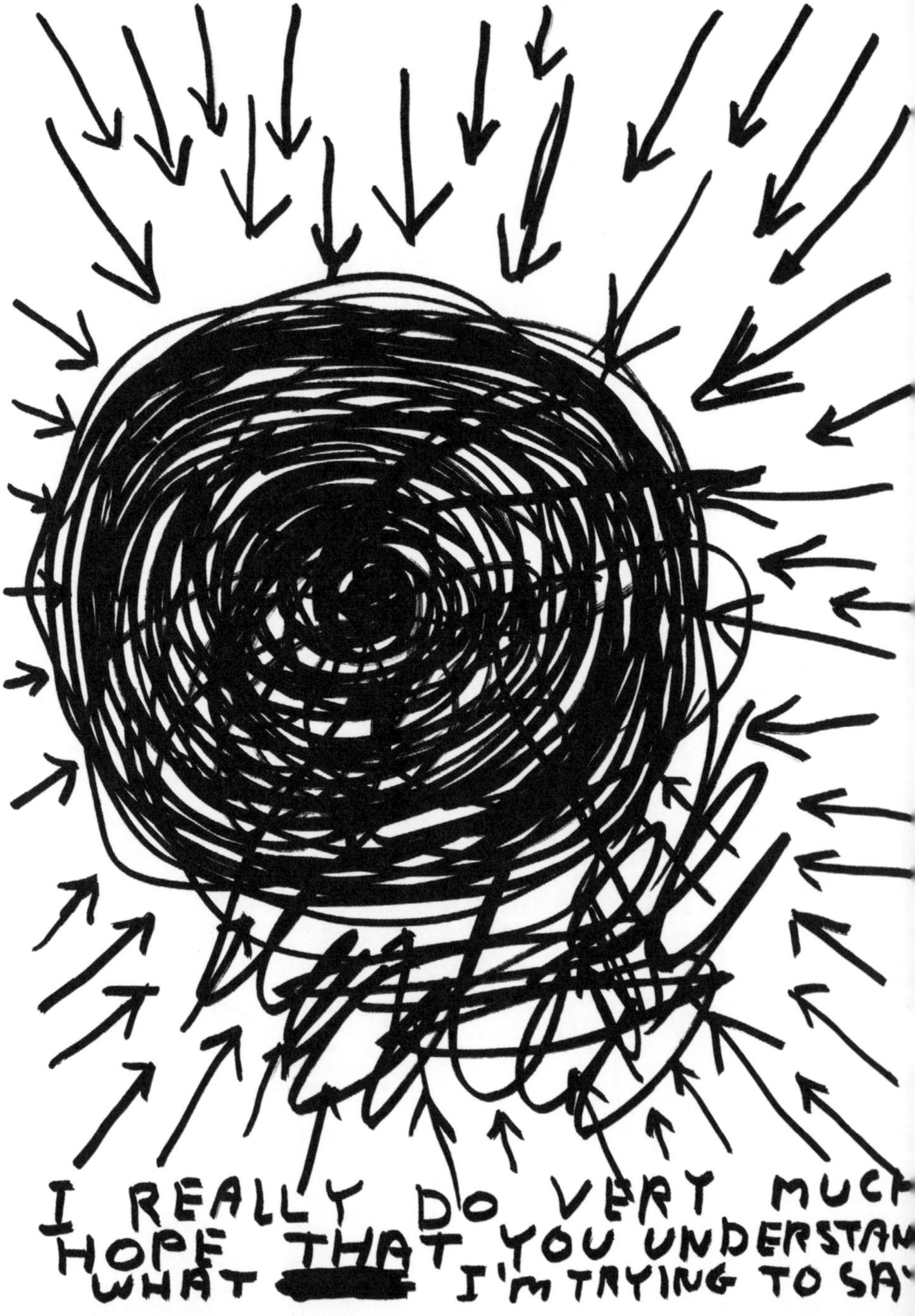
I REALLY DO VERY MUC
HOPE THAT YOU UNDERSTAN
WHAT [redacted] I'M TRYING TO SA

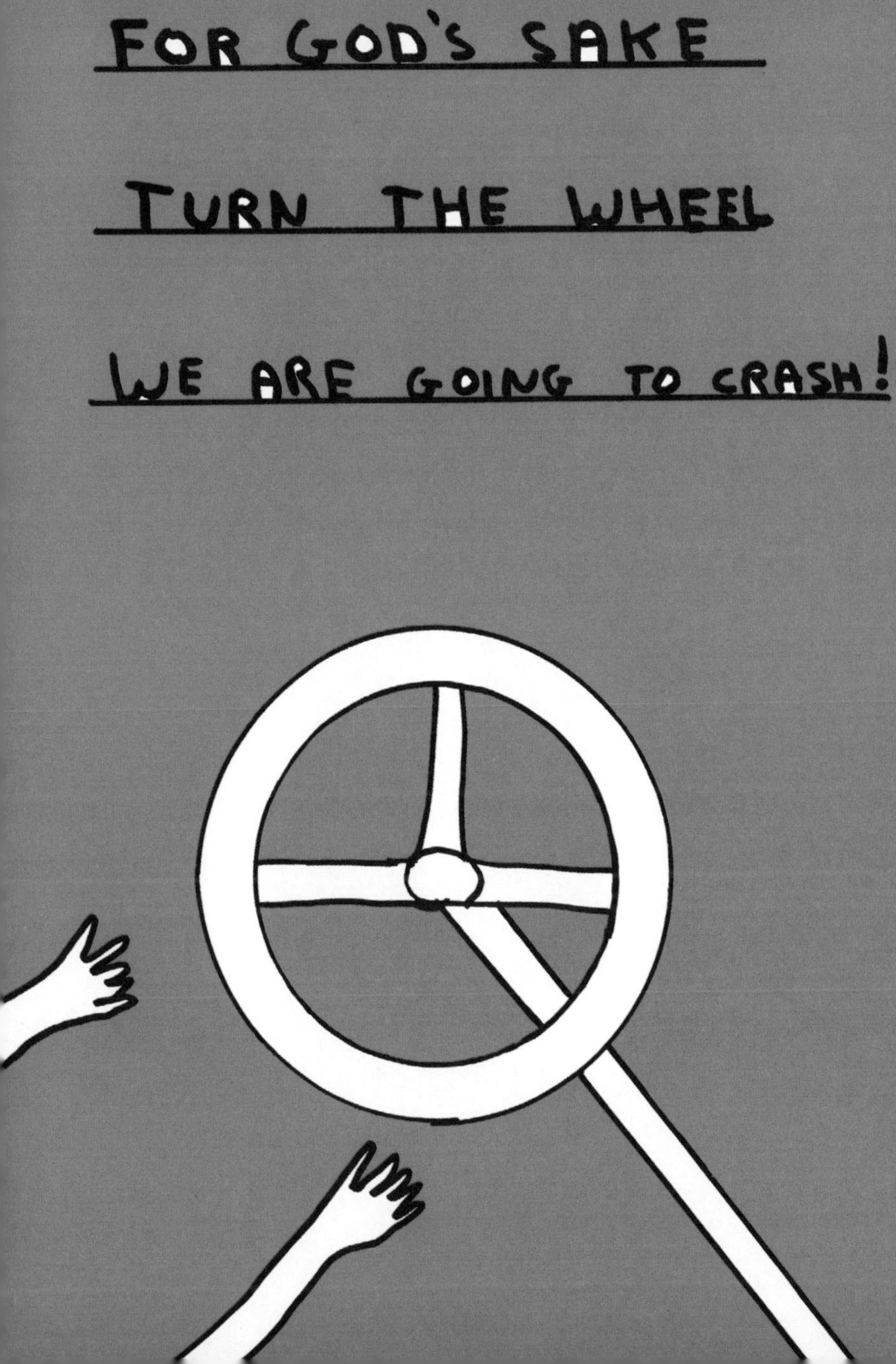
FOR GOD'S SAKE
TURN THE WHEEL
WE ARE GOING TO CRASH!

HOW TO BECOME A PSYCHIATRIST

WOULD YOU LIKE TO BECOME A
PSYCHIATRIST?
IT IS AN INTERESTING JOB
AND IS WELL PAID
THERE IS A SHORTAGE OF
PSYCHIATRISTS
BECOMING A PSYCHIATRIST IS EASIER
THAN YOU MIGHT THINK
WHY NOT GIVE IT A TRY?